A gathering of LACE

gathered by **Meg Swansen**
edited by **Elaine Rowley**

Photography by **Alexis Xenakis**

published by  **BOOKS**

PUBLISHER
Alexis Yiorgos Xenakis

CHIEF EXECUTIVE OFFICER
Benjamin Levisay

EDITOR
Elaine Rowley

KNITTING EDITOR
Ann Denton

TECHNICAL ASSISTANT
Mary Lou Eastman

FASHION DIRECTOR
Nancy J. Thomas

PHOTOGRAPHER
Alexis Yiorgos Xenakis

PUBLISHING DIRECTOR
David Xenakis

PRODUCTION DIRECTOR
Dennis Pearson

GRAPHIC DESIGNER
Bob Natz

BOOK PRODUCTION MANAGER
Andrew Holman

DIGITAL COLOR SPECIALIST
Daren Morgan

ILLUSTRATIONS
Carol Skallerud

PRODUCTION ARTISTS
Jason Bittner
Jay Reeve
Lynda Selle

SEVENTH PRINTING 2008, FIRST PUBLISHED IN USA IN 2000 BY XRX, INC.
PO BOX 965, SIOUX FALLS, SD 57101-0965

ISBN 10: 1893762246
ISBN 13: 9781893762244

Produced in Sioux Falls, South Dakota, by XRX, Inc., 605.338.2450

Printed in China

CONTENTS

DEDICATION

How would it look, do you think, if everyone, old and young, would sit down together to knit for a while? Laughter and merriment and riddles and questions and folktales and anecdotes from each person's life would blend together in the stitches. Then later, when you recalled these events that have gone through your own fingers stitch by stitch, they would speak their own quiet language: Do you remember? Do you remember?

Hermanna Stengard, *Gotlandsk Sticksom,* 1925.
Translated by Lark Books and reprinted in *The Mitten Book.*

PREPARING TO KNIT LACE

You may have heard that lace knitting is nothing but a series of yarnovers and corresponding decreases. This is true. But within that simple definition lie myriad variations.

YARN OVER & DECREASES Yarn over is usually abbreviated yo, or simply shown as ▣ in a chart. Whatever the abbreviation, this looping of wool over the needle creates a hole in the knitted fabric. The manipulation of the wool varies slightly in different knit and purl situations (see drawings, left). Even in this rudimentary form, the loop of wool is an increase and makes one new stitch. You also may find yourself being instructed to make numerous stitches out of one or more yarnovers. A Herbert Neibling design calls for a triple yarnover (wrapping the wool around the needle three times) and on the subsequent round you are to (k1, p1) 6 times into each of the 3 loops before removing them from the needle—18 sts. This is a graphic example of how extraordinarily flexible lace knitting can be. Imagine increasing 18 sts in one great bulge like that…but it works beautifully, and the resulting lace is dramatically lovely.

Standard single decreases will lean either to the right or to the left. The universal favorite right-leaning decrease is knit two stitches together, abbreviated *k2tog*. To veer to the left, the most common lace decrease remains slip one, knit one, pass slipped stitch over *(sl1-k1-psso)*. You may want to experiment with an alternative method: slip 2 sts (one at a time) knitwise, insert the left needle into them and knit them together. This slip-slip-knit method is abbreviated *ssk*.

A double decrease is a means of turning three stitches into one and the most common version in lace is sl 1-k2tog-psso. But remain alert as there are a number of different ways to work both single and double decreases. If a designer wants you to use a special decrease, it will be specified in the instructions such as the centered double decrease, *sl2tog-k1-p2sso* (diagram, lower right).

To maintain an even width of lace fabric, each yarnover (increase) must be balanced by a decrease. That decrease needn't be adjacent to the yo and it needn't even be in the same row or round. Lace knitting, for all its appearance of exactitude, is surprisingly relaxed. If the decrease that corresponds to a given yo is not in the same row, the stitch count may change from row to row, but eventually will resolve itself back to the original number of stitches as you prepare to knit the next vertical repeat of the motif.

If the decrease is in the same row/round as the yarnover, the location of the decrease as well as its execution will affect the final appearance. Using the example of a diamond-shaped motif: as the sides veer out from the center point, the line of yo holes will be moving to the right and to the left. The corresponding decreases can follow the lines of holes by right-leaning and left-leaning decreases; the decreases may precede the yo or follow it. The most common form is to work a right-leaning decrease (k2tog) *before* the yo and a left-leaning decrease (ssk) *after* the yo—but that is not a rule and you will occasionally come across the opposite instruction.

CHARTS If you have ever read a color pattern chart, you will have no difficulty following the graphs for lace. The chart begins at the bottom right-hand corner and, if you are knitting in the round, the lines are read from right to left. If you are working a flat piece of lace, the lines are read right to left then left to right alternately, following the line numbers on the chart.

By memorizing just a few lace symbols, you will be able to read the design on the graph and, more importantly, you can *see* the shape of the motif expressed on the chart. This is particularly useful when, for instance, you are working a double decrease to resolve the tip of a diamond; you will be able to read the preceding row of the chart, then check the knitting in your lap to make sure you are reducing the proper three stitches into one.

MARKERS, MISTAKES, and MAGNETS I highly recommend that you keep track of each row or round by mark-

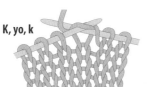

K, yo, k

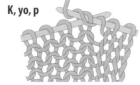

K, yo, p

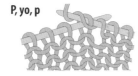

P, yo, p

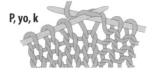

P, yo, k

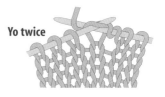

Yo twice

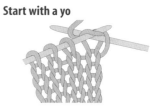

Start with a yo

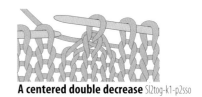

A centered double decrease Sl2tog-k1-p2sso

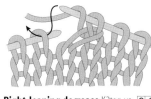

Right-leaning decrease K2tog, yo [o/]

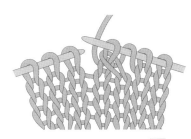

Left-leaning decrease Yo, ssk [\o]

ing off motif repeats. For instance, when knitting a circular shawl, I tie a bright red piece of wool around the needle between the first and last stitch to mark the beginning of a new round (unless I am knitting a red shawl). Then I tie a contrasting piece of wool between each quarter section of the circumference. That way I can check my accuracy four times in one round. If I have made a mistake, I will only have to backtrack one-quarter of the circle and reknit. If you are still new to lace knitting, you may feel more secure if you mark off each and every pattern repeat. It is very important to look at and read your knitting as much as you look at and read the chart.

The most common lace-knitting error seems to be omitting a yo and is usually not noticeable until the subsequent round/row. In this case, I find it perfectly acceptable to, with the tip of the left needle, scoop up the running thread between the two stitches of the preceding row and knit it as a yo. If your knitting is fairly firm, you may have to borrow wool from the stitches to the right and left to make the inserted yo of proper size.

Occasionally you will be required to shift the beginning of a round in order to keep the motifs lined up properly. You will see this symbol at the beginning of the round ←1 and it means: take the marker off the needle, knit one stitch, replace the marker. You have shifted the beginning of the round one stitch to the left (see the charts for Rippling Rainbow on p. 24 or Spiral Shawl on p. 80).

Or you may see this symbol →1 which means: slip the last stitch of the round, remove the marker, replace the slipped stitch to the left needle and replace the marker. You have shifted the beginning of the round one stitch to the right (see chart for Feather & Fan on p. 58).

Then there's the need to keep track of where you are on the chart. When reading a complex chart, I find a Magnetic Row Finder or a Post-it® invaluable.

NEEDLES AND YARN When thinking of lace, your automatic association may be: laceweight wool and multi-zero size needles. As you glance through this book however, you will see yarn ranging from super-fine Cobweb (Hazel

Carter) to worsted-weight wool (Joan Schrouder's Ljace-Kofte). From angora (Lois Young) to thickish cotton (Cheryl Oberle's Tabard). The choice of material and desired finished fabric will suggest the size needle to use: from size 000 in Sandy Terp's very fine Magical Earth Shawl, to size 7 for Joan's standard gauge sweater, to size 10 for my almost chicken-wire-gauge Spiral Shawl. You see? No rules!

GAUGE, CAST-ONS, BIND-OFFS
Gauge for garments is, as always, crucially important. Gauge for shawls, however, is subjective. When knitting a very open and loose fabric, the trickiest part may be casting on and binding off. Both cause a relatively firm, unyielding edge and are incompatible with the rest of the fabric. Try to avoid them both: a circular shawl may have 6–8 sts cast on, but binding off is eliminated by working a sideways border; or cast on invisibly for the long sides of a triangular shawl and apply a sideways border at the end; or use crochet-loops to finish a shawl. If you must cast on or bind off, be sure to do it loosely.

Speaking of casting on, I believe knitting should be totally knot-free, even unto the initial cast-on. You usually are instructed to "make a slip knot," but this may be eliminated by a simple twisted loop over the needle. Using long-tail cast-on as an example (see *Techniques*, p. 162): set your left hand as usual. With the needle in your right hand, dive down into the space between your left hand and the wool that is stretched over forefinger and thumb. Now point the needle toward yourself and up to the ceiling and you will have made a twisted loop which is cast-on stitch #1. Continue as usual.

SPLICING When it comes to joining in a new ball of wool, the usual methods are not very satisfactory for lace knitting. If you leave a few inches of both old and new ends, you will have to darn them later. If you skim them across the back, the line will show through the lace patterns; if you darn them in by duplicate stitch, you will have a noticeable thickening of fabric. The answer? Splicing. When done properly, it is totally undetectable. If you have 2-ply wool, separate the last few inches of the old skein into its individual plies and break off (do not cut) one ply several inches from the end. Repeat this procedure on the end of the new skein. Now overlap the two ends in your left palm, moisten your right palm (spit does work better than water) and rub your palms together briskly for 5 or 10 seconds...or until you can feel heat. You have fused the fibers and, because you broke off one of the plies on either end, the diameter of the wool remains constant. Sometimes I will add more twist to the spliced strand before knitting the next few stitches. OK, you may say, but what about single-ply wool? To assure a uniform thickness, untwist the last few inches of fibers on both old and new ends and d-r-a-w out the wool. Overlap and proceed as above. For the latest innovation in splicing, see Robert Powell's Backwinding on p. 24.

BLOCKING OR DRESSING LACE is critical. I remember being seriously suspicious the first time I knitted a lace shawl. How could that shriveled thing hanging off the needles ever turn into the beautiful and ethereal garment pictured in the book? To me the transformation remains thrilling and parallels the metamorphosis of a caterpillar into a butterfly.

Thoroughly wet the finished shawl (wash, if necessary) and squeeze out most of the water. You may now wrap it in a nice thick bath towel and jump on it, or, if you are not using an unspun wool, spin it in the washing machine. The shawl is now damp and ready to be blocked.

Generally speaking, lace is fairly loosely knitted, which provides plenty of leeway during blocking. I designed a baby blanket years ago which, when gently blocked, produced a 36" square crib cover. The very same item, if stretched severely when wet, made a 54" evening shawl. So, determine the size you want before blocking.

As as example, let us take a circular shawl. I like to block on the rug as it will hold pins securely, and I begin by vacuuming. Now find a full box of large, rust-proof T-pins and a measure. Flop the damp shawl onto the clean rug. Assuming that there is a scalloped lace border—or a crocheted loop edging—pin out the four compass points and measure the radii to make sure they are all the same. Now pin the eighths, the sixteenths, and the everything-in-betweens. Because lace is mostly holes, you may be surprised to learn that, unless it is a particularly humid day, the shawl will dry in a matter of hours.

If you have a sideways garter-stitch border, pinning it out will produce artificial scallops. To avoid this, I drape the damp shawl over a 4" thick dowel suspended between two cupboards, then carefully measure as described above.

Blocking wires are a newly available tool and reduce the number of T-pins required (see resource list on p. 173).

The Russian Orenburg shawls have their own particular blocking method that works well for any square or oblong shawl. See p. 78 for Sandy Terp's description of securing the scallops with string and stretching the shawl over four anchor points. For lace garments, block as you would any sweater, vest, sock, tam, etc.

In recent decades the ancient art of lace knitting has caught the attention of designers and knitters in the United States, and with little wonder. This country steadily has grown in its appreciation of, and skill in knitting—much as an individual knitter grows: innocent interest turns to hesitant beginnings which may blossom into a deep and passionate fascination for all things knitted. As our appetite to acquire new techniques and knowledge becomes keener, it is nearly inevitable that the True Knitter will eventually turn to Knitted Lace.

The frequent response to hearing the words "lace knitting" is to conjure up doilies, antimacassars*, table runners, curtain edgings, jam-pot covers, etc. I like to think this book will help to change that caricature of knitted lace into a more contemporary image.

When we first learn to knit, the discipline of lace usually stands apart and is looked at with awe. But once launched into, we see that even though it has a totally different feel from "regular" knitting, the basic moves are surprisingly elemental—but, like knitting itself, the variables of these few simple moves can occupy a lifetime or two to explore thoroughly.

Knitted lace? Or Lace Knitting? Margaret Stove, in her book, *Creating Original Handknitted Lace,* makes the following distinction between the two: "Lace Knitting is defined as a knitted fabric where there is a row of plain knitting worked alternately with a row of holes made in various ways. Whereas Knitted Lace is a knitted fabric where the holes are made on every row." Examples of each respective discipline may be found herein.

Through the 27 years of Knitting Camp and my travels across the country giving workshops, I have met some extraordinary knitters, a number of whom have been—or are going—through their Lace Period. In *A Gathering of Lace* we are pleased to offer you the cream of their design crop. The contributors, listed alphabetically, are: Eugen Beugler, Nancy Bush, Dallas Cahill, Hazel Carter, Thom Christoph, Katherine Cobey, Amy Detjen, Maureen Egan Emlet, Sidna Farley, Norah Gaughan, Medrith Glover, Sheryl Hill, Diane Hrvatin, Debra M. Lee, Susanna Lewis, Dale Long, Sally Melville, Katherine Misegades, Rachel Misegades, Katie Nagorney, Debbie New, Cheryl Oberle, Emily Ocker, Robert Powell, Gayle Roehm, Bridget Rorem, Joan Schrouder, Joy Slayton, Meg Swansen, Ann Swanson, Sandy Terp, Marilyn van Keppel, Joyce Williams, Lois Young, and Elizabeth Zimmermann.

A wealth of information, magnificent designs, and knitting pleasure awaits you in this lovely book.

Good Knitting

*Antimacassars are the lace "protectors" on the backs of stuffed chairs to prevent staining by the oil men used to wear in their hair: Macassar oil—made from the seed of the Kusam tree in Indonesia and shipped to Europe from the port city of Makassar. Isn't that a great etymology?

Amy Detjen

A Beginner's Triangle

Skill level

Easy

Finished measurements

36" – center back neck to tip

74" – long edge of triangle

44" – each short edge of triangle

Yarn

Schoolhouse Press Satakieli

(3oz/110g; 360 yds/325m; wool)

3 skeins Deep Plum #582

Needles

Size 6 (4mm) needles,

or size to obtain gauge

Extras

Stitch markers

Blocked gauge

4 sts and 8 rows to 1"/2.5cm in garter st using size 6 (4mm) needles.

The beauty of this design is that you can use any amount of yarn—just work Increase Section chart until you have used half of the yarn, then begin Decrease Section—and you can knit to any gauge that pleases you! If this is your first time knitting lace, read pages 10 and 11, where Amy Detjen answers questions about this project and lace knitting in general.

Centered Eyelet (Worked over 3 sts; 3 sts remain.)
Sl first st knitwise, k 2nd st but do not remove from LH needle, psso, yo, k2tog (3rd and 2nd sts).

Centered Eyelet Decrease (Worked over 4 sts; 3 sts remain.)
Sl first st knitwise, k 2nd st but do not remove from LH needle, psso, yo, k3tog (4th, 3rd, and 2nd sts).

Cast on 25 sts loosely. **Begin chart** Work Set-up rows A and B, then continue to work rows 1–20 of chart, working an additional 10-st rep each time through. When you are either halfway done with your yarn, the triangle is long enough, or you are bored, end the increase part of the chart after a Row 10 or a Row 20. If you end after Row 10, start the decrease part with Row 31. If you end after Row 20, start the decreasing with Row 21. Work through row 40 of chart, then rep rows 21–40 until 26 sts remain. **Begin Bind-Off** Ssk, bind off until 3 sts remain on LH needle, k2tog, then bind off remaining sts.

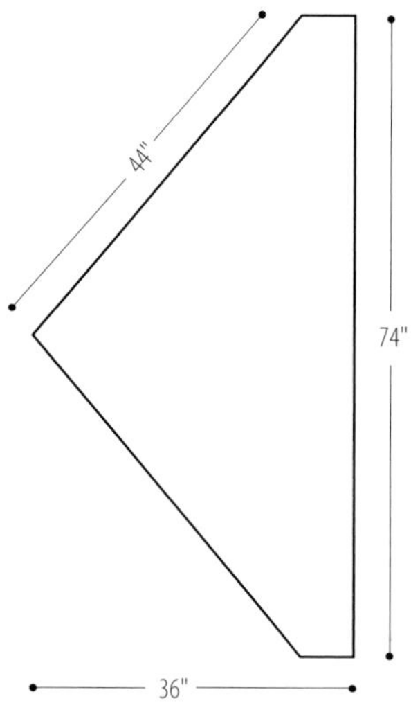
44"
74"
36"

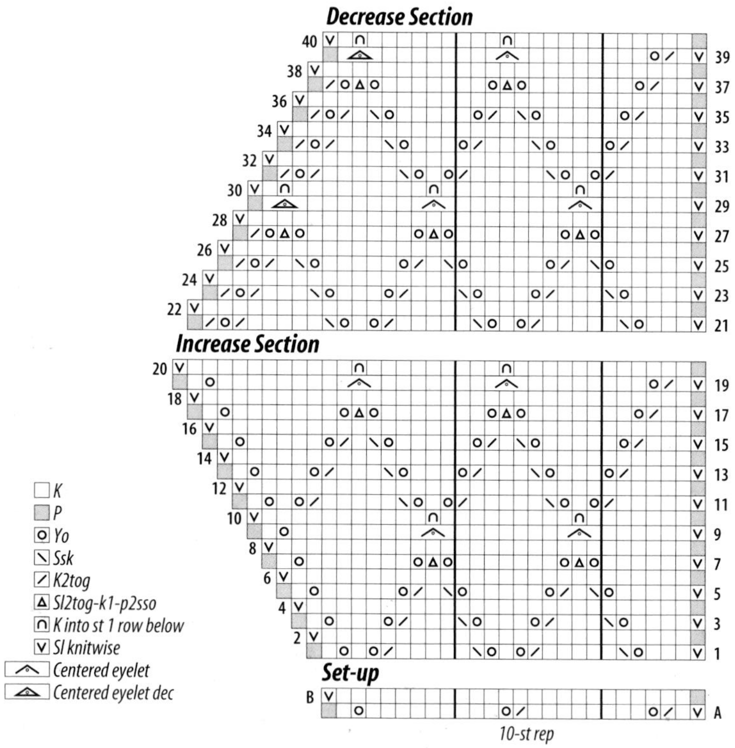
Decrease Section
Increase Section
Set-up
10-st rep
K
P
Yo
Ssk
K2tog
Sl2tog-k1-p2sso
K into st 1 row below
Sl knitwise
Centered eyelet
Centered eyelet dec

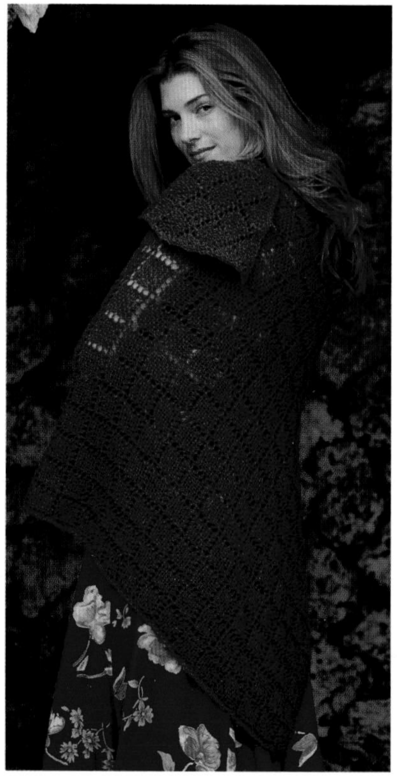

Lace—that wonderful fabric

made with light,

air and space.

Susanna E. Lewis,
Knitting Lace

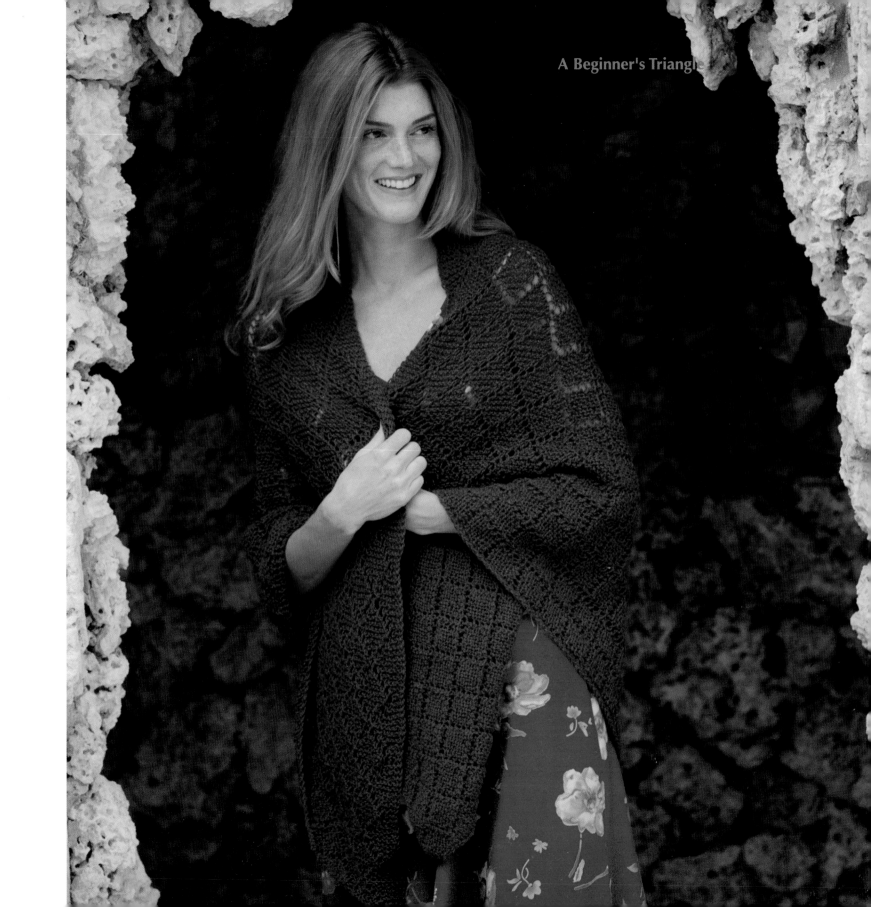

Welcome to Lace Knitting!

If you have knitted lace before, you'll no doubt find these pages rather dull. If you've not knitted lace before, they are here to help clear up some of the mystery. I am writing specifically about the Beginner's Triangle as the example here, but most of the things you'll read here apply to all lace projects.

Since I'm a knitting teacher, I tend to think in terms of questions and answers. Here are the questions I've anticipated for the knitting of the Beginner's Triangle.

Why do you call it a triangle if it doesn't have pointy corners?

I decided to start the shawl with a hefty 25 stitches on the needle. Beginning lace knitters are often intimidated by the unwieldy beginnings of a few scrawny stitches, and this is a friendly shawl, not an intimidating one. It's knitted back-and-forth with a garter stitch base, because I wanted you to feel comfortable with the needles of your choice: circular, straight, or double-pointed (although short dpn won't last long; this shawl gets wide quickly). The other reason I didn't want completely pointed sides was that I'm very hard on my knitted garments, they get slept under and over by people, cats, and dogs, wadded and stretched, and hauled around the country. I was worried about stretching out pointy corners to look like pigs' ears.

What yarn and needles should I use?

You can use practically any yarn at all for this project. The trick is to create a fabric that drapes well and has eyelets (holes) a size you like. You can knit Shetland 2-ply wool on a size 4 or 5 (3½ or 3¾mm) needle, and create a sturdy lace fabric with barely-there eyelets, or you can knit it on a size 10 (6mm) needle and have a truly delicate shawl. I used Satakieli wool because it's plush and bouncy, without being hairy. I didn't want fuzzy yarn because I really wanted to enunciate the stitch pattern. (Want to know a secret? The shawl in the photo was never blocked! There is at least one other in this book that wasn't either. The photo shoot sneaked up on me, and it looked fine just off the needles. The Satakieli is lofty and garter stitch makes a resiliant fabric; we

decided we could get away with it. I am looking forward to blocking it, though.)

How much yarn do I need?

Well, how much yarn do you have? One of the things I really liked about this triangular design is that, when you are halfway through your supply of yarn, you are halfway done with the shawl. You can find the halfway mark using yardage, number of skeins, or weight of the shawl compared to weight of the remaining yarn. Not all shawls are like that, because you often add a lace border, or the shawl is growing so that each row uses more yarn than the one before. You can use this basic pattern for those lots of luxurious yarn you bought with nothing particular in mind. If you only have a little, make a scarf. If you have tons, make a scarf and two shawls!

I'm intimidated by lace charts; how do I start?

If you haven't knitted lace, then you probably don't know exactly how to read a lace chart! It's really not difficult if you know just a few tricks. In this book, we always put the row number on the side of the chart where you begin that particular row. For example, look at the set-up rows A and B of the chart for the Beginner's Triangle. The "A" is to the right of the chart, so that row is worked from right to left. The "B" is to the left of the chart, so that row is worked from left to right. The odd-numbered rows (and A) are knitted on the right side of the shawl, and the even-numbered rows (and B) are knitted on the wrong side (or "back side" or "inside," or whatever term you like best) of the shawl.

Some lace patterns don't show the even-numbered rows, because the instructions will say "knit the knits and purl the purls" or "knit all stitches on even-numbered [or wrong-side] rows," or some other similar instructions. There's no need to chart rows with no action! This shawl has a few wrong-side rows (10, 20, 30, and 40) that have special stitches in them (enough that we decided to chart them). All other wrong-side rows are: Slip one knitwise, knit to within one stitch of the end, purl the last stitch, turn.

Take a moment, please, to look at the legend for the chart. Notice that the plain white box (for "K") is always for knit stitches. It doesn't specify which side of the knitting (right-side or wrong-side). This means that the background field for this lace is garter stitch. Now let me lead you through row A: sl 1 knitwise, k1, k2tog, yo, k8, k2tog, yo, k9, yo, k1, p1. You now have 26 stitches. All I did to write that row was to read the symbols aloud, and to type what I was reading! On to row B: sl 1 knitwise, knit to within one stitch of the end, purl the last stitch, turn. You still have 26 stitches on your needle. Next, start row 1, and you're off and running.

Some knitting patterns leave the addition or deletion of an edge stitch up to the knitter. I charted the edge stitch (purl the last stitch on every row, slip the first stitch knitwise) to make a nice braid-like edging for both sides. Don't let that edge vex you! If you prefer a different edge for garter stitch, do that instead.

What do I do when I'm done with row 20?
Keep knitting! Go back to row 1 of the chart, but do the "10-st rep" stitches an additional time. Trust me, it won't be long until you don't need the chart for much at all. You can read your knitting to see where you are.

How do I tell where I am in my knitting?
This shawl is a relatively easy one to read. First of all, look at its chart, then at the picture on the model. Notice the similarity between the diagonal lines of symbols on the chart, and the diagonal lines of eyelets on the shawl itself. On the Beginner's Triangle, you can tell which row to knit next by counting the number of plain knit stitches between the diagonal lines of eyelets, and by determining if the diamonds are currently getting larger or smaller.

Another hint is the stitch count. After you knit row 20, you have 36 stitches on your needle (counting the number of squares on the chart). Every 20 rows, you are adding 10 stitches, so after row 40, you'll have 46 stitches, after row 60, you'll have 56 stitches, and so on.

The one thing that may cause you to go astray in the pattern is forgetting to begin a new line of diagonal eyelets at the left edge of rows 1 and 11. You'll see your mistake within a few rows, but it's better to not make that mistake at all! (I did it myself about three times while knitting the shawl shown here, so remember everyone has to un-knit the occasional row!)

Why are there so many different types of decreases?
Some decreases lean to the left (ssk) and some lean to the right (k2tog). In lace knitting, these decreases are often paired with yarnovers (yo's). Doing one decrease (ssk) with one increase (yo) keeps the total stitch number from changing. When these two types of stitches are paired, they are often done in a predictable sequence to keep the line of eyelets uniform. In this shawl, the sequence is [k2tog, yo] on the right-leaning lines of eyelets, and [yo, ssk] on the left-leaning lines.

The only exception for the Beginner's Triangle is at the left edge (lower edge when worn). In the Increase Section (the first half of the shawl), all right-side rows have a yo with no accompanying decrease. That is what makes the triangle grow. In the Decrease Section, all right-side rows except 29 and 39 have a yo with a k2tog on each side. That is what makes the triangle

shrink again. (Rows 29 and 39 have used the Centered Eyelet decrease instead, keeping the eyelet line intact.)

About the Centered Eyelet
Even though this is a relatively straightforward project, it offers a rather exciting new technique. The Centered Eyelet was based on Robert Powell's *3-into-2 decrease* (the same maneuver without the yarn over, and no special treatment on the next row). I was looking for a symmetrical way to cross two diagonal lines of eyelets. I turned to my knitting library, but found no solution. I was surprised to discover that very few lace patterns have diagonal lines of eyelets that cross each other. I kept looking, because I couldn't imagine that nobody else was bothered by the asymmetry of the pivotal stitch where the two diagonal lines cross. (By the way, many knitters wouldn't care about this trivial bit, but there are those of us who fuss about the smallest things!)

Calling on my knitting friends led me to this solution. Nancy Robinson reminded me of Robert Powell's *3-into-2 decrease*, which is symmetrical (demonstrated to us at Meg Swansen's Knitting Camp). I played with it until I found that adding a yarnover in the middle of the decrease was very close to what I wanted, but there was a horizontal bar across the eyelet. Simply knitting into the row below on the backside row solved that nicely. If you knit this shawl, you can dazzle and amaze even veteran lace knitters by asking them to tell you how you did that stitch. Won't that be fun?

Right-leaning decrease K2tog, yo

Left-leaning decrease Yo, ssk

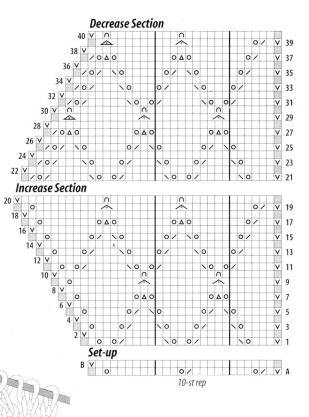

☐ K
☐ P
☐ Yo
☐ Ssk
☐ K2tog
△ Sl2tog-k1-p2sso
∩ K into st 1 row below
∨ Sl knitwise
⌒ Centered eyelet
⌒ Centered eyelet dec

Decrease Section

Increase Section

Set-up

10-st rep

Skill level

Easy–Intermediate

Size

This garment fits best if it is a custom length.
Have the person who will wear the shrug
stand with her arm slightly bent in front of
her chest. A second person should measure
from wrist bone to the bone at the base
of the neck (center back).
Multiply this measurement by 2.
You will knit the shrug about 2" less than
the sum and block it 2" longer.
For example, my wrist to center back
measurement was 30". (2x30=60)
I knit my shrug 58" long and blocked
it to 62". The width is 27".

Yarn

Schoolhouse Press Laceweight Icelandic
(1¾oz/50g; 250yds/228m; wool)
6 balls Light Gray #1026

Needles

Size 6 (4mm) needles,
or size to obtain gauge
Size 1 (2.25mm) needles

Blocked gauge

5.5 sts to 1"/2.5cm in Body chart pat
using size 6 (4mm) needles.

Construction notes

The shrug is knit with built-in I-Cord on each edge. The first and last 3 sts of every
row are the I-Cord sts, worked at row beginnings by knitting and at row endings
by slipping purlwise with yarn in front. Since they are knit only every other row,
do not knit these sts too tightly or they will "pull in" the edge. If this is happening,
you can add an extra I-Cord row occasionally as follows: k the first 3 sts, slip
them back onto the left-hand needle and knit them again; continue row.

Make 1 (M1) Make 1 by picking up running yarn before next st and knitting into
back of it (see *Techniques*, p. 162).

With smaller needles, cast on 59 sts. Work rows 1 and 2 of Rib Pattern chart for
30 rows—approx 3". Change to larger needles. **Body Increase chart:** *Row 1* (RS) K
5, work rep 8 times, work to end. Continue to work chart as established through
row 22—145 sts.

Body chart: *Row 1* (RS) Work first 8 sts of chart, work 16-st rep 8 times, work last
9 sts of chart. Work as established through row 24, then rep rows 1–24 until shrug
measures about 4–5" less than desired length, end with a chart row 11. (I repeated
the 24-row pattern 19½ times.)

Body Decrease chart: *Row 1* (WS) Working chart from left to right, work first 9 sts
of chart, work 16-st rep 8 times, work last 8 sts of chart. Continue as established
through row 22—59 sts remain. Change to smaller needles. Beginning with row 2
(WS row), work 30 rows of Rib Pattern chart. Bind off in pattern.

Finishing

Block shrug 2" longer than the measurement obtained in the beginning (see Size).
When the shrug is dry, overlap the I-Cord edges of the cuffs. Sew cuff seams with
one I-Cord border on the outside and one on the inside.

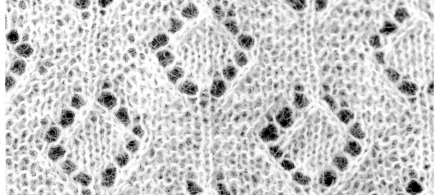

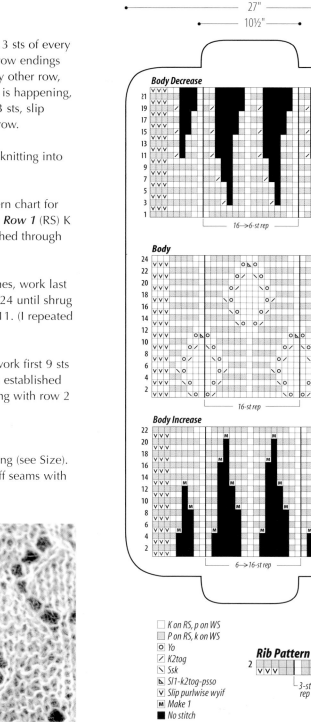

Key:
☐ K on RS, p on WS
▨ P on RS, k on WS
○ Yo
⟋ K2tog
⟍ Ssk
◪ Sl1-k2tog-psso
∨ Slip purlwise wyif
M Make 1
■ No stitch

A fair little girl sat under a tree,

Sewing* as long as her eyes

could see;

Then smoothed her work,

and folded it right,

And said, "Dear work, good night,

good night."

Richard Monckton,

Good Night and Good Morning

*We like (mentally) to substitute

the word 'knitting.'

Shrug

Construction notes

This shawl, knit on a garter st ground, has no bound-off edges. It begins with the bottom border, then sts are picked up along the inside edge of the border for the center panel and along the cast-on edge of the border for the right edging. The left and right edgings are knit at the same time as the center panel. The top border is knit last, attaching to the shawl as you go, and its end is grafted to the top of the left edging.

NOTES *1* Center motif chart only shows odd rows. Even rows are knit. *2* See *Techniques,* p. 162, for invisible cast-on and garter st grafting.

Bottom Border

With larger needle, invisibly cast on 8 sts. **Bottom Border chart** Work rows 1–16 of chart ten times, then work rows 1 and 2 once more (7 sts remain on needle)—162 rows. Do not break yarn. Place marker (pm), then pick up 88 sts along the straight edge of border as foll: 1 st in each ridge of the border, 1 st from the cast-on border, pm, then remaining 7 sts of the border—95 sts in all.

Skill level

Intermediate

Finished measurements

24"x72"

Yarn

Jamieson & Smith Jumperweight

Shetland (1oz/28g; 150yds/137m; wool)

8 skeins Gilly Green #FC46

Needles

Size 6 (4mm) needles,

or size to obtain gauge

Size 2 (2.75 mm) needles,

for picking up stitches

Optional: One size 6 (4mm) double-

pointed needle (dpn), for top border

Extras

Stitch markers

Small amount of waste yarn

Blocked gauge

24 sts and 48 rows to 5"/12.5cm.

in center motif pat using size 6 (4mm)

needle. Actually, it was just a tad

under 72 sts and 144 rows to

14.75"/36cm.

-------- Cast on at a, graft at b

A GATHERING OF LACE

When I was a young girl I read in a story
that one Cossack woman
knitted the first shawl and sent it to the
Russian Czarina, Catherine the Great.
Catherine was so impressed that she
ordered the woman be given a large sum
of money for all her life. But the Czarina
also ordered that the woman be blinded
so that no other woman could ever wear
the same shawl as the Czarina.
However, there was a
mistake in Catherine's plan.
This Cossack woman had a daughter,
also an expert knitter.

Galina Khmeleva and Carole R. Noble,
Gossamer Webs

Faux Russian Stole

Bottom Border & Left Edge

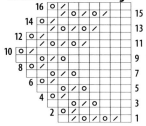

Top Border & Right Edge

Body

Next row (RS) Work row 3 of Right Edge chart (RE) on first 7 sts before marker, knit center 81 sts for body, work row 3 of Left Edge chart (LE) on last 7 sts after marker. *Next row* (WS) Work row 4 of LE, knit center 81 sts, work row 4 of RE. Continue working right and left edges as established for six more rows, keeping body sts in garter st.

Center Motif

Next row (RS) Work row 11 of RE, work row 1 of Center Motif chart (CM), work row 11 of LE. Continuing in pats as established, work rows 1–96 of CM five times, then work rows 1–46 once more. (Row 8 of edge pats completed.) Changing to garter st on center sts and continuing edge pats, work 8 more rows. (Row 16 of edge pats completed.) Remove markers.

Top Border

Beginning with RS facing, work rows 1–16 of Top Border chart (TB) ten times, joining every odd row to body and slipping the first st of every even row. (NOTE It is easier if you use a dpn to knit the odd rows.) One body st remains. Work row 1 of TB, attaching it to last st. Graft the top border to the left edge. When the grafting is complete, you will note an extra row in the pat—a glitch we couldn't solve, but it's barely noticeable.

Finishing

Sew in ends. Block.

□ K
✓ K2tog
\ Ssk
O Yo
◢ K3tog
◣ Sl1-k2tog-psso
∨ When working top border only, slip wyib
⌒ When working top border only, knit tog with 1 body st

Center Motif

81 sts

Skill level

Intermediate

Size

S-L (XL-XXL). Shown in size S-L.

Finished measurements

Width: Knitted, 24 (29)"

Blocked, 25 (30)"

Length: Knitted, 17½ (19½, 21½)"

Blocked, 18½ (20½, 22½)"

Yarn

Schoolhouse Press Laceweight Icelandic

(1¾oz/50g; 250yds/228m; wool)

4 (6) balls Beige #1038 or

Brown #0867

Needles

One size 6 (4mm)

circular needle, 24"/40cm,

or size to obtain gauge

Extras

Stitch markers

Safety pin

Stitch holders

10 yds of waste yarn

Blocked gauge

20 sts and 33 rows to 4"/10cm

in garter st using size 6 (4mm) needles.

Construction notes

The cocoon begins at the back base of the armhole *(A)*. It is knit up to the back neck, then divides for the fronts. It is knit down to the front base of the armhole *(B)*, then sts are picked up at the cast-on edge *(C)* and the balance of the garment is worked down to the hem in one piece. The rolled body edging is worked continuously around the hem, along the center fronts and around the neck. Rolled edging is also worked around armholes.

NOTES *1* Directions are for Short and Average size S-L with XL-XXL in parentheses, and with Long in brackets. Follow first figure(s) unless otherwise indicated. Any length may be worked with either width. *2* If it is not possible to work an entire k2tog-yo-yo-ssk at any time, work all affected sts as knits instead. On wider size only, after neck dec's have been worked, knit all pink chart sts at center right front edge, and knit all blue chart sts at center left front edge. *3* See *Techniques,* p. 162, for invisible cast-on and double yo.

Back Armhole to Neck

Invisibly cast on 120 (144) sts and k 3 rows. **Begin Cocoon Chart:** *Row 1* Work first 12 sts of chart, work 24-st rep 4 (5) times, work last 12 sts of chart. Continue as established, working rows 1–48 twice, then 1–22 once [1–48 twice, then 1–46 once].

Divide for Fronts

Next row: Row 23 [47] Keeping in pat, work 59 (71) sts for right front. Put the 2 center sts on a pin and the remaining 59 (71) sts on a holder for left front. Turn and work row 24 [48] on right front sts. *Dec row: Row 25 [1]* Keeping in pat, work to last 3 sts, k2tog, k1. Work dec row every odd row 10 times more. The last dec row is row 45 [21]—48 (60) sts. Turn and work row 46 [22]. *Row 47 [23]* Work sts 1–48 of chart (1–36, 13–32, then k4).

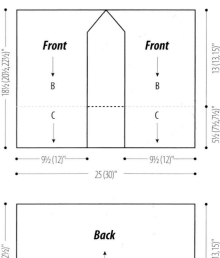

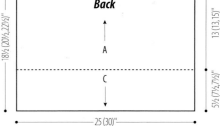

----- *Invisible cast-on*

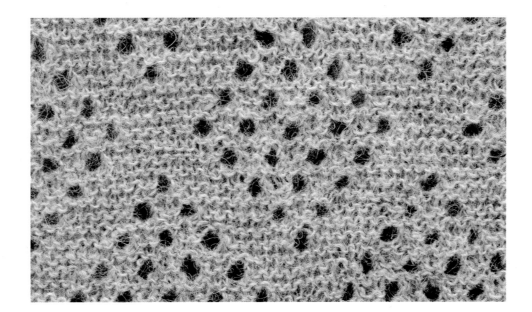

Continuing as established and remembering to alter motif for wider size, work row 48, [rows 24–48], rows 1–48, then rows 1–44. Place sts on holder. Slip 59 (71) sts from left front onto needle. Starting at neck edge, work the left front to correspond to the right front, reversing the dec shaping on odd rows at neck edge as foll: k1, ssk, work chart pat to end of row. *Row 47 [23]* Work sts 1–48 of chart (k4, then work sts 17–36, 13–48 of chart).

Join for Body
Row 45 Work across left front. Slip the 120 (144) invisibly cast-on sts from back onto the other end of the needle and knit in pat across these sts. You will be one-half st off and knitting in the opposite direction, but it isn't really noticeable. Slip the 48 (60) right front sts onto the other end of the needle and knit across them in pat—216 (264) sts. Turn and work row 46 across entire body. *Row 47* Work first 12 sts of chart, work 24-st rep 8 (10) times, work last 12 sts of chart. *For the short version of the cocoon,* continue as established, working row 48, then rows 1–40. K 4 rows. *For the average and long versions,* work row 48, rows 1–48, then rows 1–16. K 4 rows.

Body Edging
If you like the "right" side of the cocoon, knit 1 more row, place corner marker, pick up and k 1 st in each ridge of the right front, k first st on pin, place back neck marker, k 2nd st on pin, pick up and k 1 st in each ridge of the left front, place corner marker.

If you like the "wrong" side of the cocoon, don't knit another row. Instead, turn your knitting and work along edges of fronts and neck as directed above, place corner marker, k body sts across bottom edge, place corner marker.

Rnd 1 Knit, inc 1 st (by knitting in the front and back of st) before and after corner markers. Inc the back neck as foll: k to 13 sts before marker, inc in next st, (k2, inc in next st) 4 times. You are at the marker; remove it. (K2, inc in next st) 4 times, continue knitting. *Rnds 2 & 3* Knit. Bind off loosely.

Armhole Edging
Starting at the base of the armhole with RS facing, pick up and k 1 st in each ridge around the armhole. Pick up and k 1 st in the bar at the base of the armhole, place marker. *Rnd 1* K to 4 sts before marker. Inc in each of the next 3 sts, k1, slip marker. *Rnd 2* Inc in first three sts. K to end. *Rnd 3* Knit. Bind off loosely.

Finishing
Weave in ends. Block to desired measurements.

Cocoon Chart

K
Yo
K2tog
Ssk

Apart from lace stoles, scarves and
shawls, the women knitted veils
and triangular head scarves.
Silk triangular veils, knitted with
the eyelid pattern, were worn over
the face and wrapped around a hat,
and veils in fine black, white and
morrit spun yarn could be folded
and fitten into a matchbox.

Mary Smith and Christ Bunyan,
A Shetland Knitter's Notebook

Cocoon

Construction notes

This shawl is knit from the center back neck outwards. Shoulder shaping is incorporated in the first 108 rows of this shawl by yo's which do not have corresponding dec's. As the knitting progresses, note that on some rows the number of sts in the shawl increases by 4 and on others by 8.

NOTES *1* Only odd rows are shown on chart. *All even rows* K2, purl to last 2 sts, k2. *2* Work the 6-st reps on rows 13–16 and the section C reps on rows 109–188 as needed.

Shawl

With circular needle, cast on 5 sts. K 1 row. Work Row 1 of Shawl chart, placing marker just before center st. (NOTE The center st is always a knit with a yo on either side of it.) *Row 2 and all following even rows* K2, purl to last 2 sts, k2. Continue to work chart through row 16, then rep rows 13–16 until you have completed 108 rows. At the end of row 108, you should have 319 sts.

Skill level

Intermediate

Finished measurements

40" – center back neck to tip

82" – long edge of triangle

57" – each short edge of triangle

Yarn

Jagger Spun Zephyr (4oz/115g;
1175yds/1070m; 50% wool/
50% silk) Garnet

Needles

Size 4 (3.5mm)
circular needle, 24"/40cm,
or size to obtain gauge
Optional: One double-pointed
needle (dpn), size 4 (3.5mm),
for edging

Extras

Stitch marker

Rust-proof T-pins

Blocked gauge

5 sts to 1"/2.5cm in Shawl chart pat
using size 4 (3.5cm). It is difficult to state
an exact gauge for knitting lace. The
actual finished size is determined by how
vigorously the wet lace is pinned and
stretched. We find that lace stretches
about one-third larger than the
finished knitting.

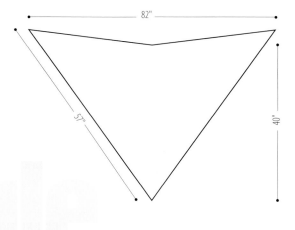

Shawl

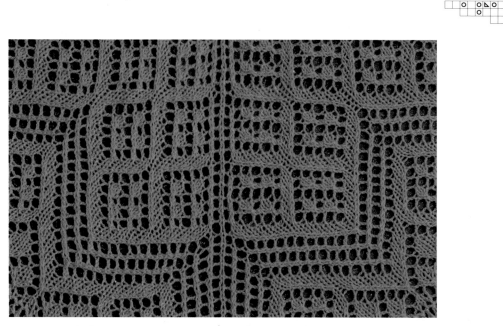

☐ K
⊙ Yo
✓ K2tog
⊠ Ssk
⊠ Sl1-k2tog-psso

When you set out
on the annual family trip naturally
you have to take your knitting;
something has to keep you sane in
face of the possibly quite ferocious
situations you will be up against in
the next two weeks.
Try a shawl. Do not scoff;
it is perfect travel-knitting,
as I have proved to myself
many times.

Elizabeth Zimmermann,
Knitter's Almanac

Lace Edging

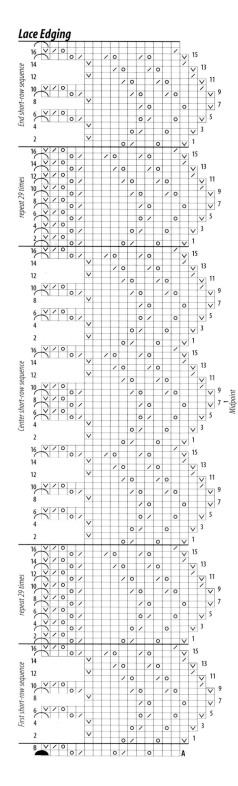

Beginning with row 109, only half of each row is charted. Reading from right to left, work A, B, C (repeat as necessary until 9 sts before marker), and D. You should now be at the center marker. Knit E as foll: yo, slip marker, k1, yo. Work 2nd half of shawl to correspond to first half: reading from right to left, work D, C, and B. There should be 2 sts remaining: end each row yo, k2. Work as established through row 188, when you should have 483 sts. Do not break yarn.

Lace Edging

(NOTES *1* It is easier to use the dpn for row A and all odd rows on edging. *2* Compensating short rows are added at beginning, middle, and end of lace edging to shape the lace gracefully. Follow the sequence of rows as given and you should reach the midpoint at the center marker. If you don't come out just right—fudge! It won't be noticeable.)

Continuing with shawl yarn on circular needle, cast on 15 sts. Work row A, knitting last st tog with 2 sts from shawl, turn. Work row B, slipping first st wyib. Continue to work Lace Edging chart as established through end short-row sequence. At this point you will be at outside edge and will have 16 lace edging sts and 1 shawl st remaining. Change to circular needle only. Using free end of circular needle, k 15 edging sts, k last edging st tog with remaining shawl st. Continuing across long edge of shawl, pick up and k 1 st for every garter ridge across the entire long edge. Carefully pick up and k 16 sts from cast-on edge of lace edging. The exact number of total sts isn't critical at this point. Turn and k across entire edge as foll: k1, k into front and back of every st until you reach last st, k1. Turn. Bind off entire edge loosely as foll: using the dpn, k1, *place st just knit back on left needle, knit this st tog with next st; rep from* until all sts are bound off.

Finishing

Weave in ends and block, using lots of pins and allowing shawl to dry thoroughly before removing pins.

□ K on RS and on WS
○ Yo
╱ K2tog
╲ Ssk
▲ S1-k2tog-psso
v Slip purlwise wyib
◠ K st tog with 1 shawl st
◖ K st tog with 2 shawl sts

Shawl

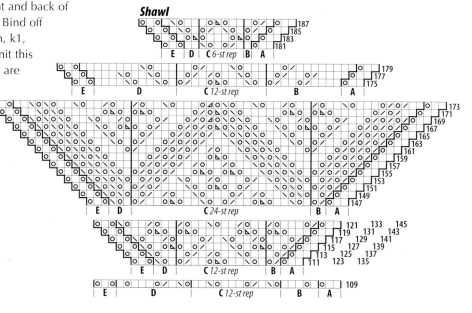

Skill level

Easy-Intermediate

Finished measurements

73" in diameter, point to point

Yarn

Jamieson & Smith Jumperweight

Shetland (1oz/28g; 150yds/138m; wool)

1 skein each:

Red #93, Orange #73, Yellow #91,

Green #79, Blue #18, and

Purple #20. 7 skeins Black #77.

Needles

Size 8 (5mm) needles in double-pointed

(dpn) and circular, 16", 24", and 60"

(40cm, 60cm, and 152cm) long,

or size to obtain gauge

One size 10½ (6.5mm) needle

for binding off

Extras

Stitch markers

Small amount of crochet cotton

or string

Rust-proof T-pins

Blocked gauge

16 sts to 4"/10cm in

St st using size 8 (5mm) needles.

NOTES *1* Shawl is knit from center outward. The center motif is an octagonal pin-wheel, changing to a chevron for the rest of the piece. *2* Change from dpn to increasingly longer circular needles as number of sts permits. *3* See *Techniques,* p. 162, for circular beginnings and sl2tog-k1-p2sso.

Shawl

With circular beginning, dpn, and black yarn, cast on 8 sts and distribute evenly. Place marker for beginning of rnd. **Begin Chart A:** *Rnd 1* Work chart 8 times around—16 sts. Continue to work chart as established through rnd 31—128 sts. Remove marker, k 3 sts, then replace marker—beginning of rnd moved 3 sts to the left. **Begin Chart B1–B2:** *Rnd 32* Work chart 16 times around—160 sts. Continue to work charts through rnd 159 as established, changing colors as indicated—800 sts at final rnd. Bind off loosely using size 10½ needle.

Finishing

Wash and block the shawl to size, pinning out each point.

Color changes in circular knitting present the ubiquitous problem of the jog, the jag, the dog-leg, or the step as it is called. The best place to hide the jog in lace or eyelet knitting is between a knit stitch and a yarn-over because the yarn-over does not appear on the same elevation as the knit stitch, but appears as the base or bottom of the knit stitch on the round above it. This is a bit of visual cheating, but it works well. However, it creates the problem of how to hide a yarn tail at a yarn-over. The way to solve this problem is by *back-winding, back-wrapping,* or *back-splicing* the tails of both colors before they are ever knitted. Do all the color changes as described on the next page. They will never come out, and you will not have to deal with all those ends. When you finish knitting, you don't have any finishing to do.

Change color between a knit stitch and a yarn over...

...and back-wind both yarns...

...for an invisible join.

Chart B2

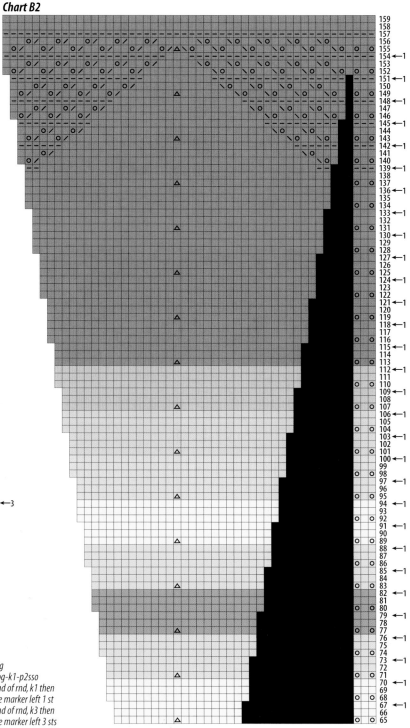

Color Changes in Lace

Here is Robert Powell's method for color changes in lace: For the first color change, k to the end of rnd 46, remove the marker and k 1 more st (indicated in the chart by ←1). *1* Break Black leaving a generous tail. Tie a bow tie marker of crochet cotton around Black yarn at the point Black yarn exits the last st knitted. Push this tie close to the st and tighten it; it marks the exact point that the color change will occur. *2* Now unpick last 10 or so sts, being very careful not to let cotton slide out of position. This will give you a length of yarn on which to back-wind the yarn tail. *3* Make a loop in Black yarn with cotton knot at center of loop. Pass a generous length of Purple yarn through this loop (A). *4* Wind Black tail back onto Black yarn, wrapping in the direction the yarn was plied (B; the "S" direction for Jamieson & Smith). After 5 or 6 wraps, separate the 2 plies in the tail. Pull on one of the plies to break it (C). Continue to wrap shorter ply around until it disappears. Pull on remaining ply to thin it out, and then wrap it around until it disappears. Untie and remove cotton. *5* Lick your fingers and rub along the yarn, then put the yarn in the palm of your hand and rub it. This will set the twist. Do the same back-wind technique with Purple tail, and then you are ready to knit (D). There are no longer any tails hanging out. As you approach the end of the rnd, adjust your tension if necessary. The last knit st should be entirely Black and the yarn-over should be entirely Purple.

- ☐ Red
- ☐ Orange
- ☐ Yellow
- ☐ Green
- ☐ Blue
- ☐ Purple
- ☐ Black

Chart B1

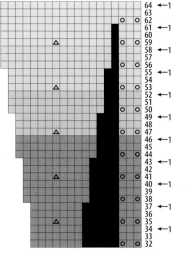

Chart A

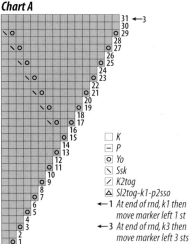

- ☐ K
- ☐ P
- ⊙ Yo
- ◢ Ssk
- ◣ K2tog
- △ Sl2tog-k1-p2sso
- ←1 At end of rnd, k1 then move marker left 1 st
- ←3 At end of rnd, k3 then move marker left 3 sts

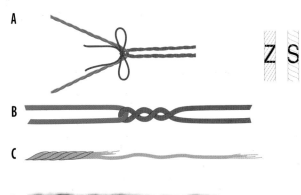

A
B
C
D

Z S

A sober black shawl hides

her body entirely,

Touch'd by th' sun an' th' salt

spray of th' sea;

But deep in th' darkness

a slim hand, so lovely,

Carries a rich bunch of

red roses for me!

Sean O'Casey,

Red Roses for Me, act IV

Skill level

Intermediate

Finished measurements

83" in diameter

Yarn

Jamieson & Smith Jumperweight

Shetland (1oz/28g; 150yds/137m; wool)

15 skeins Persimmon #125

Needles

Size 8 (5mm) needles in

double-pointed (dpn)

and circular, 16" and 24"

(40cm and 60cm) long,

or size to obtain gauge

Optional: One size 4 or 5 (3.5 or 3.75mm)

dpn, for edging

Extras

Size H/8 (5mm) crochet hook

Stitch marker

Rust-proof T-pins

Blocked gauge

16 sts to 4"/10cm in

St st using size 8 (5mm) needles.

NOTES *1* Shawl is knit from center outward. Change from dpn to increasingly longer circular needles as number of sts permits. *2* See *Techniques,* p. 162, for chain st, circular beginnings, and sl2tog-k1-p2sso.

Using circular beginning and dpn, cast on 12 sts and distribute evenly. Place marker for beginning of rnd and k 1 rnd. *1st inc rnd* *Yo, k1; rep from*—24 sts. K 2 rnds. *2nd inc rnd* *Yo, k1, yo, k2; rep from*—40 sts. K 3 rnds. *3rd inc rnd* *Yo, k2; rep from*—60 sts. K 4 rnds. *4th inc rnd* *Yo, k2, yo, k3; rep from*—84 sts. K 5 rnds. *5th inc rnd* *Yo, k3; rep from*—112 sts. K 6 rnds. *6th inc rnd* *Yo, k3, yo, k4; rep from*— 144 sts. K 7 rnds. *7th inc rnd* *Yo, k4; rep from*—180 sts. K 8 rnds. *8th inc rnd* *Yo, k4, yo, k5; rep from*—220 sts. K 9 rnds. *9th inc rnd* *Yo, k5; rep from*—264 sts. K 10 rnds. *10th inc rnd* *Yo, k5, yo, k6; rep from*—312 sts. K 11 rnds. *11th inc rnd* *Yo, k6; rep from*—364 sts. K 12 rnds. *12th inc rnd* *Yo, k6, yo, k7; rep from*—420 sts. K 13 rnds. *13th inc rnd* *Yo, k7; rep from*—480 sts. K 14 rnds. *14th inc rnd* *Yo, k7, yo, k8; rep from*—544 sts. K 15 rnds. *15th inc rnd* *Yo, k8; rep from*—612 sts. K 16 rnds.

Begin Chart A: *Rnd 1* Work 20-st rep 34 times around—680 sts. Continue to work through rnd 18 of chart as established, then remove marker, k 10 sts, and replace marker—beginning of rnd moved 10 sts to the left. *Next rnd: Rnd 1* Work 22-st rep 34 times around—748 sts. Continue to work through rnd 18 of chart, then remove marker, k 11 sts, and replace marker—beginning of rnd moved 11 sts to the left. **Begin Chart B:** *Rnd 1* Work 22-st rep 34 times around. Continue to work through rnd 18 of chart. Do not break yarn.

Crocheted Edging

(NOTES *1* The crochet edging is easier to work if raw sts are first slipped onto a smaller dpn. *2* To work slip st on 1 st, slip hook through st as if to knit, yo hook and draw through the two loops on hook. To work slip st on 3 sts, slip hook through next 2 sts as if to k2tog, then slip hook through 3rd st as if to knit, yo hook and draw through the four loops on hook.)

Using crochet hook and following markings at top of Chart B, crochet off edge sts with chain loops as foll: work slip st on the number of sts enclosed by each bracket, then work the number of chain sts indicated by the number to the left of the bracket. After final chain, join to base of first slip st and fasten off.

Finishing

Block shawl, pinning out each chain loop of the edging.

Chart A

20-st rep

22-st rep

Chart B

22-st rep

☐ *K*

✓ *K2tog*

◣ *Ssk*

○ *Yo*

♀ *K in back of st*

△ *Sl2tog-k1-p2sso*

There is nothing else knitted

that I like to dream up, plan,

knit, finish, wear, use,

or give as a gift

so much as a shawl…

A shawl can also serve as a pillow,

picnic cloth, umbrella (of sorts),

carrying bag, or seat cushion.

In a pinch, a shawl can be mosquito

netting, an evening wrap,

and a dressing gown

(or even a dressing room)

all on the same trip!

Martha Waterman,

Traditional Knitted Lace Shawls

Keep warm on cool evenings wrapped in Cat's Paws! This elegant, reversible, beaded shrug (a stole with sleeves) is knitted from cuff to cuff. The cuff is beaded in a simple lace rib in which either side works well as the public side—knitter's choice. The shrug's body is beaded and worked in an all-over Cat's Paw (a very old Shetland lace pattern) on garter st.

3-st I-Cord Selvage

K3, work in pat to last 3 sts, slip 3 sts purlwise wyif, turn. Rep to form I-Cord at end of each row.

NOTES **1** Use a dental floss threader purchased at a local drugstore to thread yarn through each bead before knitting with skein. **2** The cuffs are worked in the round, and the body of the shrug is worked flat with 3-st I-Cord selvage on the sides.

First Cuff

Thread about 175 beads onto skein. (Thread about 140 beads onto subsequent skeins.) With smaller dpn, cast on 60 sts and distribute evenly. Place marker and join. This marker indicates the beginning of each rnd and also marks the position where the shrug will be split and worked flat. **Begin Lace Rib chart** Work in chart pat until piece measures 3", end on a rnd 1.

Body

Place markers for I-Cord selvage 3 sts before and after existing marker; remove original marker; begin working flat. *Next row* Knit, inc 26 sts evenly between markers, slip last 3 sts purlwise wyif—86 sts. Turn. *Next row* Knit, inc 57 sts evenly between markers, slip last 3 sts purlwise wyif—143 sts. Turn. Change to larger dpn. **Begin Cat's Paw chart:** *Row 1* K3 (selvage sts), work next 4 sts of row, work 10-st rep 13 times, work next 3 sts of row, slip last 3 sts purlwise wyif (selvage sts). Continue to work chart as established, changing from dpn to larger regular needles after 2 or 3 pat reps for ease in working, and when piece measures 36 (38, 40, 42)" from end of rib, end on a row 6 or 12 of pat. Change to smaller regular needles. *Next row* Knit, dec 57 sts evenly between markers, slip last 3 sts purlwise wyif—86 sts. *Next row* Knit, dec 26 sts evenly between markers, slip last 3 sts purlwise wyif—60 sts. Remove markers.

Second Cuff

Thread 175 beads onto skein, change to smaller dpn, place marker for beginning of rnd, and begin working in the round. **Begin Lace Rib chart** Work in chart pat, with same side facing as first cuff, until cuff measures same as first cuff, end on a rnd 1. Bind off in rnd 1 pat.

Finishing

Weave ends invisibly. Fold shrug in half lengthwise and block to approx 12½" wide by desired length. Sew sleeve seam at each cuff to 4" or length to obtain desired fit. Sew elastic thread around cuff to tighten if desired.

Skill level

Intermediate

Finished measurements

Approximately 25" wide by 55 (58, 60, 63)" long or desired length. To calculate finished cuff-to-cuff shrug length, multiply unblocked body measurement by 1.36, then add 6" for the cuffs.

Yarn

Knit One, Crochet Too® Richesse et Soie (¾oz/25g; 146yds/133m; 65% cashmere, 35% silk) 8 (9, 9, 10) skeins Black #9900

Needles

Sizes 4 and 6 (3.5 and 4mm) needles in double-pointed (dpn) and regular, *or size to obtain gauge*

Extras

900 (1100, 1100, 1200) 6° seed beads

Beading needle or floss threader

Stitch markers

Optional: Elastic thread

Blocked gauge

36 sts to 4"/10cm in Lace Rib pat using size 4 (3.5mm) needles; 20 sts to 4"/10cm in Cat's Paw pat using size 6 (4mm) needles.

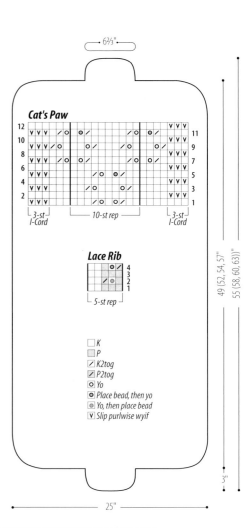

Cat's Paw

Lace Rib

☐ K
☐ P
✓ K2tog
✓ P2tog
○ Yo
◉ Place bead, then yo
◎ Yo, then place bead
v Slip purlwise wyif

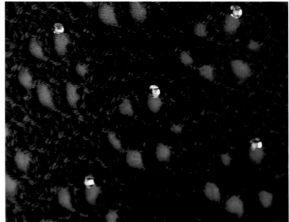

When, full of warm

and eager love,

I clasp you in my fond embrace,

You gently push me back and say,

'Take care, my dear,

you'll spoil my lace.

William Wetmore Story,

Snowdrop

Stringing Beads

*Step A: Thread one end of skein through
the loop of the floss threader.*
*Step B: Slide tip of the floss threader
through each bead, then slide bead onto skein.*
*Step C: When the desired number of beads
is threaded onto the skein, the beads are ready
to be slid into place as you knit.*

Bejeweled Cat's Paws

A GATHERING OF LACE **Traditions**

Skill level

Intermediate

Finished measurements

LARGE 47" deep by 90" wide

SMALL 24" deep by 63" wide

Yarn

LARGE Schoolhouse Press Unspun

Icelandic (3½oz/100g; 300yds/273m;

wool) 4 wheels, Silver Grey

SMALL Cashmere America 100%

cashmere 2-ply [1¾oz/50g; 437yds/

400m; cashmere) 2 skeins Oatmeal

Needles

LARGE Size 10 (6mm)

circular needle, 29"/72cm,

SMALL Size 3 (3.25mm)

circular needle, 24"/60cm,

or sizes to obtain gauge

Extras

Tapestry needle

4 markers, 3 of one color,

1 of a contrasting color

Rust-proof T-pins

Blocked gauge

LARGE 15 sts to 4"/10cm in garter st

using size 10 (6mm) needle.

SMALL 24 sts to 4"/10cm in garter st

using size 3 (3.25mm) needle.

Construction notes

This shawl is worked back and forth in garter st on circular needles, beginning at lower edge. It is edged on each side by a garter st band, and the Side Panel chart is worked on both sides of the Center Panel. The size of this shawl depends on the yarn and needles used; both shawls are made in exactly the same way.

NOTES *1* Only odd-numbered rows are charted. All even rows are worked as foll: Sl 1 purlwise, k to end. *2* See *Techniques*, p. 162, for cable cast-on, garter st grafting, and sl2tog-k1-p2sso.

Using cable method, cast on 421 sts. *Next row* (WS) K5, place marker (pm), k193 (side panel), pm, k25 (center panel), pm, k193 (side panel), place contrast color marker, k5. (NOTE Beginning with next row, the first st of every row is slipped purlwise throughout.) K 2 more rows. **Begin charts:** *Row 1* (RS) Sl 1, k4, work Side Panel chart over 193 sts, work Center Panel chart over 25 sts, work Side Panel chart again, end k5. Continue to work charts through row 192 as established, remembering to knit all even rows and to slip the first st of each row.

Next row Sl 1, k4, sl2tog-k1-p2sso, k5. *Next row* Sl 1, k to end. *Next row* Sl 1, k3, k2tog, graft the 5 sts on right needle to the 5 sts on left needle. Weave in ends and block.

It might be assumed that the finest
lace knitting would be found in rich
areas where the sophistication of
court life and the money spent on
trimmings of the latest fashion go
hand in hand. But this is not so.
It is to the most remote areas that
attention must be turned, to Iceland,
to Russia, to the Faroe Islands and to
the most northerly of the islands of the
Shetland group, Unst. It is here in
quiet homes, often far from the
nearest neighbour, that gossamer
fine wool is transformed into
cobweb-like beauty....

Rae Compton,
The Complete Book of Traditional Knitting

Center Back Panel

Side Panel

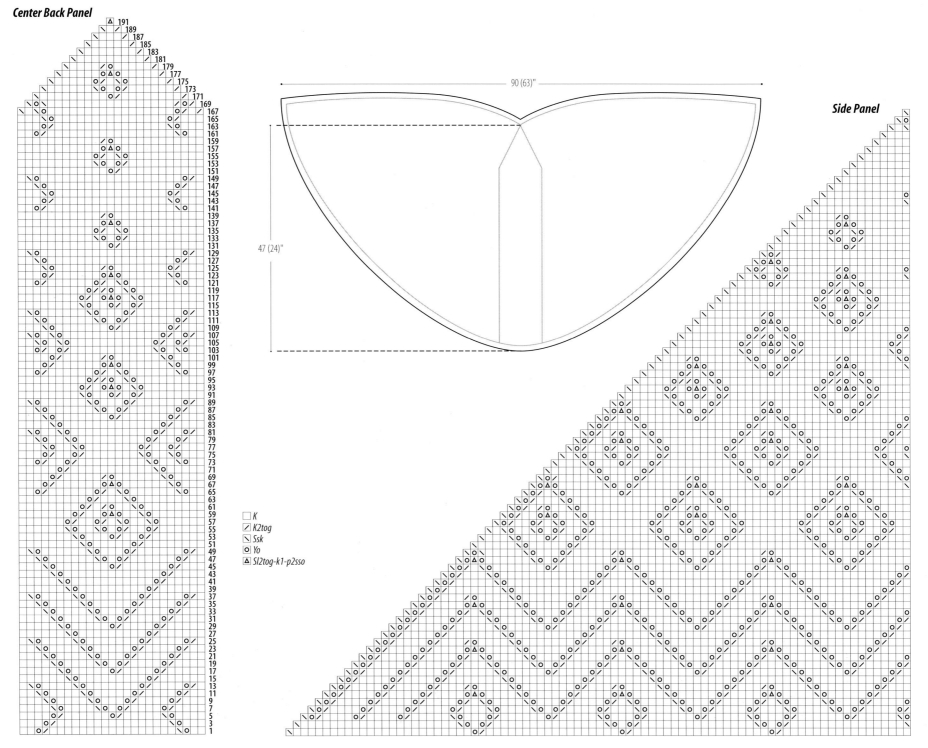

90 (63)"

47 (24)"

□ K
⊿ K2tog
◩ Ssk
⊙ Yo
▲ Sl2tog-k1-p2sso

Marilyn van Keppel

Cobweb Doily

Skill level

Intermediate

Finished measurements

17" in diameter

Yarn

Jamieson & Smith Cobweb-weight Shetland

(½oz/14g; 225yds/205m; wool)

1 skein White

Needles

Size 2 (2.75mm) double-pointed needles (dpn), preferably wood,

or size to obtain gauge

Extras

7 markers, 6 of one color and one of a contrasting color

(Yarn loops work well here.)

Rust-proof T-pins

Blocked gauge

6 sts to 1"/2.5cm in 6-st rep from chart A using size 2 (2.75mm) needles.

NOTES *1* The doily is knit circularly from the center out. *2* All even rounds are worked even in St st. *3* We do not recommend knitting this doily pattern at a larger gauge for a full-sized shawl. *4* See *Techniques,* p. 162, for circular beginnings.

Using circular beginning and dpn, cast on 7 sts and distribute evenly. Place marker (pm) for beginning of rnd. **Begin Chart A** Work rnd 1 seven times—14 sts. ***Rnd 2 and all even rnds*** Knit all sts. Work rnd 3 seven times—28 sts. While working rnd 4, pm as foll: mark the beginning of the rnd with the contrast color marker, and place the other 6 markers every 4th st. Continue to work Chart A through rnd 48, then rep rnds 25–36 once more, working two additional 6-st reps—33 sts between markers.

Change to Chart B Work in rnds, knitting all sts on even rnds as before. Beginning with rnd 15, each leaf is worked back and forth separately in rows. The first st of each odd row is slipped purlwise, and every even row is purled. After completing row 25 of first leaf and with RS facing, pick up sts along the left edge of leaf and bind off all sts loosely from this leaf and begin to work the next leaf. When all 3 leaves in a section are complete, also bind off loosely the remaining 3 sts at the end of the section; repeat the above instructions for remaining sections.

Finishing instructions

Block and fasten ends.

Chart A

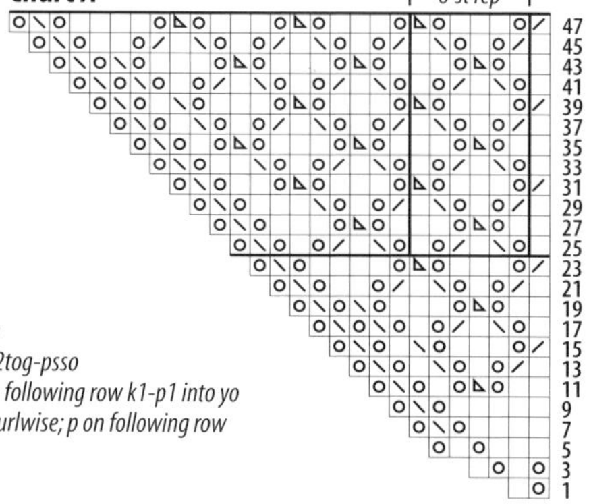

- K
- Yo
- Ssk
- K2tog
- Sl1-k2tog-psso
- Yo; on following row k1-p1 into yo
- Slip purlwise; p on following row
- No st

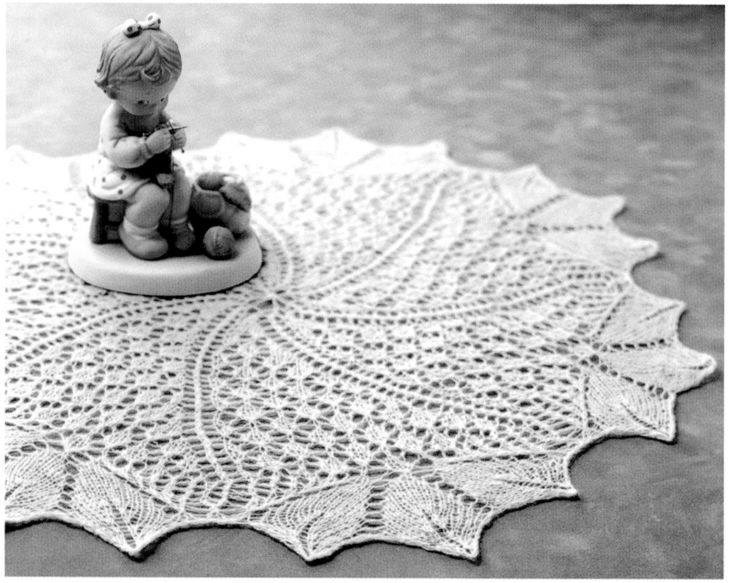

Chart B

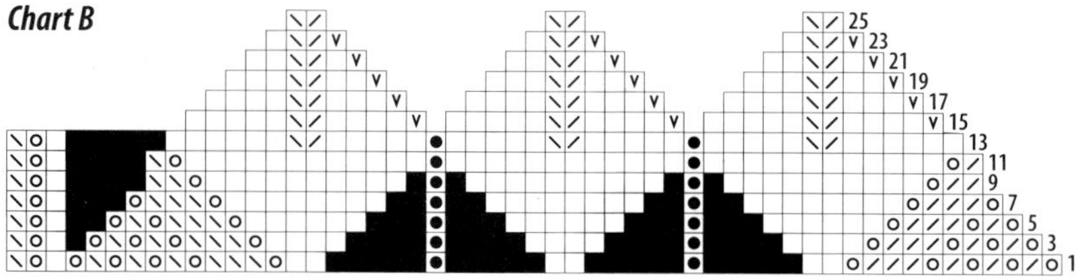

The word doily
(variously spelt doiley,
doyly, doyley and even,
erroneously, d'oily, d'oiley,
d'oyly or d'oilie)....

Tessa Lorant,
Knitted Lace Doilies

Skill level

Intermediate

Finished measurements

60" in diameter

Yarn

Morehouse Lace Yarn (1oz/28g;

230yds/209m; merino wool)

7 skeins Chocolate Brown

Needles

Size 3 (3.25mm) needles

in double-pointed (dpn) and circular,

16" and 24" (40 and 60cm),

or size to obtain gauge

Extras

Stitch marker

Point protector

Waste yarn

Rust-proof T-pins

Blocked gauge

24 sts to 4"/10cm in St st using

size 3 (3.25mm) needles.

NOTES **1** The shawl is knit circularly from the center out. After shawl is made, the sideways edging is attached as it is worked. **2** Change from dpn to increasingly longer circular needles as number of sts permits. **3** If you want a larger shawl, you can repeat Diamond Madeira chart one more time, and your shawl will increase in diameter to 92". This will require an additional 3 or 4 oz of yarn. **4** See *Techniques*, p. 162, for circular beginnings, double yo, grafting, invisible cast-on, and sl2tog-k1-p2sso.

Inc rnd

Yo, k1; rep from—number of sts doubled.

Shawl

Using circular beginning and dpn, cast on 9 sts and distribute evenly. Place marker for beginning of rnd, and k 1 rnd. Work 1st inc rnd—18 sts. K 3 rnds. Work 2nd inc rnd—36 sts. K 6 rnds. Work 3rd inc rnd—72 sts. K 12 rnds. Work 4th inc rnd—144 sts. K 4 rnds, inc 6 sts evenly over 4th rnd—150 sts. **Begin Shetland Fern chart:** *Rnd 1* Work 15-st rep 10 times. Continue to work chart as established through rnd 16. K 4 rnds, dec 5 sts evenly on first rnd—145 sts. Work 5th inc rnd—290 sts. K 4 rnds. **Begin Horseshoe chart:** *Rnd 1* Work 10-st rep 29 times. Continue to work chart as established through rnd 8, then work rnds 1–8 four times more. K 4 rnds, dec 3 sts evenly on first rnd—287 sts. Work 6th inc rnd—574 sts. K 6 rnds. **Begin Diamond Madeira chart:** *Rnd 1* Work 14-st rep 41 times. Continue to work chart as established through rnd 36. K 6 rnds. Break yarn.

Edging

Put a point protector on the left needle tip. Using a dpn, invisibly cast on 17 sts. **Begin Beechleaf Edging chart** Holding the right tip of the circular needle in your right hand and dpn in your left, work row 1 of chart as follows: K first st from dpn tog with last worked st of

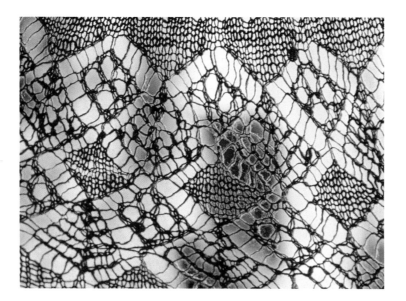

This shawl is made with Elizabeth Zimmermann's Pi Shawl shaping. I simply incorporated some traditional Shetland lace patterns into the areas between the increases.

"It's Pi; the geometry of the circle hinging on the mysterious relationship of the circumference of a circle to its radius. A circle will double its circumference in infinitely themselves-doubling distances, or, in knitters' terms, the distance between the increase-rounds, in which you double the number of sts, goes 3, 6, 12, 24, 48, 96 rounds, and so on to 192, 394, 788, 1576 rounds for all I know. Theory is theory and I have no intention of putting it into practice, as I do not plan to make a lace carpet for a football field."

Elizabeth Zimmermann,
A Knitter's Almanac

The thought beneath

so slight a film—

Is more distinctly seen—

As laces just reveal the surge—

Or Mists—the Apennine—

Emily Dickinson,

No. 210 (c.1860)

Shetland Tea Shawl

shawl, work to end of row. Every odd row of the edging pattern will start with this k2tog, joining the edging and the open sts of the last round of the shawl, and you will be working the rows back and forth from dpn to circular needle. The edging will march clockwise around the perimeter of the shawl as you work the 10-row rep of the edging 115 times. When you finish the final rep of edging chart, you will be one shawl st short, but you can fudge it with an extra darning st when you graft the two ends of the edging together. Break yarn, leaving a tail long enough for grafting. Place invisibly cast-on sts on 2nd dpn. Graft the end of the edging to the beginning.

Finishing

Weave in ends. Block, pinning out each point.

Shetland Fern

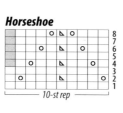

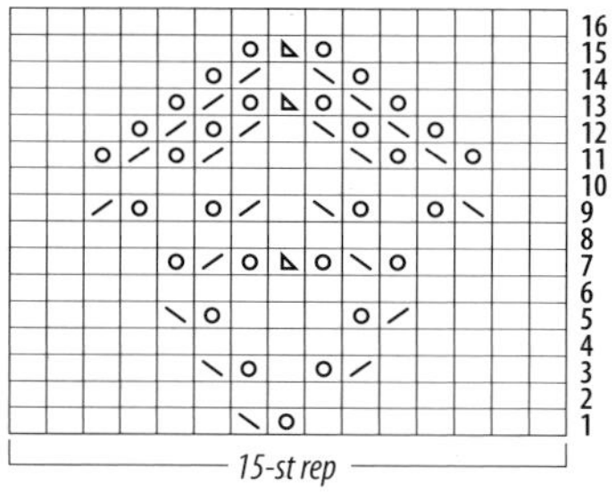

15-st rep

Horseshoe

10-st rep

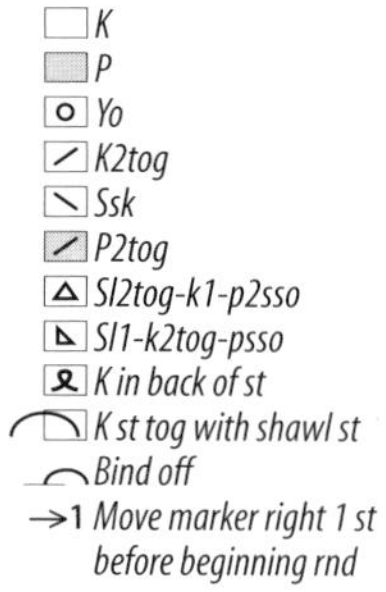

☐ K
▨ P
○ Yo
╱ K2tog
╲ Ssk
▨ P2tog
△ Sl2tog-k1-p2sso
� Sl1-k2tog-psso
ℜ K in back of st
⌒ K st tog with shawl st
⌢ Bind off
→1 Move marker right 1 st
    before beginning rnd

Diamond Madeira

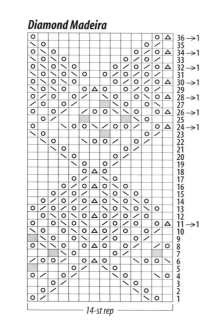

14-st rep

Beechleaf Edging

17 sts

Skill level

Experienced

Finished measurements

20" wide x 68" long. For a shorter stole or scarf, omit one or more repeats of the central panel pattern.

Yarn

Jamieson & Smith Cobweb-weight Shetland (½oz/14g; 225yds/205m; wool) 6 skeins White

Needles

Size 2 (2.75mm) needles, *or size to obtain gauge*

Optional: Two size 2 (2.75mm) double-pointed needles (dpn), for the edging

Extras

Waste yarn for cast-on

Tapestry needle

Stitch holder or waste yarn for holding stitches

Stitch markers

For dressing: Powdered starch or cornstarch, rust-proof T-pins or dressing frame, knitting cotton for lashing.

Blocked gauge

32 sts and 48 rows to 4"/10cm in garter st, using size 2 (2.75mm) needles.

Construction notes

This stole, knit on a garter st ground, has no bound-off edges. The central panel is knit first and the first border worked directly afterwards. Sts are picked up from the cast-on edge of the central panel for the second border. The vandyked lace edging can be knit with shaped and mitered corners around the periphery of the stole, or it can be knit straight, separately, and sewn on.

NOTES *1* Do not slip sts at beginning of rows unless specified. The knitting will be subject to considerable stretching during dressing; slipped sts decrease elasticity. *2* See *Techniques,* p. 162, for invisible cast-on and garter st grafting.

Central Panel

With longer needles, invisibly cast on 99 sts. K 1 row. **Begin Central Panel chart (p. 44):** *Row 1* Work first st of chart, then work 14-st rep 7 times. It may be useful to place markers after each rep. Continue to work through row 46 of chart as established, work rows 1–46 six times more, then rows 1–22 once more.

This stole is the first of three Shetland lace designs from Hazel Carter. Her comments on Shetland lace follow:

Shetlanders have been knitting for centuries, but the development of the fine knitted lace began, as far as is known, about 1830. The chief center was the northernmost island of Unst, and the craft was a source of much-needed income for the islanders, whose livelihood otherwise depended mostly, and very precariously, on fishing. After the 1939–1945 war, the lace knitting as an industry suffered a decline, and although there has been a revival, it is now a pastime rather than the means of earning a living. Some Shetland patterns are, in the words of Mary Thomas, 'lace fabric,' where a pattern row alternates with a plain row, knit or purl; others are '[true[lace' in which each row is a pattern row. Examples of the former used here are Lace Mesh, Bird's-eye, and Four Flowers (or Peerie Flea); the true lace patterns include Shetland Bead, Lace Fan (or Madeira) and Ring or Daisy. The famous Shetland Fern combines both lace fabric and true lace. Since Shetland lace has to be stretched, it is important that the fabric be elastic; hence either there is no casting on and binding off, or else they are kept to a minimum. The only suitable cast-on method is the invisible or 'temporary' cast-on, over waste yarn.

Border

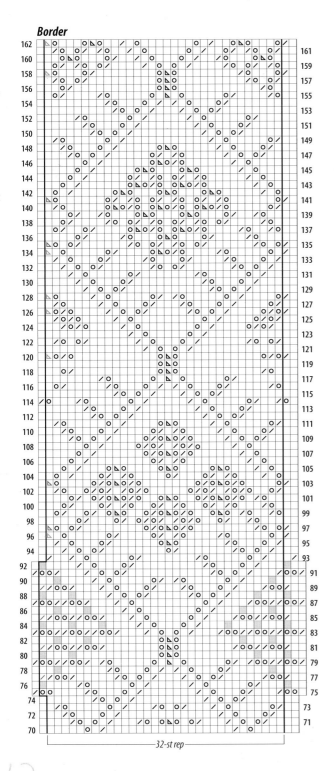

Border

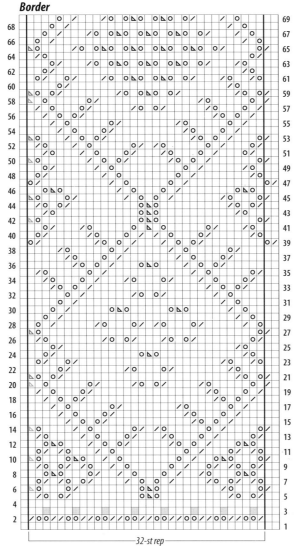

☐ K
☐ P
◉ Yo
☑ K2tog
☑ K2tog; on last repeat, k
◣ Sl1-k2tog-psso
◣ Sl1-k2tog-psso;
   on last repeat, k2tog
◣ Sl1-k2tog-psso; on first repeat, k2tog

First Border

Begin Border chart: Row 1 Work first 2 sts of chart, work 32-st rep 3 times, then work last st of chart. Continue to work through row 162 of chart as established, then k 2 rows, dec 4 sts evenly over the 2nd row—95 sts. Break yarn and place sts on a holder.

Second Border

With RS facing, pick up 99 sts from the invisible cast-on, turn and k 1 row. Continue to work as for first border. Break yarn. Work either the knitted-on edging, or the separate sewn-on edging.

Sewn-on Edging

With dpn, invisibly cast on 16 sts. **Begin Edging chart** Work 86 reps of rows 1–20, working last st of each even row as a plain knit st instead of joining to stole. This length allows for 7 reps across the top and bottom, 34 along each side and one for gathering at each corner. Place the sts from row 20 of the last rep on a holder or waste yarn, and do not break yarn until you have sewn all the edging on in case you need to add or undo some. Sew row to row along the sides, taking the needle through the bars of alternate rows, and sew 3 sts to every 4 rows along top and bottom by taking the needle alternately through one bar plus two sts, then one bar plus one st. When edging has been sewn on, graft the end of the edging to the cast-on.

Knitted-on Shaped Edging

(NOTES **1** Starting rows a–d of the Edging chart are used to establish the correct position for the final edging corner. They are identical to rows 37–40 of the Edging Corner chart. **2** The last st of each even row connects to the stole. To join the edging with a single st on top and bottom of stole, k last edging st tog with stole st. To join with two stole sts, slip last edging st, k 2 stole sts tog, psso. To join the edging at sides of stole, slip last edging st, k through next bar on stole, psso. **3** The mitering of the Edging Corner is achieved by dec the number of edging sts to 2. At the apex of the corner on row 20, sts are picked up from this dec slope through both the bars and knots. These picked-up sts are added back into the edging, 2 at a time, on subsequent incoming rows.) With dpn, invisibly cast on 18 sts.

Many women had to contend

with feeding their livestock,

helping out on the croft,

performing the duties around

the home and looking after chil-

dren—all the time continuing

to do their knitting....

The best lace knitters, however,

were unable to do the chores

around the croft since the

fineness of the lace yarn demands

the very softest of hands,

which must be treated with

great care since they are

the tools of the trade.

Sarah Don,
The Art of Shetland Lace

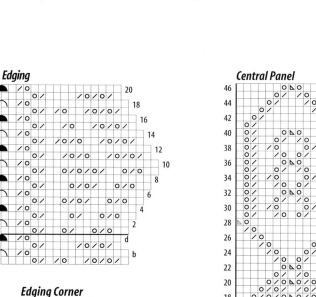

Edging

Edging Corner

Central Panel

— 14-st rep —

□ K
○ Yo
╱ K2tog
◣ Sl1-k2tog-psso
◪ Sl1-k2tog-psso; on first repeat, k2tog
◠ K st tog with 1 stole st
● On top & bottom only, k st tog with
2 stole sts; on sides, k st tog with 1 stole st
┌ Pick up and k st from slope below

Dressing Frame

20"

68"

Begin Edging chart: *Row a* Beginning by joining the edging to the open sts of the 2nd border, work starting rows a–d, then work rows 1–20 six times, adjusting if necessary so that 2 stole sts remain at the end of the last rep. Work Edging Corner chart, then work rows 1–20 of Edging chart 34 times along side of stole, adjusting if necessary so that one bar remains on the stole at the end of the final rep. Continue to work Edging Corner chart and Edging chart around the stole as established, ending the 4th corner with row 37 of Edging Corner chart. This should bring you to the starting point of the edging. Do not break the yarn. Graft the end of the edging to the cast-on.

Finishing

Wash if required and starch lightly as described under Dressing. Pin out to measurements or lash to a frame. If using a dressing frame, you might wish to add a hanging cord at one short end. The stole will dry more quickly if hung up so that air can pass through it. It will also be out of the way of your children, husband, cats, dogs, etc., who will then be less likely to trample on it or use it for claw-sharpening.

Dressing Frame (optional, see diagram)

A simple version can be made with four wooden laths, 2x6' and 2x2'. Mark 2" in from the ends of all four. Arrange them in an oblong, with the shorter ones on top, so that the marks for the measurement come together on the inside. Nail the corners together, using two nails for each corner, to hold angle firm.

Dressing Shetland Lace

An extremely important part of the making of lace is the *dressing* or blocking of the article to bring out its full beauty. If necessary the knitting may be gently washed in lukewarm water, rinsed, squeezed—never wrung— to extract excess water, then immersed in a weak starch solution. I prefer powdered starch or cornstarch (UK cornflour) to the spray kind, but there are no Shetland lace police to fine you if you want to use it. Use one heaped tablespoon (one UK dessert spoon) mixed with a little cold water. Over this, pour one pint of boiling water, stirring, then add 3 pints of cold water. Leave the knitting to absorb the starch for at least ten minutes. You may want to experiment with the quantities, depending on how stiff or soft you want the finished article to be.

Rectangular items such as shawls, stoles, and scarves are most conveniently dressed on a frame made with internal measurements of the required dimensions, to which the article is lashed with a strong but soft thread through the points. Knitting cotton is suitable for lashing, and since working with a long thread is awkward, I usually take about one yard of thread at a time, tying on further increments as required. The Shetland Baby Robe needs a dressing board (shown on p. 49), which can be readily made from stiff cardboard covered with plastic wrap. Instructions for the type of dressing apparatus needed are also given for the Shetland Lace Shawl (p. 53). It is easier to weave in ends after item is dressed and dry, but still on the dressing frame or board.

Any item sold, or given as a gift, is best accompanied by solemn warnings about the nature of Shetland knitted lace—the fact that it shrivels up to almost nothing when washed, and must be properly dressed again. Otherwise the unwary recipient may regard it as 'ruined,' and cast it into outer darkness.

Construction notes

This baby robe, knit back and forth in rows on a garter st ground, has almost no bound-off edges. The bottom edging is knit first, then sts are picked up along the inside of the edging for the skirt. At the underarm, 40 sts each side are placed on holders, more sts invisibly cast on for the sleeves, and the work continued over the shoulders, dividing for the neck. The sleeve edgings are picked up and knit last. The bodice sts at the back are grafted to those on hold, as are the cast-on to the final sts of each sleeve.

NOTES *1* The central panel chart is a half-chart. Each row, whether RS or WS, is worked from right to left to the center pivot st, then worked backwards from left to right. This center pivot st is worked only once. The 12-st rep in the first 192 rows is worked twice in each direction. *2* The short rows in the edging provide needed elasticity. Shetlanders call this process "lengthening the edge." This is most easily done by knitting (or purling—it makes no difference) the 2nd short row backwards to avoid turning the work. *3* See *Techniques*, p. 162, for double yo, invisible cast-on, and grafting.

Edging

With dpn, invisibly cast on 11 sts. **Begin Edging chart** (p. 48) Work rows A through 14, then work rows 1–14 twenty-five times more—365 rows. At the end of the last rep, you are at the inner straight edge; place the first 10 sts on a holder, then change to longer needles, placing the last worked st on one of them.

Skirt

Pick up 272 sts along the straight inner edge in a ratio of 3 sts for every 4 rows as follows: *k into the bar (not the knot; see drawing, p. 49) at the end of one row, yo, k into the next bar; rep from*—273 sts total. The skirt is divided into 5 panels by 4 vertical bands of the Column chart pat (C). The central panel is an all-over lace panel; the 4 side panels—2 each side of the Central Panel—are garter st interspersed with 6 horizontal bands of Cat's Paw chart pat. Use markers to separate the skirt pats as foll: 34 sts (side panel), 5 sts (C), 58 sts (side panel), 5 sts (C), 69 sts (central panel), 5 sts (C), 58 sts (side panel), 5 sts (C), 34 sts (side panel). It will also be helpful to mark the center st of the central panel. Skirt dec's are

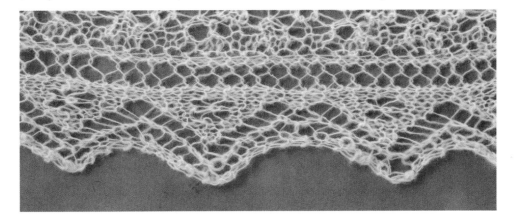

Skill level

Experienced

Finished measurements

Underarm: 20" Length: 39"

Yarn

Jamieson & Smith Cobweb-weight
Shetland (½oz/14g; 225yds/205m; wool)
6 skeins White

Needles

Size 2 (2.75mm) needles,
or size to obtain gauge
Optional: Two size 2 (2.75mm)
double-pointed needles (dpn),
for edging

Extras

Waste yarn for cast-on
Stitch markers and holders
Cardboard for dressing board,
22" x 40"
White satin double-faced ribbon: 2 yds,
⅜" wide and 1 yd, ¼" wide
Powdered starch or cornstarch
Tapestry needle
Optional: Two 12" blocking wires

Blocked gauge

32 sts and 48 rows to 4"/10cm
in garter st using size 2
(2.75mm) needles.

Robes or gowns of this kind were fashionable during the Victorian age for such events as christenings. Since they were intended as heirlooms, hence expected to be worn by babies of various sizes, they were fairly loose, and able to be fitted to the individual infant by means of draw-strings or ribbons. The preferred construction for knitted gowns had no gathers, whether at the waist or elsewhere, since this would have made it difficult to wash and dress in the future, after the gown was made up. Both of these features are replicated in the present robe, which is based on a Shetland christening gown illustrated in *The Art of Knitting*, having a front central pattern, where most of the decoration is concentrated, and which gradually decreases in width towards the waist. Instructions are also given for making a dressing board. Cardboard is preferable to wood, as the arm pieces have to be folded back when the dress is taken off the board.

Central Panel

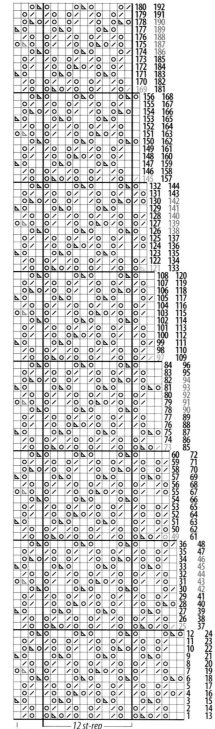

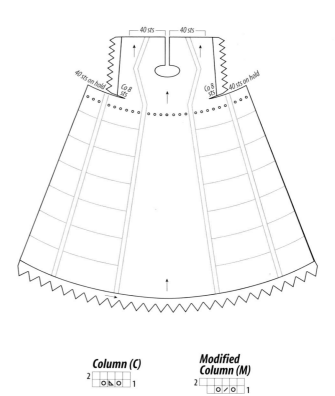

Column (C)

Modified Column (M)

K

Yo

K2tog

Sl1-k2tog-psso

Sl1-k2tog-psso on 1st half of chart row;
k2tog on 2nd half of row

K2tog on 1st row rep;
k on 2nd row rep

K on 1st row rep;
yo on 2nd row rep

Sl1-k2tog-psso on 1st row rep;
k2tog on 2nd row rep

Center st

12 st-rep

worked each side of a Column on all rows marked in blue on the Central Panel chart as follows: k to 2 sts before C, k2tog, work C, k2tog, k to 2 sts before C, k2tog, work C, work Central Panel chart (dec's in the central panel are incorporated into the chart itself), work C, k2tog, k to 2 sts before C, k2tog, work C, k2tog, k to end. The Cat's Paw (CP) rows are worked on the rows marked in pink on the Central Panel chart. Since the set-up for these rows will vary as the skirt narrows, these instructions are written out for the first half of the row up to the central panel. Work the appropriate 6-st CP rep as many times as indicated, and after central panel has been worked, reverse the instructions for the 2nd half of the row, working CP chart reps from left to right as for central panel. On odd rows in the Cat's Paw bands, all side panel sts are knit.

Rows 42 and 46 K1, CP 5 times, k2, C, k1, CP 9 times, k1, C. *Row 44* K1, k2tog, CP 4 times, yo, k3, yo, k2tog, k1, C, k1, k2tog, CP 8 times, yo, k3, yo, k2tog, C. *Rows 90 and 94* K1, CP 5 times, C, k2, CP 8 times, k2, C. *Row 92* K2tog, CP 4 times, yo, k3, yo, k2tog, C, k1, k2tog, CP 7 times, yo, k3, yo, k2tog, k2, C. *Rows 138 and 142* K3, CP 4 times, k2, C, k3, CP 7 times, k3, C. *Row 140* K2, k2tog, CP 3 times, yo, k3, yo, k2tog, k2, C, k2, k2tog, CP 6 times, yo, k3, yo, k2tog, k3, C. *Rows 186 and 190* K2, CP 4

The appeal of Shetland Lace is
obvious, yet its delicacy belies
its strength.
It allows the knitter to create
something beautifully special
which is light and warm to wear,
yet can be washed time and time
again without coming to any
harm and still maintain its
family-heirloom status.
You will have made something
which is more than just a piece
of knitting; it will be an art form,
a garment which had been
worked in the same way
generations before you,
and your participation helps
to keep this
historic craft alive.

Bea Neilson, Knitting Editor,
The People's Friend

Shetland Baby Robe

times, k1, C, k1, CP 7 times, k1, C. *Row 188* K2, k2tog, CP 3 times, yo, k3, k2tog, C, k1, k2tog, CP 6 times, yo, k3, k2tog, C. *Rows 234 and 238* CP 4 times, k1, C, k2, CP 6 times, k2, C. *Row 236* K2tog, CP 3 times, yo, k3, yo, k2tog, C, k2, k2tog, CP 5 times, yo, k3, yo, k2tog, k1, C. *Rows 282 and 286* K2, CP 3 times, k3, C, CP 6 times, C. *Row 284* K2, k2tog, CP 2 times, yo, k3, yo, k2tog, k2, C, k2tog, CP 5 times, yo, k3, yo, k2tog (which will include first st of C), C. Work skirt as established through row 339—161 sts remain.

Bodice

Rows 340–341 K across, keeping Column pat correct (this should be k20, C, k30, C, k41, C, k30, C, k20.) *Row 342* (waist eyelet row) K1, (k2tog, yo twice, k2tog) 40 times. *Row 343* Knit, working k1-p1 into double yo's. *Rows 344–349* Work as for Rows 340–341. The Columns now begin to slant toward the shoulders. This slant is created by working the Modified Column chart pat (M) plus a k2tog on the outer side edge of each M every 6th row as follows: *Row 350* K21, M, k2tog, k26, k2tog, M, k43, M, k2tog, k26, k2tog, M, k21. *Rows 351, 353, and 355* Knit. *Rows 352 and 354* K21, C, k28, C, k43, C, k28, C, k21. *Row 356* K22, M, k2tog, k24, k2tog, M, k45, M, k2tog, k24, k2tog, M, k22.

Sleeves

Row 357 K121, slip last 40 sts onto waste yarn. Using same waste yarn, invisibly cast on 8 sts for sleeve. *Row 358* K8 sleeve sts, k13, C, k45, C, k13, hold last 40 sts and cast on 8 sts for sleeve as in previous row. *Rows 359 and all odd rows through row 391* Knit all sts. **Begin Four Flowers chart (FF):** *Row 360* K21, C, k15, work row 360 of FF, k15, C, k21. Continue to work FF on center 15 sts and other pats as established through row 376, working M and k2tog's instead of C on rows 362, 368, and 374. *Row 378* K18, C, k51, C, k18. *Row 380* K16, k2tog, M, k53, M, k2tog, k16. *Rows 382 and 384* K17, C, k53, C, k17. *Row 386* K15, k2tog, M, k55, M, k2tog, k15. *Rows 388 and 390* K16, C, k55, C, k16.

Neck Opening/Right Neck Edge

Row 392 K44, bind off 9 sts, k44. The rest of the bodice is worked in two pieces, starting with the left side, and beginning at the outside edge of the sleeve. *Row 1* (WS) K14, k2tog, M, k24. *Row 2 and all even rows through row 18* Dec for neck by

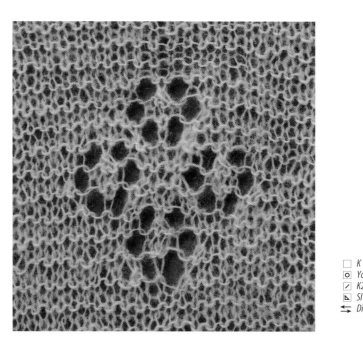

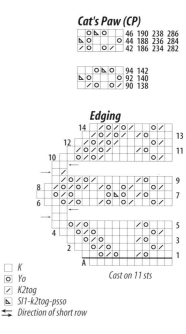

Cat's Paw (CP)

Edging

K
Yo
K2tog
Sl1-k2tog-psso
Direction of short row

Cast on 11 sts

k1, k2tog, k to end. Continue in pat, working Column as established through row 18—35 sts.

Left Shoulder and Bodice Back

Row 19 K11, k2tog, M, k18. *Rows 20, 22, and 24* Knit. *Row 21 and 23* K12, C, k18. Beginning with row 25, the Column slants toward center again. This slant is created by working M plus a k2tog on the center edge of each M every 6th row. Eyelets are worked at center back on rows 40 and 64 for ribbons. *Row 25* K13, M, k2tog, k16. *Row 26 and all even rows through row 36* Inc for neck by inc 1, knit to end. Continue in pat, working Column as established through row 37. *Row 38* Cast on 7 sts, k to end—48 sts; end of neck inc's. *Rows 39 and 41* K15, C, k28. *Row 40 (1st center back eyelet)* K2, yo, k2tog, knit to end. *Rows 42 to 63* Continue in pat, working Column as established. *Row 64 (2nd center back eyelet)* K2, yo, k2tog, knit to end. *Rows 65–78* Continue in pat, working Column as established. (Row 77 should be k21, C, k22.) Row 78 ends at the outer edge of the sleeve. Do not break yarn.

Sleeve Edging

Slip all but last worked st to waste yarn. Using same waste yarn, invisibly cast on 11 sts—12 active sts total. Turn and k10, k2tog. **Begin Edging chart** Work row 1 of chart. *Next row* Work row 2 of chart, knitting the last st of chart tog with the adjacent bar at the end of a sleeve row. Continue to work 14-row rep of chart a total of 8 times as established, joining edging to sleeve at the end of each even row. Adjust if necessary by knitting into the same bar twice so that you end with a row 14 of the chart. K 1 row and break yarn, leav-

Four Flowers (FF)

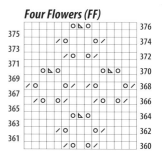

ing about a 12" tail. Transfer sts to the end of the holding yarn with the back bodice sts, making sure you begin with the inner side of the edging (sts now oriented properly for grafting).

Right Neck and Bodice
Beginning at neck edge, work right side of neck, shoulder, and bodice back to correspond to left, reversing all shaping and pattern placement. Row 77 should end at the outer edge of the sleeve. Place lower back bodice sts on holder, then work sleeve edging as for left side.

Neck Edging
This is optional, since babies do not have very much neck, but it is attractive and useful for maintaining the shape of the garment between wearings. With RS facing and beginning at center back neck, pick up and k 76 sts evenly around neck. K 1 row. *Row 2* (K2tog, yo twice, k2tog) 19 times. *Row 3* Knit, working k1-p1 into double yo's. *Row 4* Knit. Bind off loosely.

Finishing
Starting from the back opening edge, graft together (in one continuous graft) the 40 held sts and cast-on sleeve sts—including edging sts—to the sts from the bodice back and the final sts of sleeve and sleeve edging.

Starting from 15 ridges below waist eyelet row and working down to edging, using overcasting seam as shown, sew lower center back seam. Do not fasten off at beginning or end of seam, but leave a 12" tail each end for loosening or tightening during and after dressing.

Dressing
Make a dressing board by cutting the cardboard according to the diagram and cover it with plastic film. It is useful to pierce a hole in the top and run a hanging thread through it. Follow instructions for starching as given on p. 44 of Sampler Stole; put robe on dressing board and lash together the points of the edging on sleeves and bottom of robe, bringing together each point with the corresponding one on the opposite side of the board. Either (i) run blocking wires through each

side of the back opening, and fix the wires together at top and bottom by tying them together, or with elastic bands or paper clips, or (ii) whip the edges together temporarily with a contrasting thread. It is easier to sew in ends after the dressing. If possible, hang up to dry.

When dry, the robe needs to be taken off carefully. Take out the blocking wires or temporary seam at the back and the lashing of sleeves and bottom. Gently pull off one of the sleeves. Bend back sleeve board at the dotted line. Repeat for the other sleeve. The robe can now be slipped upwards off the board.

Cut ⅜" ribbon into one 36" and two 18" lengths. Thread long piece through the waist eyelets and tie at the back. Slip each short piece through a pair of the back eyelets from underneath, to tie on top. Thread the ¼" ribbon through the neck eyelets and tie at the back. Trim ends to length required, cutting the ribbon ends slantwise. If desired, thread ribbon through the faggoting of the sleeves.

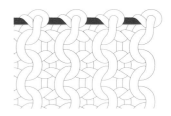

Overcasting Seam

To pick up stitches for the skirt, knit into the row-end bars of the edging (indicated in red, above).

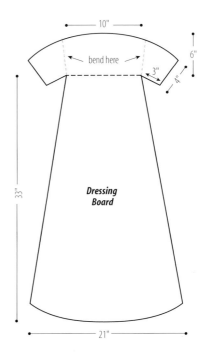

Dressing Board

49

Skill level

Experienced

Finished measurements

54" square

Yarn

Jamieson & Smith Cobweb-weight

Shetland (½oz/14g; 225yds/205m;

wool) 10 skeins White

Needles

Size 2 (2.75mm) needles,

or size to obtain gauge

Optional: Two size 2 (2.75mm)

double-pointed needles (dpn)

for edging

Extras

Stitch markers

Waste yarn for cast-on

4 stitch holders or

yarn for holding stitches

For dressing: Powdered starch

or cornstarch,

rust-proof T-pins or dressing frame,

knitting cotton for lashing to frame

Blocked gauge

32 sts and 48 rows to 4"/10cm in

garter st using size 2 (2.75) needles.

This shawl, notably the border pattern, was inspired by one in the Victoria and Albert Museum, London. It was used at the christening of my grandson, Ross Walker, in May 1992. The construction is traditional: it is worked on a garter stitch ground without bound-off edges. The vandyked edging is worked widthwise for one side (Edging 1), stitches picked up along the inner edge for the border (Border 1), and the border worked towards the central square, decreasing every row. The central square is knit without breaking yarn. Three more sections of edging and border are worked and then sewn or grafted in place around the remaining sides of the central square.

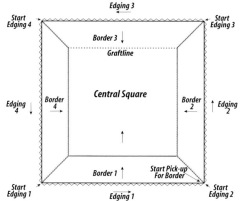

NOTES **1** The additional pairs of 2-st rows in both the Border and the Edging charts provide necessary elasticity for the diagonal edges. Shetlanders call this "lengthening the edge." This is most easily done by knitting (or purling—it makes no difference) the 2nd short row backwards to avoid turning the work. **2** See *Techniques*, p. 162, for invisible cast-on and garter st grafting.

Edging
Invisibly cast on 2 sts. **Begin Edging chart** Work rows 1–12 of chart, work rows 13–32 twenty-one times, then work rows 33–44 once—444 rows total. Do not break yarn. Pick up and k 365 sts along

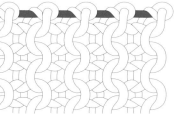

To pick up stitches for the border, knit into the row-end bars of the edging (indicated in red, above).

Shetland Lace Shawl

…Charles, who was my cousin

ten years younger than I…

was very delicate, always

passing from critical illness

to critical illness, so that he was

always brought downstairs

wrapped in an enormous white

Shetland shawl, in which he sat

at the piano, with his puny little

legs dangling, as unable to touch

the pedals as his tiny hands were

to span an octave.

Vita-Sackville West

from *Portrait of a Marriage*

by Nigel Nicolson.

straight edge—approximately 5 sts for every 6 edging rows—as foll: (k into bar) twice, *(k into bar, yo) twice, k into bar; rep from*, end (k into bar) twice. **Next row** Knit, dec 4 sts evenly—361 sts.

Border
Begin Border chart: *Row 1* (RS) Work first 97 sts of chart, work 56-st rep 3 times, then work last 96 sts of chart. Continue to work chart through row 91 as established, working dec's each end of every row from Row 2 onwards—81 sts. K 2 rows, inc 2 sts evenly—183 sts. **Begin Dewdrops chart:** *Row 1* (WS) Work first st of row, work 4-st rep 44 times, work last 2 sts of row. Work rows 2 and 3 of chart as established.

Central Square
Begin Central Square chart: *Row 1* (RS) Work first 2 sts of row, work 20-st rep 9 times, then work last st of row. Continue to work chart as established through row 46, work rows 1–46 four times more, then work rows 1–37. K 1 row and place sts on a holder or on waste yarn. Make 3 more sections of Edging and Border.

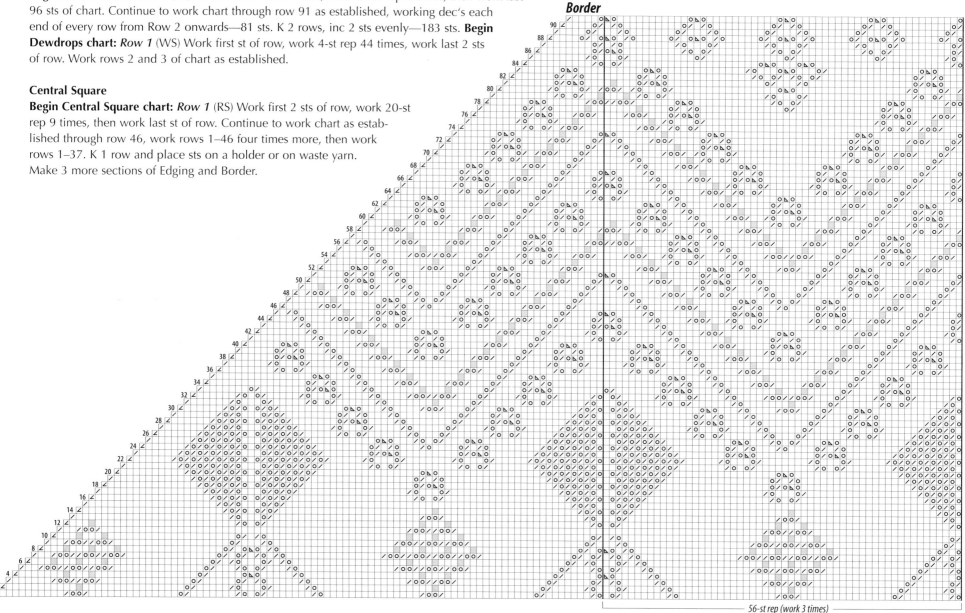

Border

56-st rep (work 3 times)

Finishing

Graft live sts of Border 3 to live sts of the Central Square. Sew live sts of Borders 2 and 4 to the row-end bars on the sides of the Central Square, using Overcasting Seam, as shown below. You may find it easier to sew up the corner seams (including the cast-on and bound-off sts of the edging) while the dry shawl is still on the frame.

Overcasting Seam

Dewdrops

└ 4-st ┘
rep

Edging

Dressing

Finish as described on page 44 of Sampler Stole, using a frame with internal measurements of 54" square. A set of four 6-foot wooden laths will work well, nailed together at the corners.

☐ K
☐ P
⟋ K2tog
⟋ K2tog on all but last rep;
   on last rep, sl1-k2tog-psso
○ Yo
◣ Sl1-k2tog-psso
◣ Sl1-k2tog-psso; on last rep, k2tog
◣ Sl1-k2tog-psso; on first rep, k2tog
⟉ K into front and back of st
⟋ K2-k same 2 sts back to
   edge-then k these sts tog
↞ Direction of short row

Central Square

└── 20-st rep ──┘

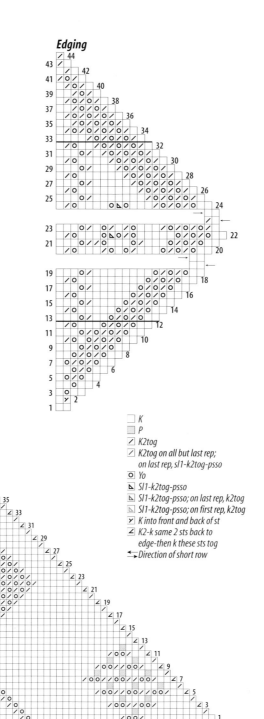

A GATHERING OF LACE **Points of Departure**

NOTES *1* Shawl is worked from the center outward in eight equal segments. Change from dpn to increasingly longer circular needles as number of sts permits. *2* Chart shows odd rnds only. Purl the purl sts and knit the knit sts on even rnds. *3* It may be helpful to mark beginnings of sections. *4* The blue and oatmeal shawls pictured are identical except that the oatmeal incorporates an eyelet cable detail every third scallop. *5* See *Techniques,* p. 162, for circular beginnings, double yo, and chain st.

Shawl

Using circular beginning and dpn, cast on 8 sts and distribute evenly. Place marker for beginning of rnd. **Begin Chart 1** K 2 rnds. *Rnd 3* Inc 1 st in each st around by k1-p1 in each st—16 sts. K 1 rnd. *Rnd 5* *Yo twice, k2; rep from* 7 times. K1-p1-k1 into double yo on following rnd—40 sts. Continue to work each rnd of chart 8 times around shawl as established through rnd 60. **Begin Charts 2A and 2B:** *Rnd 61* For the oatmeal shawl, *work 2A once, work 2B twice; rep from* 7 times around. For the blue shawl, work 24 reps of 2B around. Remember to purl the purl sts as well as knit the knit sts on even rnds. Continue to work through rnd 190 of chart(s) as established. Do not break yarn.

Edging

Using crochet hook and following markings at top of Charts 2A & 2B, crochet off edge sts with chain loops as foll: slip hook through the number of sts enclosed by each bracket, yo hook and draw through all loops on hook, then work the number of chain sts indicated by the number to the left of the bracket. After final chain, join to base of first chain and fasten off. Block to measurements, pinning out each chain loop.

Skill level

Intermediate

Finished measurements

68" in diameter

Yarn

Jamieson & Smith Laceweight Shetland

(1oz/28g; 225yds/205m; wool)

10 skeins Oatmeal #L202 or Blue #L35

Needles

Size 5 (3.75mm) needles

in double-pointed (dpn)

and circular, 16", 29",

and 60" (40, 72, and 150cm) long,

or size to obtain gauge

Extras

Size B/1 (2.5mm) crochet hook

Stitch markers

Rust-proof T-pins

Blocked gauge

19 sts and 30 rows to 4"/10cm

in St st using size 5

(3.75mm) needles.

Feather & Fan Shawl

...the real **Red Letter Day** for me

was learning to knit

my first lace pattern.

This was 'Feather and Fan'

as my grandmother

always called it,

or 'Old Shale,' according

to the Shetland tradition.

She wrote this down for me

as I was now at school and

well into learning to read,

and I will never forget

my delight at being

initiated into the meaning of

knitting pattern abbreviations.

Margaret Stove,
Creating Original Hand-Knitted Lace

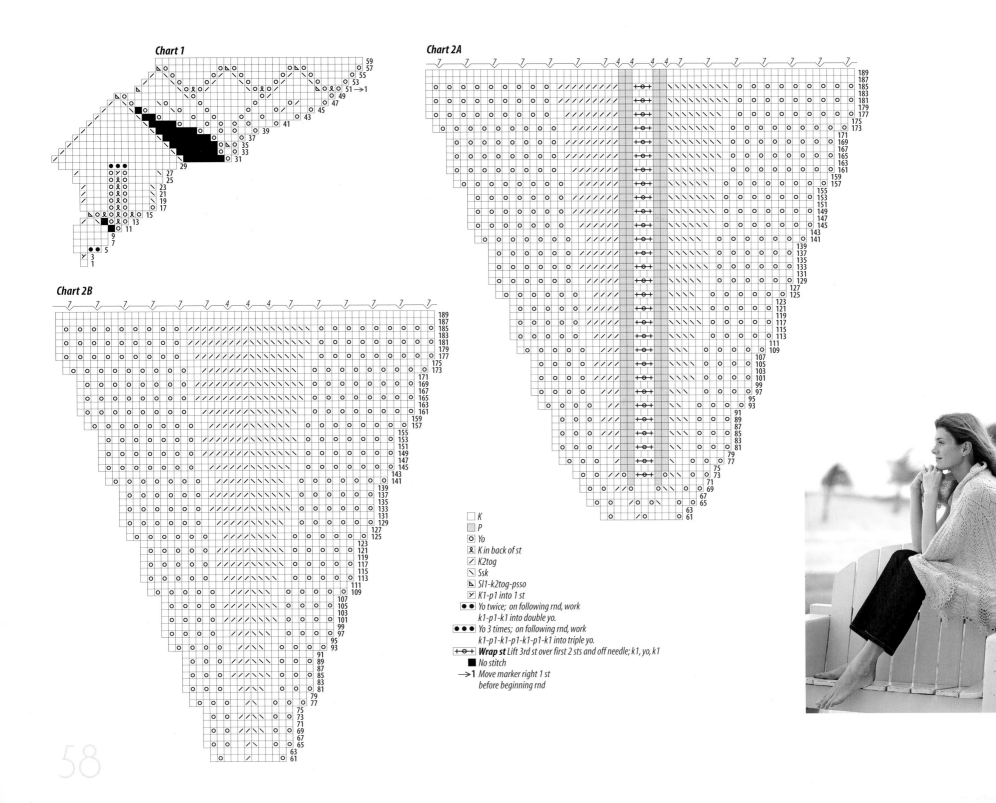

Chart 1

Chart 2A

Chart 2B

□ K
▨ P
◉ Yo
⅄ K in back of st
⟋ K2tog
⟍ Ssk
⟁ Sl1-k2tog-psso
⅄ K1-p1 into 1 st
●● Yo twice; on following rnd, work
k1-p1-k1 into double yo.
●●● Yo 3 times; on following rnd, work
k1-p1-k1-p1-k1-p1-k1 into triple yo.
┼◉┼ **Wrap st** Lift 3rd st over first 2 sts and off needle; k1, yo, k1
■ No stitch
→1 Move marker right 1 st
before beginning rnd

Skill level

Intermediate

Finished measurements

72" square

Yarn

Jamieson & Smith Laceweight Shetland

(1oz/28g; 225yd/205m; wool)

16 skeins Pale Green #L151

Needles

Size 6 (4mm) needles in double-pointed

(dpn) and circular, 24" and 42"

(60 and 105cm) long,

or size to obtain gauge

Extras

Stitch markers

Waste yarn

Point protector

Rust-proof T-pins

Blocked gauge

25 sts and 28 rows to 4"/10cm

in 34-st rep of Chart 2 using

size 6 (4mm) needles.

NOTES *1* Shawl is knit from center outward in four equal segments. Change from dpn to increasingly longer circular needles as number of sts permits. After shawl is made, the sideways edging is attached as it is worked. *2* Before rnd 39, chart indicates odd rnds only. Knit all sts on even rnds 2–38. After rnd 39, work chart for all rnds. *3* It may be helpful to mark beginnings of sections. *4* Shift the beginning of rnd as indicated on chart. *5* See *Techniques*, p. 162, for circular beginnings, invisible cast-on, and grafting.

Shawl

Using circular beginning and dpn, cast on 8 sts and distribute evenly. Place marker for beginning of rnd, and k 2 rnds. **Begin Chart 1:** *Rnd 3* Work chart 4 times around. Continue to work through rnd 66 of chart as established, remembering to knit all sts on even rnds through rnd 38. **Begin Chart 2:** *Rnd 67* *Work beginning of rnd once, work 34-st rep once, work to end; rep from* 3 times. Rep rnds 67–82 six times more, each time working an additional rep of the 34-st rep—178 rnds have been worked. **Begin Chart 3:** *Rnd 179* *Work beginning of rnd once, work 32-st rep 7 times, work to end; rep from* 3 times. Take care when working rnd 179 as there are several instances where there are two unexpected adjacent ssk's (highlighted in color). Continue as established through rnd 194.

Edging

Put a point protector on the right needle tip. Using a dpn, invisibly cast on 12 sts. **Begin Edging chart** Beginning at a shawl corner with working yarn and RS facing, work row 1 of chart, knitting last edging st tog with next shawl st on left needle. Turn and work row 2. The end of every odd row of the edging pat will join the edging to 1 or 2 shawl sts, and you will be working the rows back and forth from the dpn to the circular needle, moving counter-clockwise around the shawl. Continue to work through row 6, then work the 16-row rep around shawl, fudging if necessary so that row 15 of the chart is centered at each corner, and ending 4th side of edging with rows 23–28 of chart. Slip cast-on sts onto a 2nd dpn and remove waste yarn. Graft end of edging to beginning.

Finishing

Weave in all ends. Block to a square.

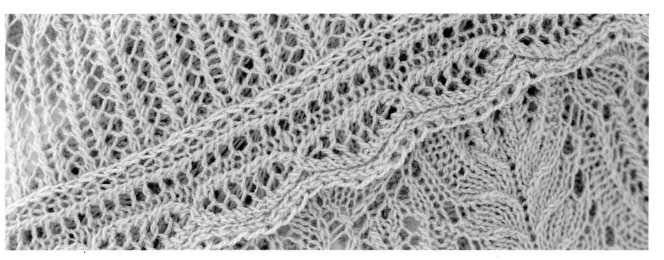

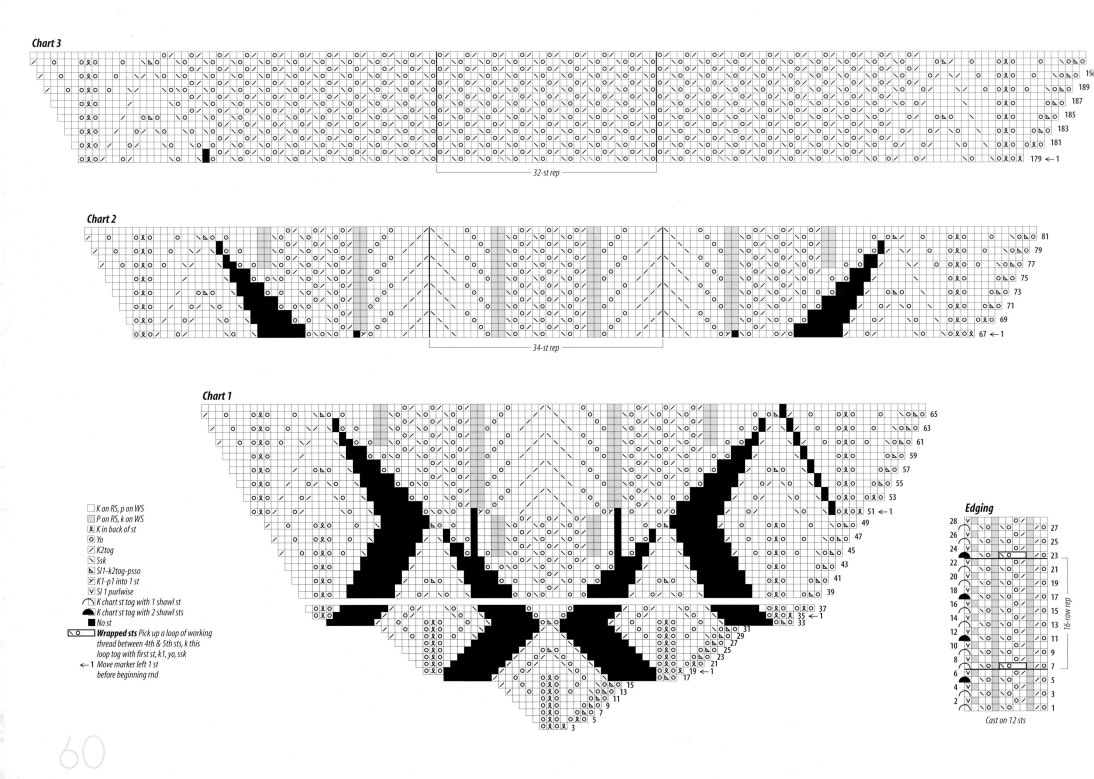

Chart 3

32-st rep

Chart 2

34-st rep

Chart 1

K on RS, p on WS
P on RS, k on WS
K in back of st
Yo
K2tog
Ssk
Sl1-k2tog-psso
K1-p1 into 1 st
Sl 1 purlwise
K chart st tog with 1 shawl st
K chart st tog with 2 shawl sts
No st
Wrapped sts Pick up a loop of working thread between 4th & 5th sts, k this loop tog with first st, k1, yo, ssk
←1 Move marker left 1 st before beginning rnd

Edging

16-row rep

Cast on 12 sts

A GATHERING OF LACE

Did the first lace knitter
awake one cold winter morning,
gaze in wonder at the
frost flowers on her
window pane, and rush
to pick up her needles?
Or did the first lace knitter
stand upon a sandy shore,
wondering at the foamy waves
spreading among her toes,
then rush into her rude home
to seize her needles?

Shirl the Purl,
Canada Knits

NOTES: *1* Shawl is knit beginning with center back diamond. Sts are then picked up to knit the two side panels, and the border is picked up and knit last. *2* Charts A and C show pat rows only. All odd rows are purled on Chart A. All even rnds are knit on Chart C. *3* See *Techniques*, p. 162, for chain st, double yo, M1, and sl2tog-k1-p2sso.

Center back diamond

With larger needles, cast on 2 sts. **Begin Chart A:** *Row 1* (WS) Purl this and all other WS rows. Continue to work chart as established through row 111, then rep rows 68–111 three times more, each time working two additional 20-st reps—223 sts. Continue to work through row 287 of chart, then rep rows 244–287 three times more, each time working two fewer 20-st reps. Place remaining 67 sts on a holder. Break yarn.

Left Side Panel

With larger needles and RS facing, pick up 141 sts evenly spaced between **b** and **c** at left back. **Begin Chart B:** *Row 1* (WS) Work first 2 sts of chart, work 34-st rep 4 times, work last 3 sts of chart. Continue to work rows 1–28 of chart as established 12 times (336 rows). Purl 1 row. Place all sts on a holder.

Right Side Panel

Work as for left side panel.

Chart A, Part 1

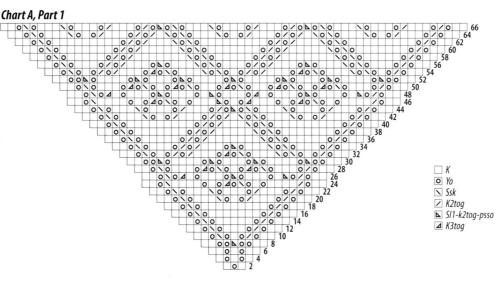

☐ *K*
⊙ *Yo*
◊ *Ssk*
☑ *K2tog*
◣ *Sl1-k2tog-psso*
◺ *K3tog*

Skill level

Experienced

Finished measurements

See schematic, p. 65.

Yarn

Jamieson & Smith Cobweb-weight Shetland

(½oz/14g; 225yds/205m; wool)

16 skeins White #L1

Needles

Size 2 (2.75mm) needles,

or size to obtain gauge

Size 0 (2mm) circular, 48"/120cm

long, for border

Extras

3 extra-large stitch holders

or spare needles

Stitch markers

Rust-proof T-pins

Size 10 (1.3mm) steel crochet hook

Blocked gauge

38 sts and 59 rows to 4"/10cm

in 20-st rep of Chart A using

size 2 (2.75mm) needles.

The inspiration for this shawl came from a variety of sources. I was invited to a wedding at which the guests were encouraged to come in ethnic dress. Being of Irish descent, my first thought was lace. I've always loved the deep V shaping on the back of a triangular shawl, but was drawn more to the way a rectangular shawl draped over the arms and down the front of the body. I was reminded of a shawl of similar shaping I had seen, and decided to combine the two ideas for a more feminine and formal look. The lace edging was adapted from a pattern passed down from my grandmother and was added last. I love the way the shawl looks, and the way I feel when I wear it.

Shetland lace...is an

exotic, fragile flower,

closer in spirit

to the Mediterranean than

the stormy seas of Britain.

Alice Starmore and Anne Matheson,

Knitting from the British Islands

Border

With smaller needle, RS facing, and beginning at **a**, pick up and k 382 sts to **d**; place marker (pm); knit between **d** and **e** dec 11 sts evenly spaced (130 sts remain); pm; pick up and k 224 sts to **c**; knit sts from center back holder dec 7 sts evenly spaced (60 sts rem); pick up and k 224 sts to **f**; pm; knit between **f** and **g** dec 11 sts evenly spaced (130 sts remain); pm; pick up and k 382 sts to **a**; pm and join—1532 sts. **Begin Chart C: Rnd 1** Work to rep, work 42-st rep 9 times, work to end of rnd. You should be at the marker at **d**. The sts of the chart outside the rep will form corners, so these should only be worked at marker positions. Continue to work chart as established, working 42-st rep of chart 3 times between **d** and **e**, 12 times along neck edge to **f**, 3 times between **f** and **g**, and 9 times to **a**. Continue to work through rnd 50 of chart, knitting all even rnds. Do not break yarn.

Edging

Using crochet hook and following markings at top of Chart C, crochet off edge sts with chain loops as foll: slip hook through the number of sts enclosed by each bracket, yo hook and draw yarn through all loops, work 9 chain sts. After final chain, join to base of first st and fasten off.

Chart B

```
27  28
25  26
23  24
21  22
19  20
17  18
15  16
13  14
11  12
 9  10
 7   8
 5   6
 3   4
 1   2
```

— 34-st rep —

Chart C

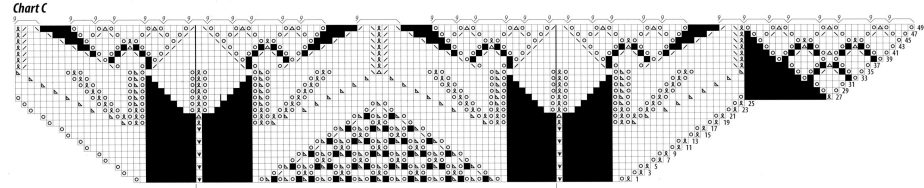

— 42→58→ 48-st-rep

Finishing

Carefully weave in all loose ends. Gently wash shawl according to yarn label directions and roll in towels to remove excess moisture. Block shawl to dimensions given, placing one T-pin at center of each ch-9 loop. Draw gently on shawl, moving pins as necessary, until blocked to size. Allow to dry completely. Put on your most gorgeous dress and then your new shawl.

"Dance modest but triumphant jig."
Elizabeth Zimmermann

Even though the angles differ, the border treatment on the corner of a side panel (d) is the same as that on the apex of the center diamond (a).

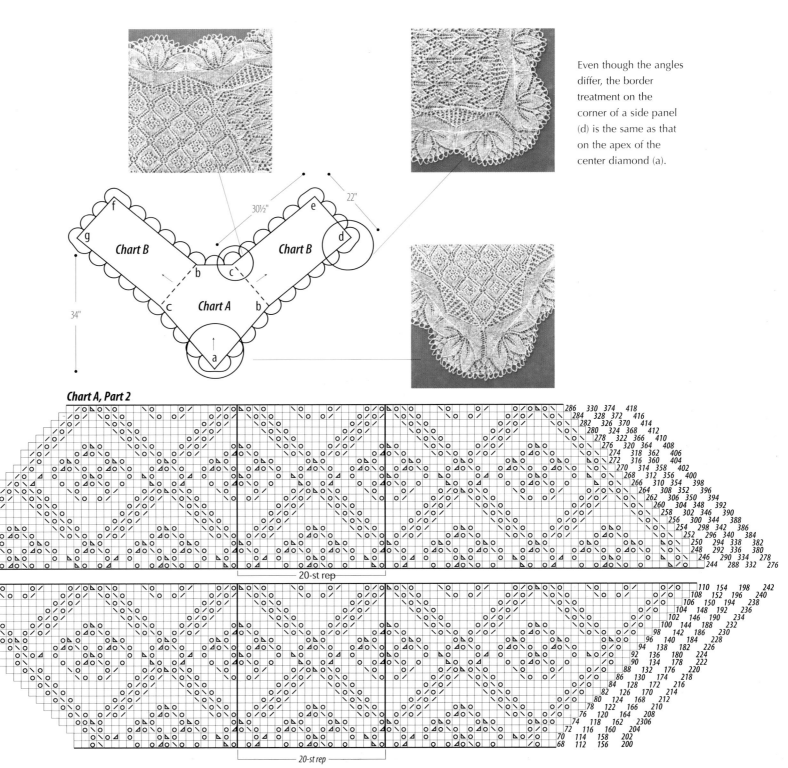

Chart A, Part 2

Key:
☐ K on RS, p on WS
▨ P on RS, k on WS
⊻ K in back of st
○ Yo
⟍ Ssk
⟋ K2tog
⟋ Yo first time; k2tog on other rows
△ Sl2tog-k1-p2sso
◺ Sl1-k2tog-psso
◹ Ssk on last rep; sl1-k2tog-psso on others
■ No st
⊻ M1-k1-M1

20-st rep

Skill level

Adventurous

Finished measurement

59" in diameter, unblocked.

80", blocked

Yarn

Jamieson & Smith Cobweb-weight

Shetland (½oz/14g;

225yds/205m; wool)

17 skeins Natural

Needles

Size 2 (2.75mm) circular needle,

40"/100cm long,

or size to obtain gauge

Optional: One size 2 (2.75mm)

double-pointed needle (dpn)

Extras

Cable needle (cn), for edging

Smooth cotton yarn such as Coats &

Clarks Speed Cro-Sheen for casting on

Tapestry needle

Stitch markers

Blocked gauge

28 sts and 56 rows to 4"/10cm in

garter st, using size 2 (2.75mm) needles.

Construction notes

This shawl, knit on a garter st ground, has no bound-off edges. It begins with a central octagon (A, see drawing below). Sts are picked up along the outside edge of the octagon for the border (B), which is knit in the round. The edging, invisibly cast-on then worked together with the border, eliminates the hundreds of border sts and is knit in rows (C): a splendid time to perfect purling backwards instead of turning the work every row.

NOTES *1* The background pattern in the center section is a multiple of 14 plus 1. St markers placed before the first yo and then every 14 sts across the row will make it easier to keep track through the complicated chart. I prefer to use waste cotton for markers, as it takes up little space and does not stretch or distort the fabric. *2* After the center section is worked, sts will be picked up and worked all along the perimeter of the octagon. To make this easier, wrap a piece of cotton waste yarn along each edge as you turn to knit the next row (see drawing, p. 96). This can be done either by using one long piece of yarn on each edge, or by using separate pieces of yarn for the increase section, the straight section, and the decrease section on each edge. The invisible cast-on will provide the 7th section of sts; the working needle will contain the 8th. *3* The size and shape of the holes created by yo's in the center section and the braid pattern are controlled by knitting into the back of the st two rows directly above the yo. While it is not strictly necessary to do this, the pattern looks more nearly symmetrical left to right and top to bottom if this is done. Similarly, when a dec occurs two rows above a yo, I twist the st which falls directly above the yo before completing the dec. There is no separate symbol given when this occurs; it is a matter of choice to twist the st or not. I argue for consistency throughout. *4* See *Techniques*, p. 162, for double yo, knitting on, invisible cast-on, purling backwards, and grafting.

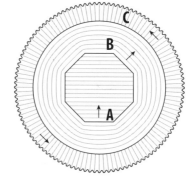

One of the most satisfying knitting experiences for me is creating something for a baby. I particularly like knitting a lace shawl to wrap a small new person in the snug warmth of soft wool. The center of this baby shawl is a pattern I designed for my daughter Ingrid's bridal veil. Three elements in the Celtic-style knot intertwine endlessly; one represents Ingrid, one her husband, Tony, and the third represents the marriage which unites the two. I placed the knot on a faint but persistent background pattern to remind Tony and Ingrid that a marriage takes place in the context of family and community. On Ingrid's veil, I used the knot in a square; here, I have put it in an octagon. Each of the eight sides of this shawl features a large crown topped by four hearts; a baby is the king or queen of its parents' heart. I love the idea of placing a baby on the center of the shawl and seeing a crown above its head! I devised a wing pattern and a tree pattern and combined them to make the crown. There is a saying that the only lasting gifts we can give our children are roots and wings. Even if they are not visible, the roots are what keep a tree upright and stable; wings are visually uplifting, reminding us that each of us can soar.

In 1893 a beautiful lace shawl
knitted by Marion Nisbet of Unst, was
displayed at the Chicago Exhibition.
The correspondent, trying to describe the
shawl, stated: It is impossible to give an
adequate idea of the fineness of the
thread and the delicacy and perfection
of the work, but the thread,
fine it seems as human hair,
has all been spun twice, and if you
untwist a strand of it you will find that it
consists of two threads twisted together.
Twelve miles of wool (a single yarn)
are knitted into this wonderful shawl;
and the centre as well as the border
is richly patterned. It took the best part
of two years to knit.

Linda G. Fryer,
Knitting by the Fireside & on the Hillside

Heart Instructions ♡

Rnd 1 Sl 1, place next st on cable needle (cn) and hold in front, replace sl st on LH needle, k2tog, yo twice, replace st from cn to LH needle, ssk.

Rnd 2 P1, drop 1 yo, sl remaining yo to RH needle purlwise, yo from back to front across needle, duplicating existing yo, p1.

Rnd 3 K2tog, sl 2 yo's wyif, yo, ssk.

Rnd 4 P1, sl 3 yo's, yo, p1.

Rnd 5 K2tog, sl 4 yo's wyif, yo, ssk.

Rnd 6 P1, sl 5 yo's, yo, p1.

Rnd 7 K1, sl 6 yo's wyif, yo, k1.

Rnd 8 P1, (k1-p1-k1) in top yo, k1 through all 7 yo's, (k1-p1-k1) in top yo, p1.

Rnd 9 K3, ssk, pick up left side of bottom st in just-completed ssk and sl to LH needle, k2tog, k3.

☐	*K*
⊙	*Yo*
☑	*K2tog*
↘	*Ssk*
℞	*K in back of stitch*
◿	*Ssk- place back on LH ndl- pass next st over- sl back to RH needle (dec 2)*
◹	*Sl1-k2tog-psso*
♡	*See Heart Instructions*
■	*No stitch*

Braid and Sawtooth Edging

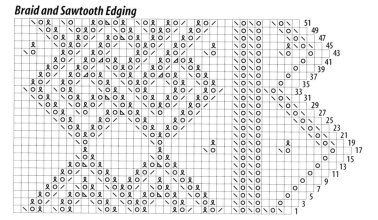

Crown and Feather Border

98 sts

5 sts

A. Octagon

Begin Ingrid's Bridal Knot chart: *Row 1* (RS) Invisibly cast on 102 sts. **Row 2** (WS) Knit this and all following even rows, following M and B instructions as indicated. Continue to work chart through row 492, making sure to knit the first st of rows 147–348. There should be 247 sts on the needle at row 147, dec to 101 sts at the end of row 492. Do not break yarn.

B. Border

The Crown and Feather Chart will be worked 8 times around the octagon, one rep for each side. The right section of the chart—the feather—is centered on the first st of each side: a point of the octagon. Although the 8 sides of the octagon are nearly identical in length, they vary in number of sts. This will be corrected in the first set-up rnd. When picking up, there should be about 72 sts for each diagonal section and 101 sts for each side section. If your st count is off from this by one or two sts, don't be concerned. Adjust as necessary during the first set-up rnd. If you have used waste yarn to pick up sts as you knit, you may either transfer them to the needle you are using or leave them on the string to be worked as you go. If you decided to wait until the octagon was complete before picking up sts, pick up the bars at the edges of the rows (see drawing on p. 50). **Border set-up:** *Rnd 1* Each side needs to be brought to 102 sts: 5 sts for the feather and 97 sts for the crown. The set-up for each side will begin with [k2, yo, place marker (pm)] and end with [pm, yo, k1]. These 5 sts (which begin as 3 sts), separated by markers and straddling the points of the octagon, become the feather. For the crown, 49 single sts (created by an evenly spaced combination of k1tbl, k2tog, and k3tog, depending on the starting st count) must alternate with 48 yo's. Begin rnd with the working sts from the center of the octagon: k2, yo, pm, [k2tog, yo] 24 times, [k3tog, yo] once, [k2tog, yo] 23 times, k2tog, pm, yo, k1. Work remaining sides similarly. Work to final st on last section, yo, knit last st and sl back to LH needle. Bring yarn over LH needle to front (creating a duplicate yo), sl yo and next st (from crown pat) from RH needle to LH needle. Bring yarn between the 2 needles and to the back (wrapping yo and crown st), sl crown st as if to knit back to RH needle. (Final crown st has been wrapped and beginning of rnd has been moved to match beginning of chart.) **Border set-up:** *Rnd 2* Purl this rnd, purling first yo and its duplicate tog and inc 1 st in the center st of each crown section—98 sts between markers. When you reach the last st in the rnd, slip the wrap off the st and sl both to LH needle with the wrap to the left of the real st, making sure the real st remains backwards on the needle. Purl these tog tbl. **Begin Crown and Feather Border chart:** *Rnd 1* Work 8 times around. *Rnd 2* Purl this and all foll even rnds, following heart instructions where indicated. Continue to work chart as established through rnd 106. Do not break yarn.

C. Edging

At the end of rnd 106, the border will consist of 15 feather sts and 122 crown sts. *Feather* The feather sts will be joined together with rows 1–32 (16 RS rows) of the edging chart. This means there will be 1 RS row where the joining ssk must be worked with a previously eliminated st, not a live st. *Crown* The crown sts will be joined together with edging rows 33–52, repeated almost 13 times. This means that 122 sts must be eliminated over 129 RS rows. Therefore, 7 ssk's, evenly spaced, must be worked with previously eliminated sts rather than live ones.

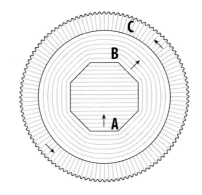

Begin Braid and Sawtooth Edging: *Row 52* Invisibly cast on 38 sts onto LH needle with working yarn. With RH needle or single dpn, work as foll: **Row 1* (RS) Work to last st of chart, ssk (last edging st tog with first feather st of border). *Row 2* (WS) For this and all following even rows, purl backwards, or turn and knit. Continue to work through row 32 as established, remembering to work the ssk at the end of one RS row with a previously eliminated st. At this point, all feather sts should be eliminated. *Row 33* Work to last st of chart, ssk (last edging st tog with first crown st of border). Continue to work through row 52 of chart, then continue to rep rows 33–52, eliminating 122 crown sts; rep from* around shawl. When 1 st remains, you should have completed the 50th row of the edging chart. Graft the working sts to the bottoms of the invisible cast-on as if knitting the 51st row.

Blocking

I have stretched the shawl only slightly in blocking, so that the thermal qualities of the garter st lace are retained. For future use as a grown-up shawl, per Elizabeth Zimmermann's excellent suggestion, the shawl can easily be stretched to be 80 or more inches across.

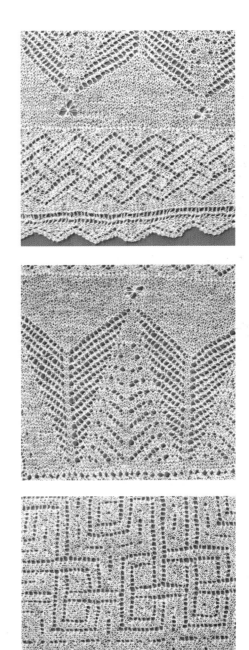

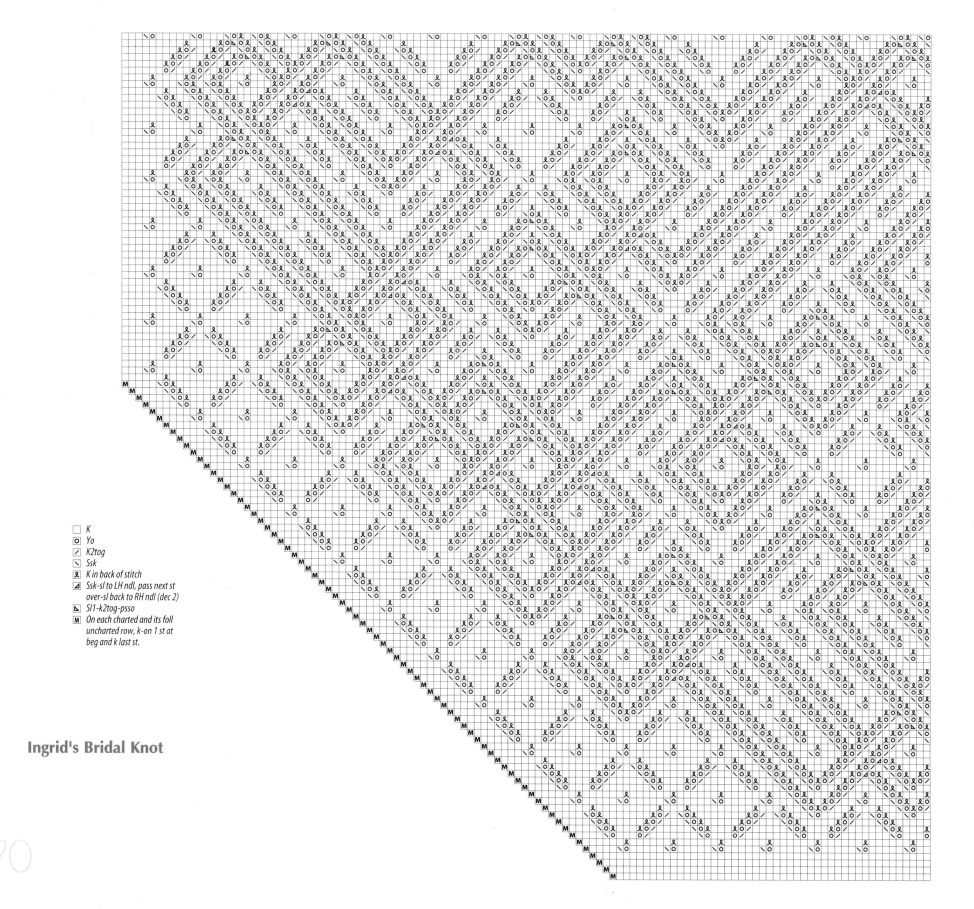

K

⊡ Yo

⊿ K2tog

⊠ Ssk

⊠ K in back of stitch

⊿ Ssk-sl to LH ndl, pass next st
over-sl back to RH ndl (dec 2)

⊾ Sl1-k2tog-psso

Ⓜ On each charted and its foll
uncharted row, k-on 1 st at
beg and k last st.

Ingrid's Bridal Knot

247
245
243
241
239
237
235
233
231
229
227
225
223
221
219
217
215
213
211
209
207
205
203
201
199
197
195
193
191
189
187
185
183
181
179
177
175
173
171
169
167
165
163
161
159
157
155
153
151
149
147
M 145
M 143
M 141
M 139
M 137
M 135
M 133
M 131
M 129
M 127
M 125
M 123
M 121
M 119
M 117
M 115
M 113
M 111
M 109
M 107
M 105
M 103
M 101
M 99
M 97
M 95
M 93
M 91
M 89
M 87
M 85
M 83
M 81
M 79
M 77
M 75
M 73
M 71
M 69
M 67
M 65
M 63
M 61
M 59
M 57
M 55
M 53
M 51
M 49
M 47
M 45
M 43
M 41
M 39
M 37
M 35
M 33
M 31
M 29
M 27
M 25
M 23
M 21
M 19
M 17
M 15
M 13
M 11
M 9
M 7
M 5
M 3
1

71

Ingrid's Bridal Knot

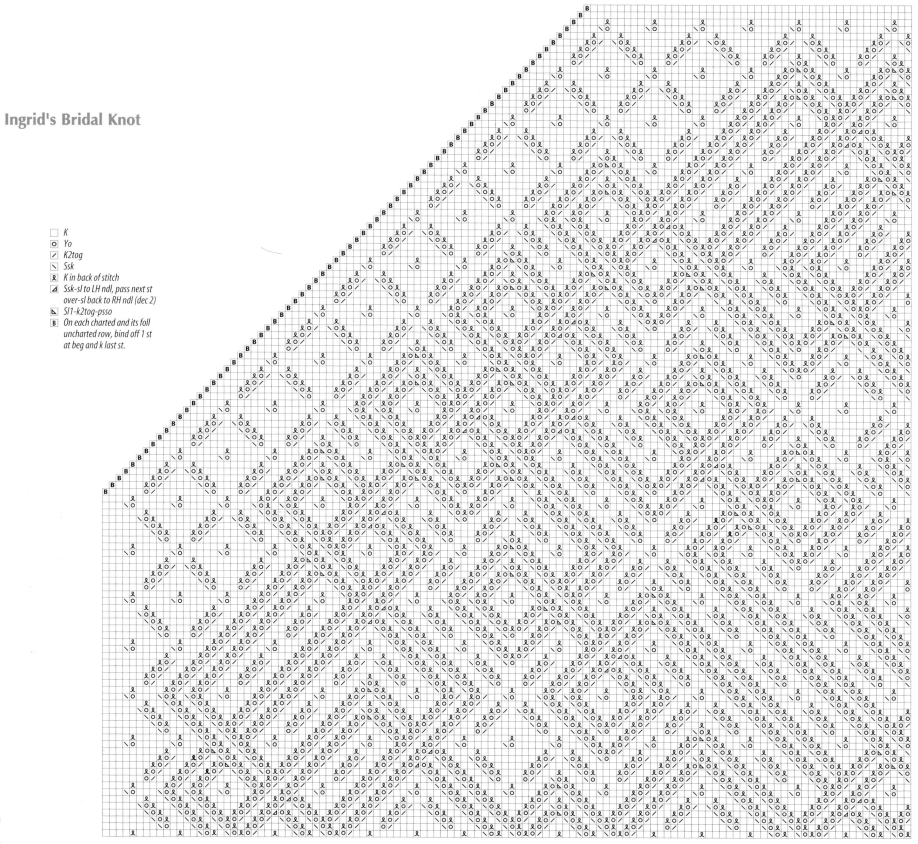

□ K
○ Yo
∕ K2tog
＼ Ssk
ℛ K in back of stitch
◿ Ssk-sl to LH ndl, pass next st
  over-sl back to RH ndl (dec 2)
↘ Sl1-k2tog-psso
B On each charted and its foll
  uncharted row, bind off 1 st
  at beg and k last st.

Skill level

Experienced

Size

42" square

Yarn

The original shawl was made in a
very thin (2/48) blend of wool and
silk that is no longer available.
In a thicker yarn, maybe a 2/24 or 2/25,
and a size O (2mm) needle, it would be
about 60" square. Jagger Spun makes
a variety of these yarns;
allow 6-8oz of these fine yarns.

Needles

Size 000 (1.5mm) needle in double-
pointed (dpn) and circular, 16", 24",
and 42" (40, 60, and 105cm) long,
or size to obtain gauge

Extras

Stitch markers

Waste yarn

Tapestry needle

Rust-proof T-pins

Blocked gauge

36 sts and 52 rows to 4"/10cm in St st,
using size 000 (1.5mm) needles.

Celtic symbolism celebrates the earth; the never-ending vine
embracing all, the evergreen trees with their promise of immortality,
the magic of the unicorn, the compass points and intertwined knots
showing our interdependence on each other. The center circle
shows the seas, the mountains, sky and, at the very center, the feminine moon reminds us of the source of life and creativity.

Notes on the designs
The vine pattern used on the edging is a classic pattern, called "Print
o' the Wave" by Sarah Don and Gladys Amedro or "Leaf Lace" by
Barbara Abbey. The evergreen trees are a variation of Barbara
Walker's "Christmas Trees" given in the first *Treasury of Knitting
Patterns*. The unicorns are done with a wonderful technique I call
"Carried Eyelet" that I learned from an old *Anna* magazine. It allows
the knitter to use any square graph in an eyelet pattern. The chart for
the unicorn is original. The Celtic Knot is Barbara Walker's in her
Second Treasury. She calls it "Scrolls" and credits Dorothy Reade.
You probably recognized the water in the center section as a varia-
tion of the Shetland pattern called "Feather and Fan;" the remaining
patterns are original.

NOTES *1* When swatching for your shawl, start by doing a couple of
reps of the edging. Stretch it out and check the density carefully. You
need a good contrast between the solid parts and the holes. Now is
the time to change needle size or even yarn. If you don't *love* the
swatch, you probably won't like the project! *2* The edging of the shawl
is knit first, then its end grafted to its beginning. Sts are picked up
along the straight inside edge, and the shawl is knit circularly from
the outer edge inward, first with corner dec's to form a square, then
with random dec's to form a central circle. *3* The edging is worked
back and forth on a pair of short needles. The body of the shawl will
require progressively shorter circulars, finishing with dpn at the center. *4* See *Techniques*, p. 162, for invisible cast-on, grafting, sl2tog-
k1-p2sso, and sssk.

Edging
(NOTES The edging consists of two parts: a garter st scallop done on
10–14 sts and a St st vine pattern done on 23 sts. The scallop is a
16-row rep and the vine is a 12-row rep, so it takes 48 rows to work
three scallops and four vines.)
Using dpn, invisibly cast on 33 sts. **Begin Edging chart:** *Row A* (WS)
Work first 23 sts of row, place marker to separate the two parts of

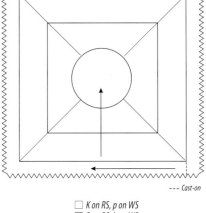

--- *Cast-on*

☐ K on RS, p on WS
▨ P on RS, k on WS
⊻ Slip purlwise wyif
⊘ K2tog
△ Sl2tog-k1-p2sso
⊙ Yo

Edging

Cast on 33 sts

Knitting is an effective medium

through which you can express

your individuality. . .

Everywhere we look we find

inspiration: forged iron

grillework, lacelike in design;

cross sections of stem

structures; spider webs;

elevated train trestles and

their shadow patterns....

Mary Walker Phillips,
Creative Knitting

the edging, k to end. Rep rows 1–48 of chart as established 47 times, then work rows 1–46 once. Break yarn, leaving an 18" tail.

Grafting the ends
Place 33 sts from invisible cast-on onto dpn, removing waste yarn. There will be 34 sts on your working needle with the yarn coming from the scalloped side. Making sure edging is not twisted, graft ends together using garter st graft on scallop part of edging, then remove marker and use St st graft on vine part of edging.

Body
(NOTES *1* Evergreen Trees, Celtic Knot, Compass Points, and Mountain and Sky charts indicate pat rnds only. Work all unmarked rnds in knit. *2* Work dec rnd as specified every other rnd for square portion of shawl.)
With longest circular needle, beginning anywhere on inside (vine side) of edging, and using the loops formed by slipping the first st of each even edging row, pick up and k 1 st for every two rows of the edging as foll: *K 287, place marker (pm), k1 for corner, pm; rep from* 3 times, using a different color for final marker to indicate beginning of rnd—1152 sts (287 sts each side plus 4 corner sts).
Begin Evergreen Trees chart *Work rnd 1 of chart, working 16-st rep 15 times; rep from* 3 times around. *Work rnds 2–4* of chart as established. *Rnd 5* (dec rnd): *Ssk, work to 2 sts before marker, k2tog, slip marker (sm), k1, sm; rep from* 3 times. Continue to work chart through rnd 54, working dec rnd every odd rnd, and working 16-st rep 14 times each side beginning with rnd 32. (This will cause rnds 32–54 to be offset.) When chart is complete, there should be 231 sts each side plus corner sts. **Begin Unicorn chart:** *Rnd 1* Ssk, k1, work last 2 sts of chart 13 times (26 sts), pm, work rnd 1 of chart 3 times, placing marker between each rep of chart, work last 2 sts of chart 10 times (20 sts), k2 (but work k2tog instead on all following odd rnds), sm, k1, sm—230 sts each side plus corner sts. Continue to work through rnd 60 of chart as established, working dec's both sides of corners every odd rnd, keeping corner sts in St st, and working 2 or 3 sts each side of corners in St st for ease in working dec's. When chart is complete, there should be 172 sts each side plus corner sts. *Next rnd:* Work a purl rnd with dec's as for rnd 3 of Evergreen Trees chart, k 1 rnd, then work one more purl rnd with dec's—168 sts each side plus corner sts. **Begin Celtic Knot and Compass Point charts:** *Rnd 1* K31, pm, work rnd 1 of Celtic Knot chart, pm, k17, pm, k10 for North, pm, k17, pm, work Celtic Knot,

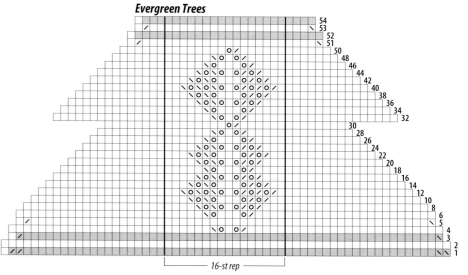

Unicorn

60-st rep

Evergreen Trees

16-st rep

pm, k31, sm, k1, sm, *k31, pm, work Celtic Knot, pm, k17, pm, k9 for East (South on 2nd rep), pm, k18, pm, work Celtic Knot, pm, k31, sm, k1, sm; rep from* once; k31, pm, work Celtic Knot, pm, k16, pm, k11 for West, pm, k17, pm, work Celtic Knot, pm, k31, sm, k1, sm. Continue to work in pats as established, beginning charts for Compass Points on rnd 21, and remembering to work corner dec's on even rnds. When rnd 56 of Celtic Knot is complete, there should be 112 sts each side plus corner sts—452 sts. This is the end of the square portion of the shawl. From now on, all dec's should be positioned randomly (keeping dec's away from corners and nearer center of sides to round out the circle). *Next rnd:* P, dec 2 sts randomly each side, removing all markers except the beginning of rnd marker—444 sts. *Next rnd:* K, dec 8 sts—436 sts. *Next rnd:* P, dec 8 sts—428 sts. *Next rnd:* K, dec 8 sts—420 sts. **Begin Water chart:** *Rnd 1* Work 21-st rep 20 times around shawl. Continue to work chart as established through rnd 14—360 sts. **Begin Mountain and Sky chart:** *Rnd 1* Work 90 sts of chart 4 times. Continue as established through rnd 28, knitting all sts on even rnds—240 sts. *Next rnd* P, dec 6 sts. K 1 rnd. *Next rnd* P, dec 6 sts—228 sts. Now would be a good time to change to dpn: place 76 sts on each of 3 needles and knit with the 4th. **Begin Moon pat** On each rnd from now on, work yo-sl 1-k2tog around, dec approx 8 sts each rnd by substituting a k3tog or sssk for the k2tog. This pat needs to be very irregular, so stack the dec's, group them, skip rnds—anything to keep it irregular. Check appearance of pattern every couple of rnds, adjusting as necessary. When approx 8 sts remain, break yarn, leaving an 8" tail, and thread it through a tapestry needle, running it around through all sts twice. Work in the tail, but do not cut thread until after blocking.

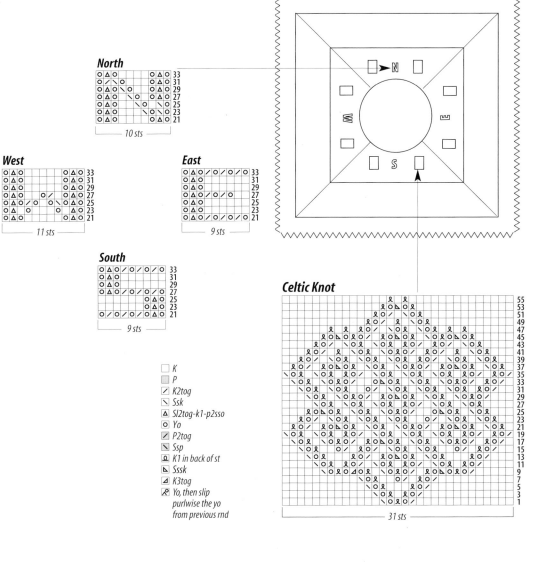

- ☐ K
- ☐ P
- ☑ K2tog
- ◹ Ssk
- △ Sl2tog-k1-p2sso
- ○ Yo
- ◺ P2tog
- ◸ Ssp
- ℧ K1 in back of st
- ◿ Sssk
- ◹ K3tog
- ℛ Yo, then slip purlwise the yo from previous rnd

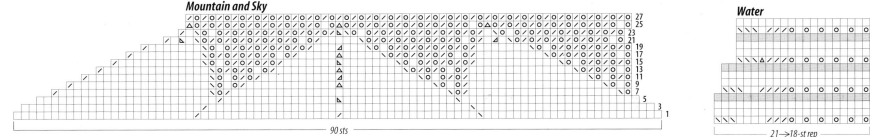

The Russian technique for blocking shawls

Here is a *magic* way to block square, rectangular, or triangular pieces. When you have finished knitting, neaten any ends, but do not cut them until after blocking.

Take a very long piece of smooth string or yarn (no color!) and thread a needle with it. Go around your shawl threading the string through every point of your scallops. Make sure you are consistent in the direction of the needle—up through every point, or down through every point. When you get to a corner, leave a long loop. As you go along, pull out the knitting so the string is not at all tight. When you are all the way around, tie the ends together. Arrange the string so it is fairly loose on the sides and has loops at every corner.

Prepare a bed or carpet by putting down a cotton blanket or sheet and have some pins ready. Wash or wet your knitting. Gently squeeze out excess water. Find a friend—this takes four hands—each of you takes two adjacent corner loops and standing over the prepared surface, gently p-u-l-l.

You will be surprised to see how your work will grow and how evenly it squares up. Lay it on the surface and pin it in its outstretched position. I find that usually I don't need to pin every point, especially if I want the scallops to be rounded a little bit, which I usually do. A few pins holding the string out and straight is all that is needed. Protect from children and cats and let dry. Remove string, cut any ends, and you are done!

For a triangular piece, you only need three hands, of course. If your shawl has rounded corners, leave the corners out of the threading and pin them out after stretching and pinning the rest.

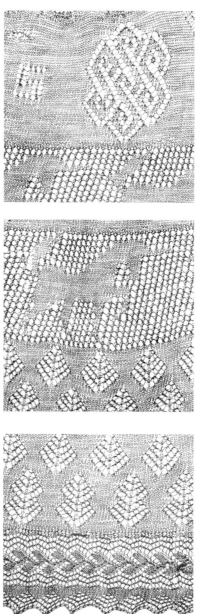

Skill level

Intermediate

Finished measurements

80" in diameter for the cream

version with 7 spokes and a deep border;

72" in diameter for the teal blue version

with 8 spokes and a shallower edging.

Use finer needles for a smaller,

less lacy shawl.

Yarn

Schoolhouse Press Laceweight Icelandic

(1¾oz/50g;250yds/228m; wool)

6 balls of Teal #9809 or

7 balls of Cream #0851

Needles

Size 10 (6mm) needles in

double-pointed (dpn) and

circular, 16" and 24"

(40 and 60 cm) long,

or size to obtain gauge

Extras

7 (8) yarn loop markers,

6 (7) of one color and one of a

contrasting color to mark the

beginning of the rnd

Waste yarn

Rust-proof T-pins

Blocked gauge

14 sts to 4" in Spiral pat using

size 10 (6mm) needles.

The circle shawl begins in the center and maintains a steady 7- (or 8-) point swirling increase throughout. Knitting the first few rnds with 6–8 sts on three or four dpn can be challenging. I recommend bamboo or wooden dpn as they have more surface friction than aluminum, enamel, or nickel, and the wool will cling to them in a more secure and comforting fashion.

To determine when you have reached your wanted length, snag a passer-by to measure the radius as you grab the beginning (center) of the shawl in one hand, your working needle in the other and stretch the knitting fiercely. The more loosely you knit, the more the shawl will stretch when blocked. During your very first lace shawl, you may be discouraged as you observe the shriveled knitting hanging from your needle. Persevere. You will be rewarded as you take scores of T-pins, flop the freshly washed, damp shawl down onto the rug and metamorphose that thing into a resplendent butterfly by pinning out each scallop of your chosen lace border. It will dry in a matter of hours.

NOTES *1* The shawl is knit circularly from the center out. Begin with dpn and change to the 16" circular needle when possible; end with the 24" needle. *2* Instructions are for a 7-point inc, with an optional 8-point inc in parentheses. *3* As you are establishing your lace reps, tie a loop marker around the needle between each rep. That way you can check your accuracy in increments each rnd and never have to rip back more than one rep. *4* Only odd-numbered rnds are charted. All even rnds are knit, working (k1-p1) into each double yo from the rnd before. *5* See *Techniques*, p. 162, for circular beginnings, double yo, invisible cast-on, and garter st grafting.

This pretty ladder pattern is from an Icelandic lace book, *Príhyrnur Og Langsjöl,* and I wanted to see how it would look in a spiral. It is a simple design and reps are added when the increased sts build up to k5. It is quite exciting to add the 2nd full rep, then the 3rd. By the 4th addition the rhythm of the design—the song of the shawl—will have become ingrained in your cortex and you can knit on auto-pilot.

Note that the chart shows only 5 ladder reps, but you will continue adding reps to each section until you are within "x" number of inches from wanted radius.(The number to fill in for "x" will be determined by the width of the final border design you choose.) Then bring the lace ladders to points by following the last 7 rows of the chart. If you decide to knit the 7-point inc version, choose a deep lace edging to prevent the inc points from making seven blips around the periphery.

Shawl

Using circular beginning and dpn, cast on 7 (8) sts and distribute as evenly as possible. **Begin Spiral chart** Work Rnd 1 seven (eight) times, placing markers between each rep—14 (16) sts. Continue as established through the Center section, then begin working the Spoke section. The yo-ssk-yo at the end of each chart line forms the 7 (8) spokes of the shawl. When each group of plain sts builds up to k5, a new 6-st ladder rep (ssk, k1, yo, yo, k1, k2tog) is formed on the next rnd. Decide how deep you want your shawl to be. The cream shawl has 10 ladder pats between each of the 7 spokes, a wide edging, and is 80" in diameter. The teal blue version has 8 ladder pats between each of the 8 spokes, a narrower border, and is 72" in diameter. Both were knitted loosely on a size 10 (6mm) needle. Work through rnd 70 of the Spoke portion of the chart (5 ladder pats), then continue to work additional reps of rnds 59–70 as many times as you wish, each time working one more 6-st ladder pat. Resolve the ladders into points by working chart rnds 71–84, and working more 6-st reps if necessary. Do not break yarn if working Cream Edging.

Edgings

For the cream edging, invisibly cast on 20 sts. Work row A of Cream Edging chart, uniting last st of edging to first shawl st by a k2tog through back loops. Work the 10-row rep of the edging around the shawl, continuing to join the edging to the shawl on each incoming row. Work the very last shawl st on a row 10 of the edging (fudge if necessary by knitting edging sts together with 2 shawl sts), then graft the last row to the cast-on edge.

For the teal edging, invisibly cast on 19 sts. Work 6-row rep of Teal Edging chart around the shawl, joining the edging to the shawl on each incoming row, and grafting the last row to the cast-on edge when complete.

Finishing
Block and fasten ends.

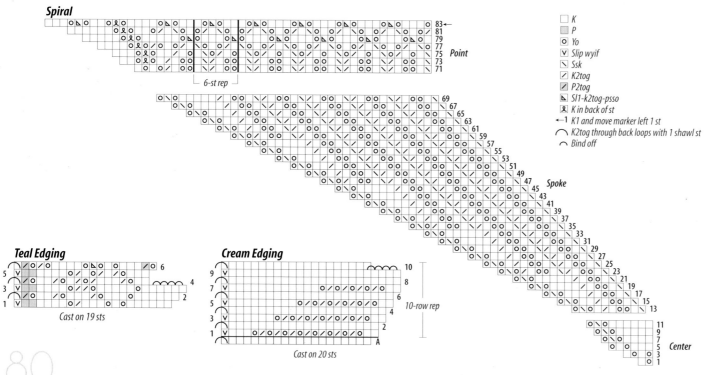

Spiral

Point

6-st rep

Spoke

Center

Teal Edging

Cast on 19 sts

Cream Edging

Cast on 20 sts

10-row rep

	K
	P
o	Yo
V	Slip wyif
\	Ssk
/	K2tog
/	P2tog
⋏	Sl1-k2tog-psso
Ω	K in back of st
←1	K1 and move marker left 1 st
⌒	K2tog through back loops with 1 shawl st
⌒	Bind off

Lace Knitting depicts the height
of the knitter's art,
as it is inspired by the desire to
reproduce as near as possible
the art of the lace-maker.

Mary Thomas,
Mary Thomas's
Book of Knitting Patterns

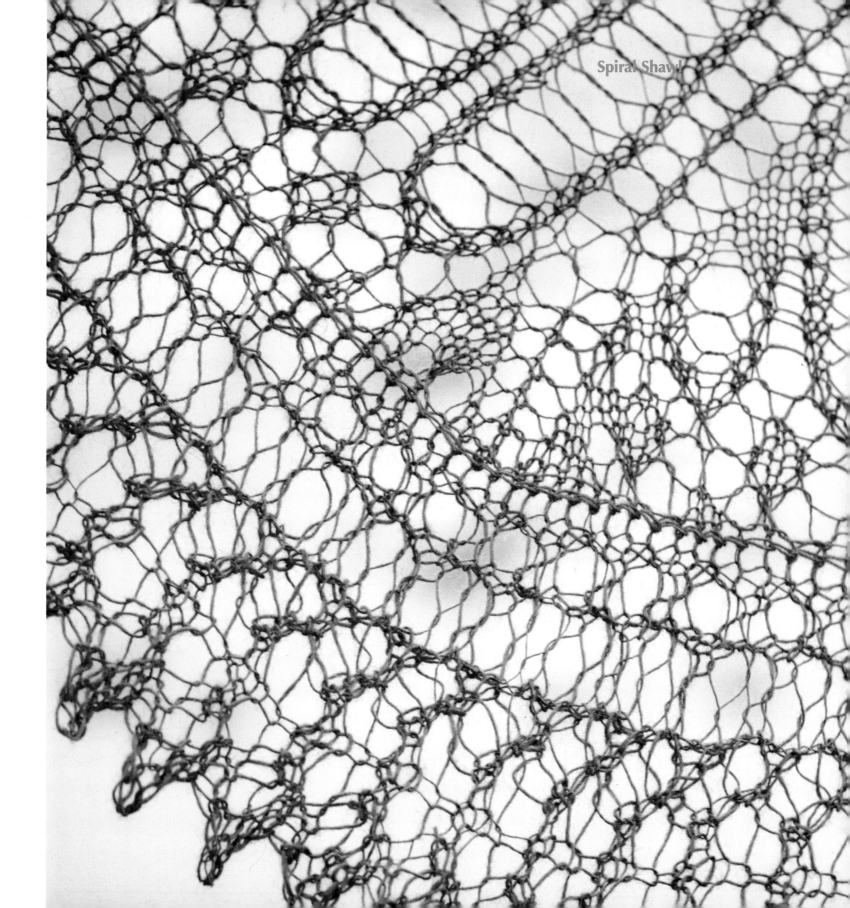

Skill level

Intermediate

Finished measurements

66–68" in diameter

Yarn

Schoolhouse Press Laceweight Icelandic

(1¾oz/50g; 250yds/228m, wool)

5 balls Cranberry #9154

or Slate #0008

Needles

Size 10 (6mm) needles in

double-pointed (dpn) and circular, 16"

and 24" (40 and 60 cm) long,

or size to obtain gauge

Extras

7 yarn loop markers, 6 of one

color and one of a contrasting color

to mark the beginning of the rnd

Tapestry needle

Rust-proof T-pins

Blocked gauge

14 sts to 4"/10cm in St st using

size 10 (6mm) needles.

This design spirals at twice the rate of the preceding shawl and is more like a Nautilus shell. Again, you will quickly memorize the simple increase technique and may decide to add different lace patterns in between the swirls.

Two versions are shown: the slate blue sample is decorated only by the increase lines and the narrow edging; the burgundy shawl has a simple (yo, k2tog) design in every other segment.

NOTES *1* The shawl is knit circularly from the center out. Begin with dpn and change to the 16" circular needle when possible; end with the 24" needle. *2* The basic spiral design is one I have seen in a number of old lace doilies. It causes you (in each section) to inc 3 sts on every other rnd and dec 1 st every rnd. Thus you gain 8 sts overall every 2nd rnd. *3* The optional mesh pat, worked every other segment in the burgundy shawl, is indicated in color on the body chart. *4* See *Techniques*, p. 162, for circular beginnings, double yo, and EZ's Sewn Cast-Off.

Shawl
Using circular beginning and dpn, cast on 8 sts and distribute as evenly as possible. **Begin Body chart:** Work Rnd 1 eight times, placing markers between each rep—16 sts. Continue to work chart as established through rnd 36, then rep rnds 35 and 36, each additional rep working 1 extra st, until you are within 4–5" of total wanted radius. In my case, I knitted until I had 63 sts in each section.

Border
This rep may be adjusted in case you want a larger or smaller shawl. The number of sts in the rep remains static, containing one dec and one inc. The inc is worked as a double yo, into which just 1 st is knitted on the next rnd. This giant hole provides enough extra fabric to permit the points to stretch out when blocked. Since I had 63 sts in each segment and my border rep is 7 sts wide, I had 9 reps in each segment. You may add or subtract from the plain knit part of the border to make your border fit evenly into the number of sts you have in each spiral. Make sure you line up the k2tog to continue the established shape. After working rnd 10, bind off very loosely using EZ's Sewn Cast-Off.

Finishing
Block and fasten ends.

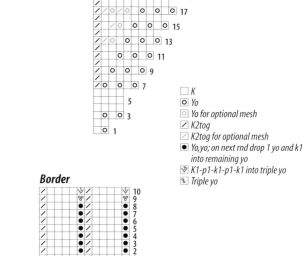

Body

☐ *K*

⊙ *Yo*

○ *Yo for optional mesh*

╱ *K2tog*

╱ *K2tog for optional mesh*

● *Yo,yo; on next rnd drop 1 yo and k1 into remaining yo*

⊻ *K1-p1-k1-p1-k1 into triple yo*

⅋ *Triple yo*

Border

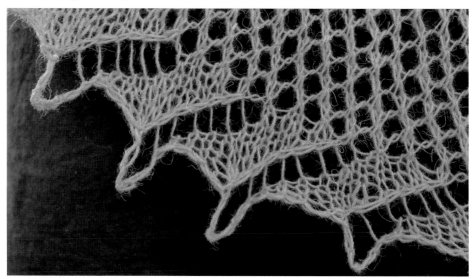

Everything in the house tatted and

doilied in the great art of the place,

designs of lace waves and floe ice,

whelk shells and sea wrack,

the curve of lobster feelers,

the round know of cod-eye,

the bristled commas of shrimp

and fissured sea caves,

white snow on black rock,

pinwheeled gulls,

the slant of silver rain....

Annie Proulx,
The Shipping News

Skill level

Intermediate

Size

One size, easily modified

Finished Measurements

Underarm circumference

of garments shown: 46"

Length: 30"

Changing needle size, number of

knitted-up sts, and blocking give

considerable room for adjustment.

Yarn

Schoolhouse Press Laceweight Icelandic

(1¾oz/50g; 250yds/228m; wool):

4 balls Electric Blue #9803

or Cranberry #9154

Needles

Size 8 (5mm) circular needles,

16" and 24" (40 and 60 cm),

or size to obtain gauge

Double-pointed needle (dpn),

for I-Cord

Extras

Stitch markers

Waste yarn

Optional: Crochet hook for working

Phoney Seams

Blocked gauge

15 sts to 4"/10cm in garter st using size

8 (5mm) needles.

These elegant garments may be worn summer or winter, and knit up surprisingly quickly; the key being fine wool (such as Spun Icelandic Laceweight or Shetland Jumperweight) and large diameter needles. They are knitted in two sections with minimal—if any—sewing. The garter st yoke is worked back and forth—with Elizabeth's Phony Seams for detail—sideways from dropped-shoulder to dropped-shoulder, scooping out the neck as you go. (You may choose to put a lace pat in place of the garter st.) The lace sleeve sections are worked down on circular needles. The body sts are then picked up from the selvage of the yoke—and here is where you decide how wide you want the body to be, knitting up the appropriate number of sts, and working down, in a tube, to wanted length: sweater? tunic? dress?

A word about fine wool on thick needles: if you have ever knitted a shawl in laceweight wool on size 10 or 13 needles, you will remember that the shrivelled bit of lace that hung from your needles became transformed into a large, beautiful expanse once it was properly blocked. I have not gone to such an extreme for this garment, but I did use a size 8 needle (and I knit very loosely), anticipating the considerable stretch I would get upon wetting and blocking the tunic. The advantage of loosely knitted lace is that—when wet—it is very malleable. The Icelandic Laceweight knits up beautifully, becoming softer after washing, and each tunic used just 4 balls of wool.

I will give you the numbers I worked with—and the approximate gauge. Length may easily be changed by adding or subtracting repeats of section C of the lace pattern. Since the style is free-hanging and oversized, you have quite a bit of leeway.

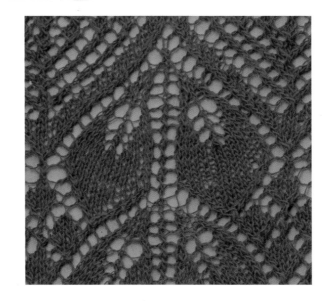

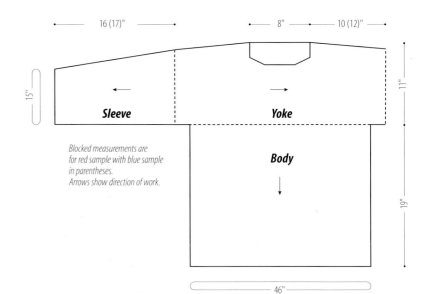

*Blocked measurements are
for red sample with blue sample
in parentheses.
Arrows show direction of work.*

Let me grow lovely,

growing old—

So many fine things do;

Laces, and ivory, and gold.

And silk need not be new.

Karle Wilson Baker,

Old Lace: Let Me Grow Lovely,

NOTES *1* The yoke of the tunic is worked in garter st (knit back and forth). 2 rows of knit = 1 ridge of garter st. If you wish to break up the garter st with a bit of detail, work Elizabeth Zimmermann's Phony Seams (shown on samples) down the center st, and again at 18 sts in from each selvage as follows: drop the st in question down to the cast-on. With a crochet hook, hook up 2 ladders at a time. I work this trick every 3–4" as I go. If you decide not to include the Phony Seams, it may be helpful to mark knitting so as to distinguish RS from WS rows. *2* Only odd rnds are shown on Lace chart. Knit all even rnds. *3* See *Techniques,* p. 162, for backward-loop cast-on, cable cast-on, invisible cast-on, sl2tog-k1-p2sso, and St st grafting.

M1 Make 1 by picking up running yarn before next st and knitting into back of it (see *Techniques,* p. 162).

Picot Bind-Off Work regular bind-off to first double dec of Lace chart, *return st on RH needle to LH needle, cast 3 (or 4) sts onto LH needle using the cable cast-on, bind off to next k1b or double dec in the chart and rep from*.

YOKE
With 24" needle, invisibly cast on 59 sts. Work back and forth in garter st for 5 rows, slipping the first st of each row purlwise for a chain-st edge.

Shape shoulder
Next row (RS) Sl 1, k27, M1, place marker (pm), k3, pm, M1, k28. Continue as established, inc 1 st each side of center 3 sts at markers every 4th RS row 9 times more—79 sts (more for a deeper yoke). Work even until piece measures (slightly stretched) about 10 (12" for longer-sleeved blue tunic) from cast-on, ending with a WS row and noting how many ridges you work after the final inc.

Shape front neck
Next row (RS) You now have 39 sts each side of the center st. Work to within 7 sts of the center st. Turn. Work back. *Work to within 2 sts of last turn. Turn again and work back. Rep from* 4 times more. Place those 17 abandoned sts onto a thread or st holder and work back and forth on remaining 22 sts for 30 rows. *Next row* (RS) Cast on 2 sts (by backward loops) at end of each neck-edge row 5 times, then cast on the final 7 sts. Put all 39 sts on a thread and break the wool. (The two neck selvages will look a bit ratty—but don't worry; we will cover that all up with Elizabeth's Applied I-Cord at the end.)

Back neck and 2nd shoulder
Next row (RS) Work even a corresponding number of ridges (27 in my version) on 40 sts for yoke back. At the end of the last WS row, join Back to Front again (79 sts), work same number of ridges as between final shoulder inc and beginning of neck shaping, then work shoulder dec's to correspond to inc's: dec 1 st each side of 3 center sts every 4th RS row 10 times—59 sts—then work 5 more rows, ending with a WS row.

LACE SLEEVE
Switch to the 16" needle and join the sts into a circle. K 1 rnd, dec 3 sts evenly—56 sts.

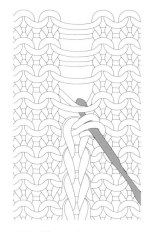

EZ's Phony Seam
Drop stitch. With crochet hook, hook up 2 ladders at a time.

Begin Lace chart: *Part A* Work first st of rnd 1, work rep twice, then work last st of rnd 1. Work 23 (or more, 31 on blue tunic) more rnds as established, remembering to knit all even rnds—at least 6 complete reps of Part A. Work Parts B and C of chart, then work rnds 35–43 of Chart C once more. Work 4 rnds (2 ridges) of garter st by k 1 rnd, p 1 rnd. Work Picot Bind-Off. Pick up invisibly cast-on sts from yoke, removing waste yarn, and work second sleeve.

BODY

(NOTE If you wish your body section to be other than 46" around, you may pick up and work more or fewer sts than these instructions indicate. Part A begins as a 27-st rep. Determine the number of body sts you need and mark the center st of F and B yoke. Since it is unlikely your wanted number of sts will be evenly divisible by 27, do not worry about it; knit up whatever number of sts *you* need and divide the leftover sts in half, keeping them in St st at each side "seam.") For a 46" measurement, I needed 81 sts across each Front and Back, so counted 40 sts from the marked center-back and knitted up 40 sts into the chain of the yoke selvage, then 1 center st, and 40 sts to the other underarm—81 sts total (3 reps). Rep for Front—162 sts total. **Begin Lace chart:** *Part A (Rnd 1)* Work rep 6 times. Work 15 (or, for longer sleeve, 19) more rnds of Part A as established. Work Part B of chart, then Part C. Choose your wanted length by repeating Part C as often as you like, ending at rnd 43. Work a garter st border with Picot Bind-Off as for sleeves.

FINISHING

Sew up the garter-st section of the underarms (whatever ridges may be left over from knitting up for the body—if any).

Neck edge

With RS facing and beginning at a shoulder or center back, pick up all sts around the neck.

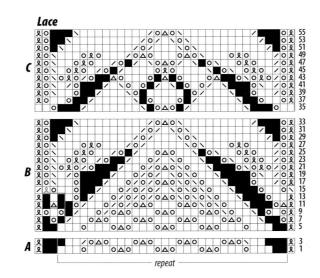

Lace

Work Elizabeth's Applied I-Cord as follows: cast on three I-Cord sts and place them on the pick-up needle, *k2, k2tog tbl (the last I-Cord st and one of the picked-up sts). Slip the three sts back to pick-up needle, and rep from* around. Graft end to beginning. Darn in all ends.

BLOCKING

Now comes the fun: soak the tunic in the sink (and/or wash if necessary). Squeeze out excess water. Spin in the washing machine (or put into a salad basket and swing around your head). Vacuum a nice, clean, tunic-sized spot on the rug, and flop the thing down. It is a good idea to have a sketch of the garment with the wanted dimensions jotted down. You will now mold the tunic to the jotted dimensions. Both body and sleeves will have become alarmingly long and narrow. Put both hands into the sleeves from the cuff, and stretch sideways quite fiercely. The blue version has longer sleeves (more garter st rows in the yoke as well as more repeats of Part A of Lace chart) than the red. Tug and coax until it is the shape you want. Since you can see through the garment, line up the Front and Back patterns with each other. Pin out the Picot points at lower edges. It will dry quite quickly.

□ K
○ Yo
ℛ K in back of st
ℛ No st on last rep; k in back of st on others
╱ K2tog
╲ Ssk
△ Sl2tog-k1-p2sso
■ No stitch

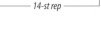

Pearl-Barred Scallop

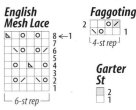

14-st rep

NOTES *1* The body is worked circularly up to the armholes, then the front and back are worked back and forth separately. The only seams are at the shoulders. Bind off the shoulders together for a totally no-sew garment. *2* If you wish to make a longer Tabard, simply add one repeat each to the Pearl Barred Scallop and English Mesh patterns. This will add approx 2½" in length. *3* See *Techniques*, p. 162, for 3-needle bind-off.

BODY

With larger needle, cast on 280 sts. Place marker (pm) for side seam and join. Work 4 rnds of Garter St chart. **Begin Pearl Barred Scallop chart** Work rnds 1–12 twice. **Begin English Mesh chart** Inc 2 sts on first rnd only, one after marker and another after 140th st (282 sts), work rnds 1–8 three times. Work 4 rnds of garter st, dec 2 sts on last rnd—280 sts. **Begin Fir Cone II chart** Placing second side seam marker between 140th & 141st sts, work rnds 1–16 once, then 1–15 once.

Divide Front and Back

Next rnd Inc 1 st at beginning of rnd, then work rnd 16 of chart to side seam marker. Place 141 sts just worked onto holder for front. Inc 1 st after marker, and continue to work rnd 16 of chart to end—141 sts.

BACK

Begin Fir Cone I chart Work rows 1–16 of chart once. K 5 rows, dec 1 st on last row—140 sts. **Begin Faggoting chart** Work rows 1–2 six times. K 5 rows, dec 1 st on last row—139 sts. **Begin Spider chart** Work rows 1–12 twice. K 4 rows. Place all sts on hold.

FRONT

Work as for back through row 9 of the first rep of the Spider chart. *Next row* (RS) Continuing in pat, work 49 sts. Place next 41 sts on holder for front neck. Attach second ball of yarn and continue in pat to end. Working both sides at same time, dec 1 st each side at neck edge every other RS row 3 times as foll: Work to 3 sts before neck, k2tog, k1. On other side of neck, k1, ssk, work to end. When neck shaping is complete, work even in pat as for back—46 sts each shoulder.

Shoulders

Join shoulders using 3 needle bind-off as foll: With WS tog, bind off 46 sts of left front shoulder tog with same number of sts of left back shoulder. Repeat for right shoulder. Leave center 47 sts from back on hold for neck.

BANDS

Beginning at left shoulder seam with RS facing and smaller needle, pick up and k 18 sts along left front neck edge, 41 sts from front neck holder, 18 sts from right front neck edge, and 47 sts from back neck holder—124 sts. Pm, join, and work 8 rnds of Garter St chart beginning with a purl rnd. Bind off loosely in knit. Beginning at underarm with RS facing and smaller needle, pick up and k 108 sts around armhole. Pm, join and work 8 rnds of Garter St chart beginning with a purl rnd. Bind off loosely in knit. Repeat for other armhole.

BLOCKING

Wash garment gently and lay it out to dry, matching finished measurements.

Skill level
Easy

Sizes
S (M, L). Shown in size M.
The instructions are identical for each size. Different sizes are obtained by changing needle size.

Finished measurements
Underarm: 43 (47, 51)"
Length: 18¾ (20, 21¼)"

Yarn
1100 (1200, 1400) yds sport-weight wool or mercerized cotton

Needles
FOR SMALL Size 2 (2.75mm) circular needles, 24"/60cm,
FOR MEDIUM Size 3 (3.25mm) circular needles, 24"/60cm,
FOR LARGE Size 4 (3.5mm) circular needles, 24"/60cm,
or size to obtain gauge
FOR ALL SIZES 16"(40 cm) circular needle two sizes smaller for bands

Extras
Stitch markers
Stitch holders

Blocked gauge
SMALL 26 sts and 33 rows to 4"/10cm in St st, using size 2 (2.75mm) needles.
MEDIUM 24 sts and 31 rows to 4"/10cm in St st, using size 3 (3.25mm) needles.
LARGE 22 sts and 29 rows to 4"/10cm in St st, using size 4 (3.5mm) needles.

English Mesh Lace

6-st rep

Faggoting

4-st rep

Garter St

Spider

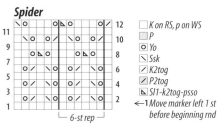

6-st rep

☐ K on RS, p on WS
☐ P
☉ Yo
╲ Ssk
╱ K2tog
╱ P2tog
╲ Sl1-k2tog-psso
←1 Move marker left 1 st before beginning rnd

Fir Cone I (flat version)

Fir Cone II (circular version)

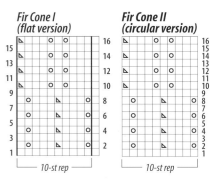

10-st rep   10-st rep

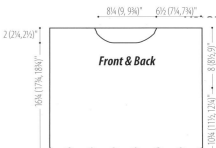

Front & Back

8¼ (9, 9¾)"   6½ (7¼, 7¾)"

2 (2¼, 2½)"

16¾ (17¾, 18¾)"   8 (8½, 9)"

10¾ (11½, 12¼)"

43 (47, 51)"

Greek, sir, is like lace; every man

gets as much of it as he can.

James Boswell,
Life of Johnson

Skill level
Intermediate

Sizes
P (S, M, L, XL, XXL).
Shown in size M.

Finished measurements
Underarm 41½ (45, 48, 51, 54½, 57½)"
Length 26 (27½, 28, 28, 29½, 30)"

Yarn
Schoolhouse Press Québécoise
(3½oz/100g; 210yds/190m;
wool) 7 (8, 8, 9, 10, 10)
skeins Aqua #42

Needles
Sizes 6 and 7 (4 and 4.5 mm)
circular needles, 16" and 29"
(40 and 72 cm),
or size to obtain gauge
One set each sizes 5 and 7
(3.75 and 4.5 mm)
double-pointed needles (dpn)

Extras
Stitch markers
4 stitch holders
4–5 yds waste yarn
Tapestry needle

Blocked gauge
5 sts and 7 rnds to 1"/2.5cm in Simple
Eyelet pat using size 7 (4.5mm) needles;
5 sts and 7 rnds to 1"/2.5cm in OXO
and Zig-Zag pat for yoke using
size 6 (4mm) needles.

NOTES *1* All charts show #'s on right edge for working in rnds. These charts may also be worked back and forth in rows. *2* The st in the second row/rnd above each yo (except for the yo's in Beaded Eyelet) is a k1b. When the st that will need the k1b will also be involved in a dec, twist the st before completing the dec. *3* Make a chain selvage at the side edges of armhole and neck by slipping the first st of each row purlwise. *4* Yoke chart shows body sts on one edge for smallest size only. There will be 8 additional sts at underarm for each size, and the eyelet positions on rows 1–18 may not match chart. *5* See *Techniques*, p. 162, for invisible cast-on, 3-needle bind-off, grafting, and ssp.

Inc 1 On RS, k1, then k into top st of double dec in row below. On WS, p into top st (as viewed from RS) of double dec in row below, then p1.

BODY
With 29" size 6 needle, invisibly cast on 208 (224, 240, 256, 272, 288) sts, join and place marker (pm), being careful not to twist. K 10 rnds. Work 2-st rep of Eyelet Row chart around. Change to size 7 needle and k 10 more rnds, remembering to k1b above the yo's in the second rnd. Slip cast-on sts to smaller needle and hold to back of larger needle, removing waste yarn. To make hem, k st from the front needle tog with st from back needle. Make sure the two sts being knitted tog are vertically aligned. K 2 more rnds. **Begin Simple Eyelet chart:** *Rnd 1* Work 8-st rep of chart 26 (28, 30, 32, 34, 36) times. Continue to work through rnd 12 of chart as established, then work 12-rnd rep until piece measures 14½ (14½, 15½, 15½, 16½, 16½)" from turned hem, end with a rnd 6 or rnd 12. K1 and move marker 1 st to left, marking next st (the one above a yo) as the side seam st. While working foll rnd, pm after 104 (112, 120, 128, 136, 144) sts for opposite side seam. **Begin Beaded Eyelet chart:** *Rnd 1* Work 2-st rep of chart around, then con-

The name, Ljace-Kofte,
is a play-on-words.
The ljus kofte is a traditional
Norwegian sweater,
worked in two or three
colored stranded patterns.
The lower body and sleeves
often have a simple dotted
design, hence the ljus
(translates as lice).
The yoke and upper sleeves are
made of horizontal bands of x's
and o's (actually, diamonds),
zig-zags, and/or
smaller diamonds.
I took it as a personal
challenge to come up with
a lace version.
I modified the drop-shoulder
by indenting the armholes
somewhat. I also chose not to
cut the armholes, and knitted the
sleeves down from the armhole.

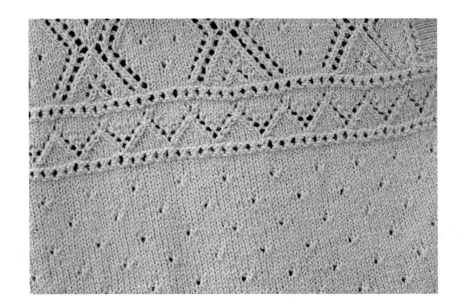

Lace knitting is a universal favorite because it offers so much variety in shape, design, and texture, and because its results—however simple the pattern—are so lovely.

Barbara G. Walker,
Charted Knitting Designs

Ljace-Kofte

continue to work rnds 2 and 3 as established. Change to size 6 circular needle. **Begin Zig-Zag chart: *Rnd 1*** Work sts 6–8 (2–8, 6–8, 2–8, 6–8, 2–8) of chart, work 8-st rep of chart around, end sts 1–5 (1, 1–5, 1, 1–5, 1). Referring to Yoke chart for pat placement, continue to work chart as established through rnd 13 or until appropriate underarm position as shown on Yoke chart. At underarms, place side seam st plus 5 (9, 13,17, 21, 25) sts each side of side seam marker on holders, leaving 93 sts for front and 93 sts for back on all sizes.

BACK

Working back and forth in rows and remembering to slip first st of each row for selvage, continue to follow Yoke chart through row 78. Change to size 7 needle. Work rows 63–65 again. Work 4 rows St st. **Begin Simple Eyelet chart: *Rnd 1*** Work selvage st, work 8-st rep 11 times, work first 2 sts of rep, k2. Continue to work chart as established until armhole measures 9 (9½, 10, 10, 10½, 11)" or slightly less. Place sts on holder.

FRONT

Work as for back through row 78. Change to size 7 needle. Continuing to follow chart, work 39 sts, place center 15 sts on holder, join second ball of yarn and work to end. Continue to work both sides of neck at same time through row 110, following pat placement as indicated for eyelet pat. **Begin Beaded Eyelet chart: *Row 1*** Work selvage st, work 2-st rep to last st, k1. Continue to work rows 2 and 3 as established. Turn work inside out and bind off front and back shoulders tog firmly by 3-needle bind-off. Bind off back neck sts firmly, dec 4 sts evenly across back neck during bind-off by k2tog.

SLEEVES

(NOTES *1* Sleeves are worked from armhole down. At the end of the 2nd and all following rows, work the last st of sleeve tog with an underarm st by p2tog at end of WS rows and ssk at end of RS rows, maintaining chain selvage. When all underarm sts have been joined, work sleeve circularly, working a k2tog over the first and last sts of sleeve at end of first rnd. This st should be marked as the underarm seam st. *2* When working dec's and lace patterning at same time, observe the following rule: if the dec will eliminate one of the sts needed to work the eyelet, don't make the eyelet. Work in St st instead. *3* The garment may be tried on at any time to adjust the length of the sleeves and the rate of decreasing.)

With RS facing and 16" size 7 needle, pick up and p 1 st in every chain along armhole edge, turning chain selvage to RS. Count your sts. Subtract your st number from target st count of 91 (95, 99, 103, 107, 111). Turn and k, inc evenly across to bring your st count up to target. This inc row will also serve as the first row of the Beaded Eyelet pattern. **Begin Beaded Eyelet chart: *Row 2*** (RS) K1, work 2-st rep across. Turn and k for 3rd row of chart. Work 4 rows St st. **Begin Simple Eyelet chart: *Row 1*** (RS) To center the chart, begin with st 1 (7, 1, 7, 1, 7) of rep, work through end of rep, work 8-st rep 7 (8, 8, 9, 9, 10) times more, work first 3, (5, 3, 5, 3, 5) sts of rep. Continue to work chart as established. AT SAME TIME, beginning with rnd 7 of chart, work a pair of sleeve dec's every 6th row/rnd by k2tog at beginning of row (or after seam st at beginning of rnd) and ssk at end of row/rnd.

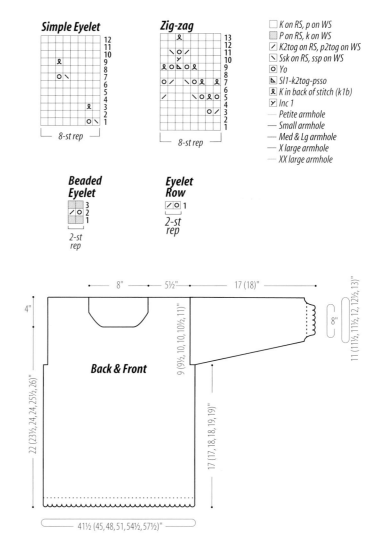

When sleeve measures approx 1½" less than desired length—approx 50 (50, 52, 54, 54, 56) sts—dec evenly down to 40 sts or amount desired for a roomy cuff. P 1 rnd. K 10 rnds, then, using size 5 dpn, work Eyelet Row around. Work 10 more rnds, then break yarn, leaving long tail. With a tapestry needle, form hem by joining live sts to inside of sleeve using whip st or grafting. Elastic may be inserted into casing before joining hem, or an opening may be created for later elastic insertion by binding off 5 sts before joining the rest of the sts for the hem.

Yoke

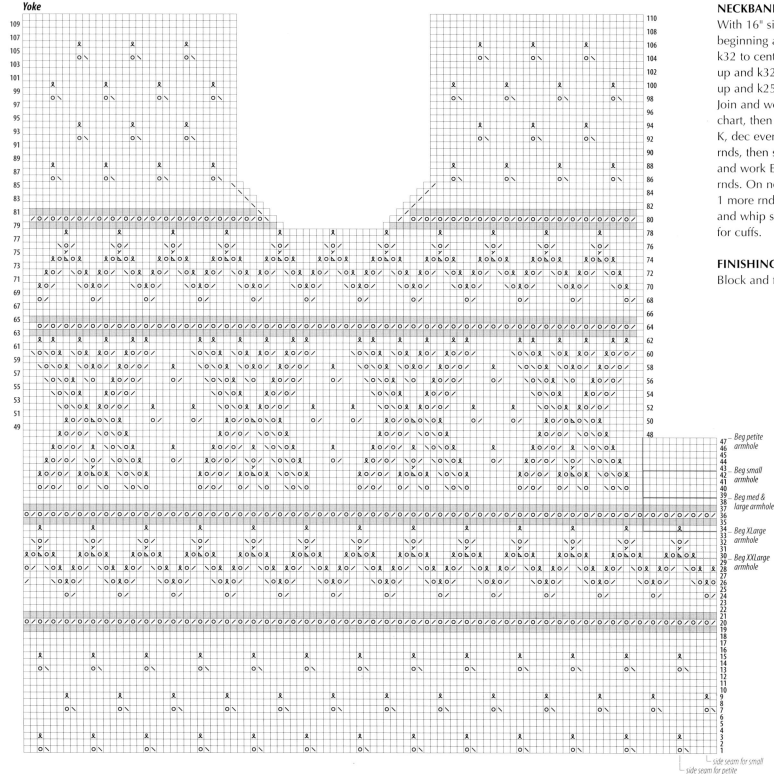

NECKBAND

With 16" size 7 needle, RS facing, and beginning at left shoulder, pick up and k32 to center front, k15 from holder, pick up and k32 to right shoulder, then pick up and k25 across back neck—104 sts. Join and work rnd 1 of Beaded Eyelet chart, then work rnds 2 and 3. *Next rnd* K, dec evenly to approx 84 sts. K 9 more rnds, then switch to shorter size 6 needle and work Eyelet Row chart around. K 8 rnds. On next rnd, inc back to 104 sts. K 1 more rnd. Break yarn, leaving long tail and whip st or graft live sts to inside, as for cuffs.

FINISHING

Block and fasten ends.

Beg petite armhole
Beg small armhole
Beg med & large armhole
Beg XLarge armhole
Beg XXLarge armhole

side seam for small
side seam for petite

Skill level
Experienced

Sizes
One size

Finished measurements
Underarm 56", buttoned
Length 28"

Yarn
Jamieson & Smith Jumperweight
Shetland (1oz/28g;
150yds/137m; wool) 4 skeins each:
Dark Brown Fleck FC44 (A),
Spice Fleck 1281 (B),
Cafe au lait FC17 (C);
3 skeins Darkest Chocolate 5 (D);
2 skeins Med Brown FC60 (E);
1 skein each: Oatmeal F202 (F)
and Straw FC43(G)

Needles
Size 5 (3.75 mm) needles in
regular and double-pointed (dpn)
or size to obtain gauge

Extras
Small amount smooth (preferably
cotton) contrasting color waste yarn
Stitch markers
Two spare needles,
smaller than working needles
Two ½" buttons or I-Cord buttons
(see p. 99)

Blocked gauge
Each square, worked in Chart 1,
using size 5 (3.75mm) needles
measures 7"x 7".

NOTES *1* Test for color fastness when blocking. See finishing instructions. *2* Only RS rows are shown on Chart 1; all WS rows are purled. *3* See *Techniques*, p. 162, for ssk, sssk, M1L, M1R, sl2tog-k1-p2sso, cable cast-on, grafting open sts to cast-on edge, and 3-needle bind-off.

Options
1 If you would like to use different colors, use the placement diagrams to "color" on and plan the placement of your colors. Each triangle takes approx 25 yds of yarn and each color used for I-Cord edging takes approx 75 yds. *2* You may make each square, joining squares as you go, using Rick Mondragon's *sliding loop* technique for joining, so there is very little seaming to do. The technique is explained in general on this page; see p. 99 for how to use it to join the squares. *3* You may make each square separately and then sew them together, working in one-half st from edge and checking flexibility of seams carefully. This will result in garment being less than 1" smaller around and slightly shorter than specified.

Attached I-Cord
(Thanks to Joyce Williams for this variation on Elizabeth Zimmermann's method.) With 2 dpn, cable cast on 3 sts. *K2, sl 1, yo, pick up and k 1 st as specified, pass sl st and yo tog over the picked-up st. Push sts to other end of dpn; rep from* as specified.

Rick Mondragon's Sliding Loop

1 Mark the turning thread as you knit
At the beginning of each row, bring working yarn around a length of contrast yarn.

2 Knit up a sliding loop Insert a free needle in the first turning thread and pull up a loop of the next working yarn.

3 Work two rows with sliding loop
Remove loop from needle and turn work.
Using the yarn supplied by the sliding loop, cast on. Turn and, continuing to work with yarn from sliding loop, work back to the turning thread. Continue pulling up a loop in each turning thread and working two rows with yarn from loop.

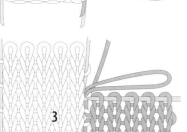

It isn't the gown compels me

Condone this venial sin;

It's the pretty face above the lace,

And the gentle heart within.

Eugene Field,

The Tea Gown

Patchwork Lace Jacket

BODY

NOTE Each square is worked from Chart 1, changing colors at row 46 (a WS row) so it appears as 2 right triangles. See placement diagrams for the color to be used for each "triangle" and the direction in which each square is worked. (You may work the squares in a different order and direction as long as the color and orientation of triangles remain the same.)

Square 1

With B, cast on 1 st. Work Chart 1 rows 1–45, remembering to purl WS rows and marking turning st at each side with contrasting yarn if using the sliding loop method. Change to A and separate lengths of contrasting yarn and work Chart 1 rows 46–89. Fasten off. (Leave approx a 12" tail where you may need to sew or weave a seam or neaten a corner.)

Square 2

With E, cast on 1 st. Work Chart 1 rows 1–45, marking turning st at left edge and joining right edge to A portion of square 1. With D, work Chart 1 rows 46–89, marking turning sts at both edges with separate lengths of contrasting yarn.

Continue to work squares 3–32 in this manner as shown on placement diagram. Note that after every 4th square is worked (and after square 21), there is one edge seam to be sewn.

Body Placement Diagram

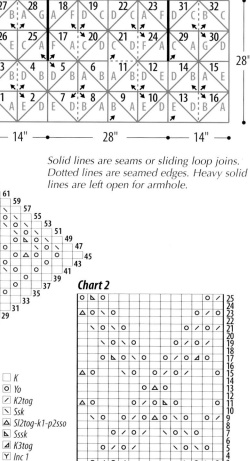

Solid lines are seams or sliding loop joins. Dotted lines are seamed edges. Heavy solid lines are left open for armhole.

Chart 1

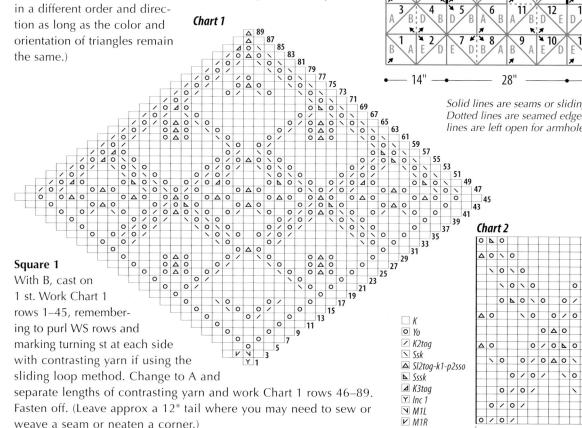

Chart 2

☐ K
◉ Yo
✓ K2tog
◢ Ssk
▲ Sl2tog-k1-p2sso
◣ Sssk
◭ K3tog
⅄ Inc 1
◥ M1L
◩ M1R

14-st rep

Sleeve Placement Diagram

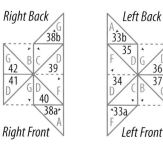

Join shoulders

Right shoulder

If you have used the sliding loop joining, work 3-needle bind-off as foll: With RS facing, insert a spare needle into each marked turning st along the top of square 23 and into about half of the sts along the top of square 22—33 sts total. Insert other spare needle into turning sts along the top of square 31 and half of those along square 32—33 sts total. With RS tog, work 3-needle bind-off with a size 5 needle. If special join technique has not been used, sew shoulder squares across same positions, working 1 st in from edge.

Left shoulder

Work to correspond to right shoulder.

LEFT SLEEVE

Square 33 This square is shown on the placement diagram as 2 triangles, but is worked as a square: rows 1–45 of Chart 1 are marked 33a on the diagram, and rows 46–89 are marked 33b. Work as before, then sew edges for sleeve seam.

RIGHT SLEEVE

Work as for left sleeve.

Try jacket on and evaluate sleeve length.
If the sleeves are long enough (or will be when blocked), work 2 rnds of attached I-Cord as foll: Use C for first rnd and with RS facing, beginning at sleeve seam, work 80 rows (this requires picking up twice in most turning sts). Graft open sts to cast-on sts. Use A for second rnd and pick up in right half of center st of previous rnd of I-Cord, picking up in 3 out of 4 rows for a total of 60 rows. Graft open sts to cast-on sts.
If you want 3–4" more (as shown) work cuff instructions.
If you want 7" more or want a turned-back cuff, work 2 more squares in colors of your choice, then 2 rnds of Attached I-Cord as specified if no more squares were worked.

CUFF

Work 2 rnds of Attached I-Cord except work second rnd

picking up a st in every row from rnd 1 for a total of 80 rows. With dpn and C, pick up and k 70 sts in right half of center st of last rnd of I-Cord (skipping every 8th row), place marker. **Begin Chart 2: Rnd 1** Work 14-st rep 5 times. Continue to work rnds 2–25. Work 2 rnds of Attached I-Cord. Use A for first rnd and k 1 st from the lace edge instead of picking up and knitting a st. Work 60 rows: k2tog from the lace edge every 6th row. Use C for second rnd, picking up in right half of center st as before in every row.

Right sleeve

Work as for left sleeve except use A for rnd 1 of I-Cord on shortest and longest options and C for second rnd. Use A for Chart 2 of cuff. Use C for first rnd of I-Cord at bottom of cuff and A for second rnd.

FINISHING
I-Cord edging

With RS facing, dpn, and C, beginning at right front lower edge at side seam, work Attached I-Cord, picking up twice in one turning st and once in the next (3 rows of I-Cord for every 2 sts), to the corner, k3, push sts to other end of dpn and k (1 row unattached I-Cord), work 1 row Attached I-Cord in corner st, work 1 row unattached I-Cord, continue with Attached I-Cord as before up right front until 2 squares are completed (where square 15 meets square 30), make a buttonloop by working 2½" unattached I-Cord, work Attached I-Cord to next square, rep buttonloop, work Attached I-Cord to neck edge corner, work corner as for lower corner, continue to work Attached I-Cord around neck edge, down left front and along lower edge, working corners as before. Graft open sts to cast-on sts. With A, work a second rnd of Attached I-Cord, picking up in right half of center st of every row of first rnd. Work corners as for first rnd. When buttonloops are reached, give each a half-twist and work second rnd of I-Cord over them to hold them in place.

Blocking

NOTE Be sure to block your swatch to check that dark colors won't run into the lights. If you see a color run, repeat the rinsing several times until the water appears clear before laying the item to dry. Also, putting a towel between layers during drying is helpful.

Wet block Soak in fairly hot water with a mild soap. Remove, squeeze gently, and rinse in hot water (a little fabric softener or hair conditioner may be added to soften the wool). Remove, squeeze out water, and roll in a towel. Lay flat, square up the edges, and pin to measurements, checking that each square is 7" on each side. Let dry.

I-Cord knot buttons (make 2)

With C, work 6" of unattached I-Cord. Fold in half to make a loop. Tie a simple knot with this loop, leaving a short part of the loop sticking out. Pull the loose ends through this loop and tighten knot. Sew in place with ends under I-Cord edging. Sew one long stitch through all layers of the knot to prevent it from working loose.

Join squares with sliding-loop join

NOTE Work your swatch beginning with square 1 and try the technique attaching square 2. If you like the finished swatch, you may continue with the sweater already in progress.

1 As you work each square, mark the turning thread of each row: Use a 12–14" length of contrasting color waste yarn to mark each side that is being joined. For square 1, four separate lengths will be used. At the beginning of each row (beginning with row 2) lay contrasting yarn on top of working yarn, then work row as usual. By placing the contrasting yarn every row, the turning thread of each row wraps around the contrast yarn.

2 Join square 2 to square 1: With E, cast on 1 st. Looking at Body Placement Diagram, place square 1 (with RS facing) so that the A portion is to the right of E portion of square 2 as you work. Insert your free needle into the first turning thread of square 1 from front to back and pull up a loop of the working yarn (E). Remove loop from needle and use anchored end to work row 1 of Chart 1 (inc 1), allow more yarn to flow into loop as necessary (extra can be removed). Turn work, lay a contrasting yarn over working yarn, and work row 2 (p2). Pull on the end of the yarn to close up the sliding loop and tighten square 2 to square 1. *Insert free needle into next turning thread and pull up a loop. Use loop to work next row of chart, lay contrast yarn over working yarn, work the following row, and tighten loop to remove unneeded yarn. Rep from* through row 45 of Chart 1. Cut all yarns. Change to A and start a new length of contrast yarn on row 46; use another length of contrast yarn to mark the turning threads at beginning of RS rows as well.

NOTE The process is the same whether you are joining at the left or right side of the square you are working on, or whether you are joining during the 1st or 2nd half of the square. You always insert your free needle from RS to WS to pull up the loop of yarn and you always work with the anchored end of the loop, allowing more yarn to pull into the loop from the ball.

Skill level
Adventurous

Sizes
XS (S, M, L, XL, XXL). Shown in M.

Finished measurements
Underarm
38 (41, 43½, 46, 49½, 52½)"
Length 25"

Yarn
Jamieson & Smith Jumperweight
Shetland (1oz/28g; 150yd/137m;
wool) 9 (9, 10, 10, 11, 11) skeins
Light Gray Heather #1280 (MC)
1 skein Green #141 (CC)

Needles
Size 5 (3.75mm) needles
or size to obtain gauge
Size 3 (3.25mm) circular,
16" (40cm) long

Extras
Stitch holders
Stitch markers

Blocked gauge
22 sts and 28 rows to 4"
(10cm) over Chart B, using size 5
(3.25mm) needles

NOTES *1* This sweater is worked in sections of patterns using short rows, divided by contrast color (CC) ridges. *2* The back, front, and sleeve charts show the armhole and neck shapings, short-row wrap and turn (w&t) sts, CC ridges, the chart worked in each section, and the outline of a full rep of the chart if it is not first used at an even edge. The small diagrams show the beginning and ending points for the short-row sections. *3* It may be helpful to reproduce and enlarge all or parts of these charts and chart some areas of the patterns where full reps may not be worked. *4* The sleeve chart shows only the first 64 rows. *5* See *Techniques,* p. 162, for sl2tog-k1-p2sso, short-row wrap, and 3-needle bind-off.

Picot cast-on
Make a slip knot for first st. *K1 without dropping st from LH needle, then slip the new st from RH needle to LH needle; rep from* once—3 sts. K2, pass first st over 2nd, k1, pass 2nd st over 3rd (one st remains—picot point complete)**. Slip st from RH needle to LH needle***. Rep from* to *** until specified number of points have been made. Do not slip st to LH needle at end of last rep. Turn, pick up and k 1 st in top of last picot. Pick up and k 2 sts in each remaining picot.

Picot bind-off
With sts on left needle, work from* to ** of picot cast-on, bind off 3 sts. Sl st from RH needle to LH needle; rep from*.

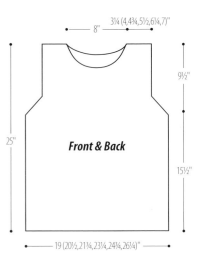

3¼ (4,4¾,5½,6¼,7)"

8"

9½"

25"

Front & Back

15½"

19 (20½,21¾,23¼,24¾,26¼)"

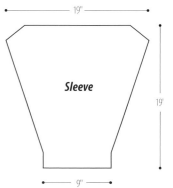

19"

Sleeve

19"

9"

A GATHERING OF LACE

Ruby Gillis smuggled three plums

over to Anne during

testament reading;

Ella May Macpherson gave her

an enormous yellow pansy cut from

the covers of a floral

catalogue—a species of desk

decoration much prized

in Avonlea school.

Sophia Sloane offered to teach her

a perfectly elegant new

pattern of knit lace,

so nice for trimming aprons.

Lucy Maud Montgomery,

Anne of Green Gables

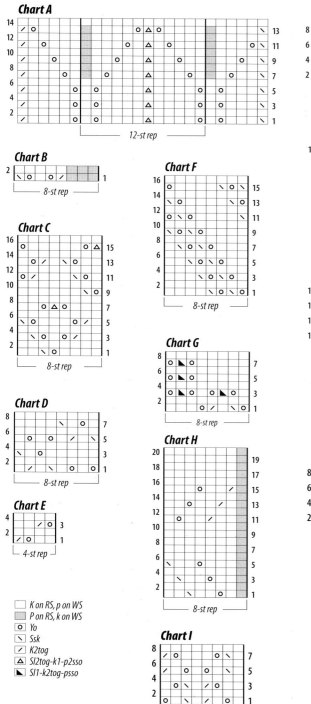

Chart A

12-st rep

Chart B

8-st rep

Chart C

8-st rep

Chart D

8-st rep

Chart E

4-st rep

□ K on RS, p on WS
▨ P on RS, k on WS
○ Yo
╲ Ssk
╱ K2tog
△ Sl2tog-k1-p2sso
◤ Sl1-k2tog-psso

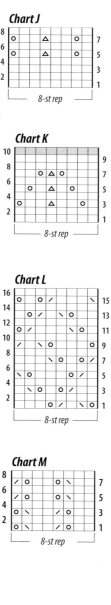

Chart F

8-st rep

Chart G

8-st rep

Chart H

8-st rep

Chart I

8-st rep

Chart J

8-st rep

Chart K

8-st rep

Chart L

8-st rep

Chart M

8-st rep

Twisted k1-p1 rib (in rnds)
Rnd 1 *K1 through the back loop, p1; rep from*. Rep rnd 1 for rib.

BACK
With larger needles and MC, using picot cast-on, make 55 (55, 61, 67, 67, 73) picot points, then pick up and k into picots—110 (110, 122, 134, 134, 146) sts. P 1 row. **Begin Chart A: Row 1** K1, work chart sts 1–6 (1–6, 0, 1–6, 1–6, 0), work 12-st rep 8 (8, 10, 10, 10, 12) times, work sts 19–24 (19–24, 0, 19–24, 19–24, 0), k1. Keeping first and last sts in St st, work chart rows 2–14 as established. With CC, k 1 row dec 4 (inc 4, 0, dec 4, inc 4, 0) sts evenly across—106 (114, 122, 130, 138, 146) sts. K 1 row. P 1 row. Change to MC and p 1 row. (NOTE The back chart begins at this point. From now on, the first and last sts of every row are kept in St st for selvages. These selvage sts are not included in any charts or instructions.) **Begin Chart B** Work 7 rows of Chart B even, then continue Chart B pat, working short rows as shown on Back chart until you are at point A. With CC, purl 2 rows. K 1 row. You are at point B. **Begin Chart C** Work Chart C pat to point C. With CC, k until you come to previous CC ridge, k1 (hiding wrap), wrap next st and turn (w&t). K 1 row. *Next row* P to wrapped st, p2. You are at point D. *Row 27* With MC, k1, w&t. *28* P1, w&t. *29* K3, w&t. *30* P4, w&t.

For Sizes XS, M, and XL ONLY: Row 31 K8, w&t. *32* P9, w&t. *33* Yo, k1, ssk, k5, yo, k1, ssk, k2, w&t. *34* P14, w&t. *35* K4, [ssk, k1, k2tog, k1, yo, k1, yo, k1] twice, w&t. *36* P22, w&t. *37* K6, [k1, yo, k1, ssk, k4] twice, k1, yo, k1, ssk, w&t. *38* P28, w&t. **Begin Chart D: Row 1** (Row 39 of Back) *Continue in Chart D pat as established, beginning with row 1, st 1, to point E, working underarm shaping as shown on Back chart**.

For Sizes S, L, and XXL ONLY: Row 31 Yo, k1, ssk, k5, w&t. *32* P9, w&t. *33* K4, yo, k1, ssk, k6, w&t. *34* P14, w&t. *35* [Ssk, k1, k2tog, k1, yo, k1, yo, k1] twice, k3, w&t. *36* P22, w&t. *37* K2, [k1, yo, k1, ssk, k4] 3 times, w&t. *38* P28, w&t. **Begin Chart D: Row 1** (Row 39 of Back) Continue as foll: K4, then work from* to ** of Sizes XS, M, and XL.

All Sizes With CC, purl (working underarm bind-off) to first CC st (point F), p1, w&t. P 1 row. K to wrapped st, k1. *Row 62* With MC, p1, w&t. *Row 63* K1, w&t. *64* P2, w&t. *65* K3, w&t. *66* P5, w&t. **Begin Chart E: Row 1** (Row 67 of Back) Work chart row 1, beginning with st 2. Continue working Chart E to point G. With CC, k to first st of CC (point H), k1, w&t. K 1 row. P to wrapped st, p1. Change to MC, k2, w&t. *Row 104* P3, w&t. *105* K1, yo, ssk, k3, w&t. *106* P9, w&t. **Begin Chart F: Row 1** (107) K3, work chart row 1, k2, w&t. Continue to work charts as established through row 152.

Shape neck
Row 153 Work in pat to center 24 sts, place center 24 sts on a holder, join 2nd ball and complete row. Working both sides at same time and continuing in pat, work neck shaping as shown on Back chart. Place remaining sts on a holder.

FRONT
Work as for back to point A, working 8 rows even of Chart B before beginning short rows. With CC, k 2 rows, p 1 row. *Row 12* With MC, p13 (17, 21, 25, 29, 33), w&t. **Begin Chart C: 13** Work chart row 1 beginning with st 4 (8, 4, 8, 4, 8). Continue to work Chart C section

Back

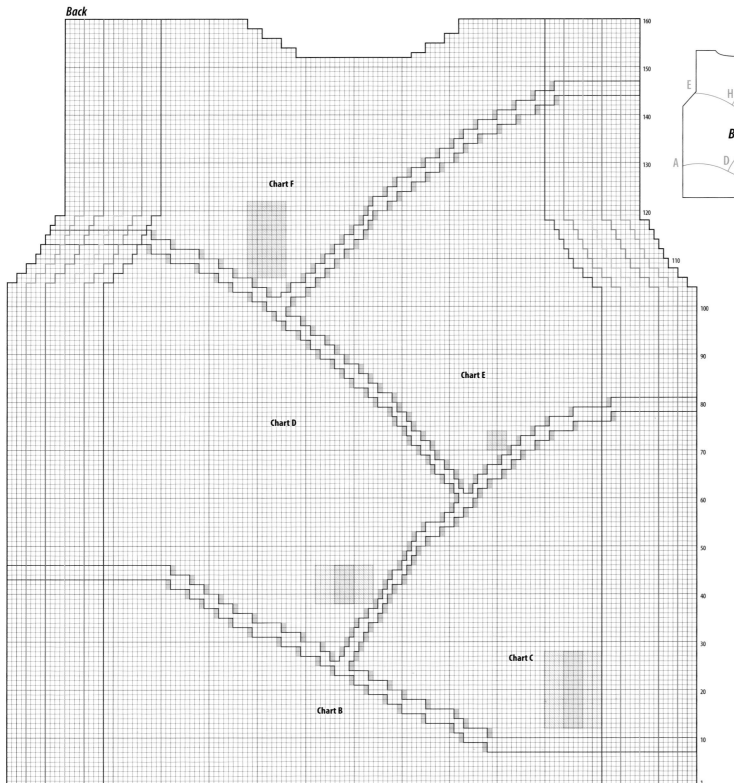

Chart F

Chart E

Chart D

Chart C

Chart B

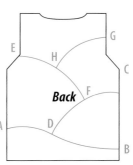

Back

to point C. With CC, purl to first CC st (point D), p1, w&t. P 1 row. K to wrapped st, k1. *Row 32* With MC, p6, w&t.

For Sizes XS, M, and XL ONLY: Row 33 K3, yo, k1, ssk, k1, w&t. *34* P9, w&t. *35* Ssk, k1, k2tog, k1, yo, k1, yo, k4, w&t. *36* P14, w&t. *37* K4, yo, k1, ssk, k5, yo, k1, ssk, k2, w&t. *38* P22, w&t.

Begin Chart D: *Row 1* (39) *Work chart row, beginning with st 1. Continue to work Chart D as established to point E.***

For Sizes S, L, and XXL ONLY: Row 33 K7, w&t. *34* P9, w&t. *35* K4, ssk, k1, k2tog, k1, yo, k1, yo, w&t. *36* P14, w&t. *37* K8, yo, k1, ssk, k6, w&t. *38* P22, w&t.

Begin Chart D: *Row 1* (39) K4, then work from* to ** as for XS, M, and XL.

All Sizes With CC, k to first CC st (point F), k1, w&t. K 1 row. P to wrapped st, p1. *Row 53* With MC, k2, w&t. *Row 54* P3, w&t. *55*, K3, yo, k2tog, w&t. *56* P7, w&t. **Begin Chart E:** *Row 1* (57) Work chart row, beginning with st 4. Continue to work chart as established to point G. With CC, p to first CC st (point H), p1, w&t. P 1 row. K to wrapped st, k1. *Row 90* With MC, p1, w&t. *91* K1, w&t. *92* P2, w&t. *93* K4, w&t. *94* P5, w&t. *95* K4, yo, ssk, k1, w&t. *96* P8, w&t. *97* K2, yo, sl2tog-k1-p2sso, yo, k1, yo, sl2tog-k1-p2sso, yo, k1, w&t. *98* P11, w&t. *99* K3, yo, sl2tog-k1-p2sso, yo, k6, w&t. *100* P14, w&t. *101* K5, yo, sl2tog-k1-p2sso, yo, k7, w&t. *102* P17, w&t. **Begin Chart G:** *Row 1* (103) Work chart row, beginning with st 7. Continue to work chart as established through row 138.

Shape neck
Row 139 Work in pat to center 12 sts,

103

place center 12 sts on a holder, join 2nd ball and complete row. Working both sides at same time and continuing in pat, work neck shaping as shown on Front chart. Place remaining sts on a holder. Join shoulders using 3-needle bind-off.

Right sleeve

With RS facing and MC, pick up and k 84 sts along straight edge of armhole. *Next row* P3, k1, [p7, k1] 10 times, pick up and p 2 sts along armhole edge. **Begin Chart H:** *Row 1* (Row 3 of Sleeve chart) K2, work 8-st rep of chart to last 4 sts, p1, k3, pick up and k 2 sts along armhole shaping. Continue to work chart as established, picking up and working 2 sts from armhole shaping at the end of each row through sleeve chart row 13—108 sts. (NOTE You are at the underarm; all required sts have been picked up.) Continuing in pat, cast on 1 st at end of next 2 rows for selvage sts, working selvage sts as for body. Work 1 row even. Dec 1 st each side of next row, then every 4th row 27 times more—52 sts. AT SAME TIME, work Chart H through row 50. *Row 51* K1, [p1, k7] twice. Do not turn. Cut yarn. Slide all remaining sts from LH needle to RH needle. Turn. With CC, p 1 row. *Next row* P2tog, p to end. *Next row* K2tog, k to end. **Begin Chart I:** *Row 1* (Row 31 of sleeve) With MC, k1, beginning with st 7, work chart row. Continue to work chart as established through row 54. Do not turn. Cut yarn and slide all sts to LH needle. *Row 8* (Row 30 of sleeve) P1, work chart row from left to right beginning with st 8. Continue to work chart through row 54. Do not turn. Cut yarn. Slide all sts to RH needle. Turn, ready for a RS row. Beginning with row 55, complete chart through row 64. Continuing to work dec's, work 24 more rows. K 1 row. With CC, p 2 rows. K 1 row.

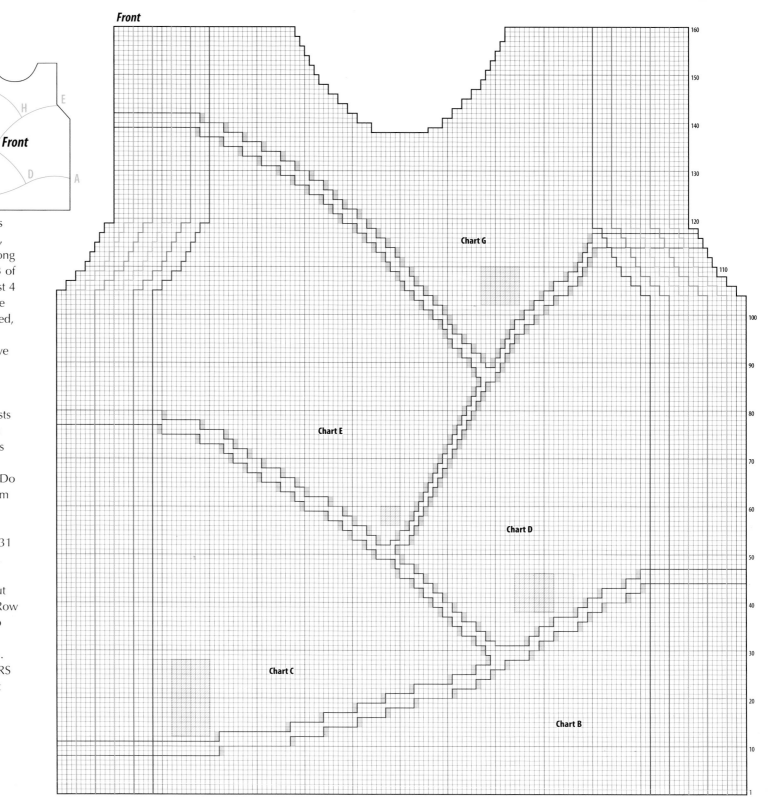

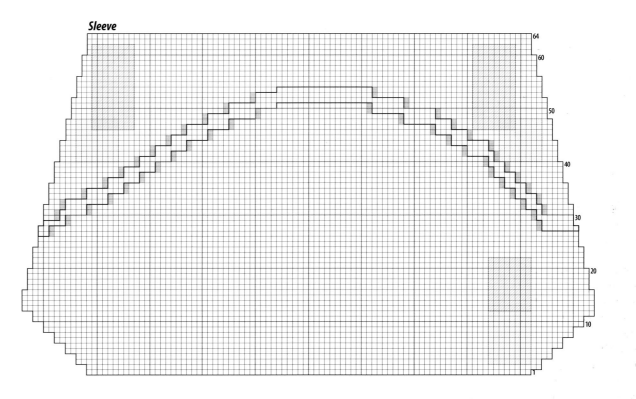

Sleeve

Begin Chart J: *Row 1* With MC, dec 1, work 8-st rep 7 times, k6, dec 1. Continue in pat as established for 42 more rows or to desired length. With CC, k 1 row, dec 4 sts evenly across—48 sts. K 1 row. P 1 row.

Sleeve edging
With MC, p 1 row. Work rows 3–8 of Chart K. Bind off using Picot bind-off.

LEFT SLEEVE
Work as for right sleeve, replacing Charts H, I, and J with K, L, and M respectively. **Begin Chart M as foll:** *Row 1* With MC, dec 1, k1, work sts 6–8, work 8-st rep 7 times, work sts 1–6, dec 1.

COLLAR
With RS facing, circular needle, and MC, beginning at right shoulder, pick up and k14 along right back neck edge, k24 from back holder, pick up and k14 along left back neck edge, k25 along left front neck edge, k12 from front holder, placing a marker between sts 6 and 7, pick up and k25 along right

front neck edge—114 sts. Join and work 8 rnds Twisted k1-p1 rib. **Divide collar** (RS and WS reversed) Work to center front marker, turn, change to larger needles and work back and forth in rows. **Begin Chart B:** *Row 1* Sl 1 wyib, p2tog, work sts 4–8 of Chart B, work 8-st rep to last 2 sts, p1, k1—113 sts. *2* Sl 1 wyib, k1, work 8-st rep to last 7 sts, work sts 8–4, k2. Work 8 more rows of Chart B, keeping the beginning and end of RS rows as sl 1, p1 and p1, k1 and the beginning and end of WS rows as sl 1, k1 and k2. With CC, k 1 row, inc 1 st in center—114 sts. K 1 row. P 1 row. With MC, p 1 row. **Begin Chart K:** *Row 3* Sl 1, work 8-st rep 14 times, k1. *Row 4* Sl 1, work to last st, k1. Keeping first and last sts as established, work chart rows 5–8. Bind off using Picot bind-off.

FINISHING
Sew side and sleeve seams. Block, pinning out each picot point.

This vest is designed to be loose and flowing. It is a seamless vest knitted from the top down. The vest may be adjusted to fit your individual size by adding or subtracting a motif across the back or at the underarm.

Seed st (over any number of sts)
Row/Rnd 1 *K1, p1; rep from*. *Row/Rnd 2* K the purl sts and p the knit sts. Rep row/rnd 2 for seed st pat.

Picot bind-off *Cast on 3 sts using chain cast-on. Bind off the cast-on sts, then bind off 3 more sts. Slip st on RH needle back to LH needle; rep from*, end by casting on 3 sts and binding them off to create a picot at each end of a straight bound-off edge. Begin but do not end with a picot if working Picot bind-off in the rnd.

NOTES *1* Only even rows are charted. All odd rows are purled. *2* When increasing in lace and when working neck edge of fronts, work sts into lace pat when there are enough sts to work both a yo and its accompanying dec. Until this is possible, work inc and neck edge sts in St st. *3* Always maintain a selvage st each side in St st, working inc sts inside the selvage. *4* See *Techniques*, p. 162, for sssk.

BACK
Using the larger needle, loosely cast on 83 (83, 103) sts. *Row 1 and all odd (WS) rows* Purl. **Begin Rose Lace chart: *Row 2 (RS)*** Working from right to left, work first 11 sts of chart, place marker (pm), work 20-st rep 3 (3, 4) times, pm after each rep, work last 12 sts of chart. Continue to work 44-row rep of chart as established until piece measures 9½ (9½, 10½)" from beginning, end with a WS row.

Skill level
Intermediate

Sizes
To fit sizes L (XL, XXL). Shown in size L.

Finished measurements
Underarm: 45 (52½, 60)"
Length: (27)"

Yarn
Jagger Spun Zephyr (silk/wool),
5 (6, 7)oz/140 (170, 200)g; 1450 (1750, 2050)yds/1300 (1600, 1850)m Blue

Needles
Sizes 3 and 4 (3.25 and 3.5mm)
circular needles 24" (60 cm) long,
or size to obtain gauge

Buttons
Nine ½" buttons. To make
lightweight coordinating buttons,
use ½" Cabone rings.

Extras
Stitch markers
Stitch holders
#22/24 embroidery needle
for making buttons.

Blocked gauge
5.4 sts and 9.6 rows to 1" over chart pat,
using size 4 (3.5mm) needle.
NOTE: 1 motif measures
approx 3.7" x 4.6"

Chain cast-on

1 *Knit into next st, then slip new st back to LH needle.

2 Repeat step 1 for each additional stitch.

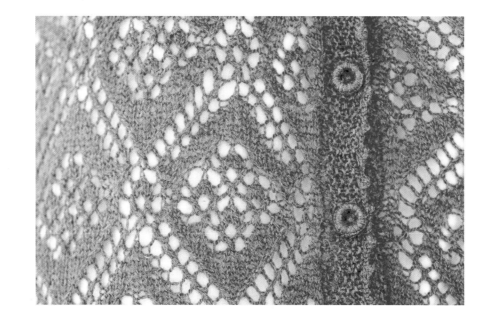

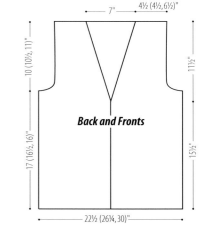

Back and Fronts

Rose Lace Vest

But Madame Bad Luck

scorns all this,

She shows no eagerness for flitting:

But with a long and fervent kiss

Sits by your bed—

and brings her knitting.

Heinrich Heine,

Das Glück Ist eine Leichte Dirne

Shape Armhole
Make a note of which patt row you are beginning so you can match your work when you do the vest fronts. Inc 1 st each side every other row 3 times—89 (89, 109) sts—end with a WS row. Work 1 RS row even in pattern, then purl 1 row. Using chain cast-on, cast on 31 (51, 51) sts at the end of this purl row for left underarm. Break yarn and place all sts on holder.

FRONTS
Work both fronts at same time. (NOTE: If you are using a cone of Zephyr, wind off enough yarn to make the right front—1¼ (1½, 1¾) oz or 350 (440, 500) yds. Use the cone to begin the left front. Otherwise, use separate balls of yarn for each front.) With larger needle and WS facing, pick up and p 22 (22, 32) from cast-on edge of back for left front. Skip center 39 sts. Pick up and p last 22 (22, 32) sts for right front. Turn work. **Begin Rose Lace chart: Row 2 (RS)** For right front, work first 11 sts of chart, pm, work 20-st rep 0 (0, 1) time, pm, then work first 11 (11, 1) sts of the 20-st rep, remembering to work edge sts in St st until these sts can be worked into chart pat. For left front, work 20-st rep 0 (0, 1) time, pm, work last 10 (10,

0) sts of 20-st rep, pm, then work last 12 sts of chart. Continue to work chart as established, inc 1 st each side at neck edge every 6 rows 12 times, then every 4 rows 9 times (21 sts over 108 rows), pm at final neck inc on each front; AT SAME TIME, when fronts measure same as back to underarm shaping, shape armhole as for back, casting on 31 (51, 51) sts at the end of final purl row on right front for right underarm. Place right front sts on holder.

Front/Back Joining
Next row (RS) Continuing neck shaping, *work in pat as established across the left front, knit across the cast-on sts of left underarm, work in pat across the back sts, knit across the cast-on sts of right underarm, work in pat across the right front. Purl 1 row, then rep from* once. (Underarm is stabilized by these 4 St st rows.) *Next row (RS)* Work in pat across all sts. All armhole sts should resolve themselves evenly into 20-st reps. Adjust if necessary. Continue in pat until piece measures 26½" from beginning or to desired length, end on a row 21 or 43 of chart.

BOTTOM BAND
Change to smaller needle and work 8 rows of seed st. With RS facing, bind off loosely in Picot bind-off. Do not break yarn.

- [ ] K
- Sl1-k2tog-psso
- Sssk
- K3tog
- Ssk
- K2tog
- Yo

Blanket Stitch

| 1 | 2 |
| 3 | 4 |

Button

Rose Lace

20-st rep

FRONT BAND
With smaller needle, RS facing, and beginning at lower right front edge, pick up and k 4 sts for every 6 rows to shoulder, picking up an extra st at neck shaping marker, pick up 39 sts along back neck, then pick up same number of sts along left front as for right front. *Next row (WS)* Work seed st to marker, inc 1 st after marker, continue in seed st to next marker, inc 1 st before marker, work to end of row. Work two more rows of seed st. Place markers on left front for 9 buttons, the first at the marker, the last ⅝" from lower edge, and 7 spaced evenly between. Continuing in seed st, work buttonholes opposite markers by yo, k2tog. When 9 rows of seed st are complete (end with a WS row), bind off loosely in Picot bind-off.

ARM BANDS
With smaller needle, RS facing, and beginning at center of underarm, pick up and k 1 st for each cast-on st at underarm and 4 sts for every 6 rows around armhole. Work 7 rnds of seed st, binding off loosely in Picot bind-off.

BUTTONS
Most ready-made buttons tend to be heavy and weigh down the front of the vest. I like to make the buttons for lace vests using the same yarn and ½" Cabone rings.
Measure 45" of yarn. Work with the yarn doubled. Work Blanket Stitch around the ring and join. Make two spokes in the center of the ring. Wrap the yarn around the spokes 4 times in an "X" pattern:
*Up at 1, down in 4,
up in 2, down in 3,
up at 4, down in 1,
up at 3, down in 2;
rep from* 3 more times.

Sew buttons to front at markers.

FINISHING
Block and fasten ends.

Skill level

Intermediate

Sizes

P (S, M, L). Shown in S.

Finished measurements

Underarm: 37 (41, 44, 47)"

Shown 27½" long with 21½" sleeves;

adjust as desired.

Yarn

Jamieson & Smith Jumperweight

Shetland (1oz/28g; 150yds/137m; wool)

9 (9, 11, 12) skeins

Dusty Rose #FC50 (MC),

3 (4, 5, 6) skeins Creme #1a (CC)

Needles

Size 4 (3.5mm) needles in double-pointed

(dpn) and circular, 16" and 24"

(41 and 60 cm) long,

or size to obtain gauge.

Extras

Stitch markers

Stitch holders or waste yarn

Blocked gauge

24 sts to 4" over St st using size 4

(3.5mm) needles.

NOTES *1* Those familiar with EPS (Elizabeth's Percentage System) will see it reflected in this design: the body circumference is 100% or [K] which stands for Key Number and equals gauge times inches around the widest part of the body. The number of sts to cast on for the cuff is approximately 20% of [K]; sleeves are increased to around 35% of [K] and the yoke is decreased to roughly 36—40% of [K] for the neck opening. On this sample, 6 sts to 1" x 41" around = 244 (adjusted down 2 sts so that when the sleeves are joined to the body, the total number of yoke sts will be divisible by the lace motif). *2* A vertical repeat of the Feather and Fan lace is 5 rnds: 1 pat rnd, 3 knit rnds, plus 1 purl rnd. *3* As I struggled (and failed) to make Elizabeth's numbers work, I was forced to analyze this lace pattern. It broke down to increasing and decreasing over two equal numbers plus a number that is one less than the other two. For example, a 20-st repeat is comprised of 7 yo's + 7 k2tog's + 6 knits, a 17-st repeat is 6+6+5, a 14-st repeat is 5+5+4, etc. *4* See *Techniques*, p. 162, for EZ's Sewn Cast-Off, M1, and St st grafting.

BODY

Using 24" needle, cast on 220 (240, 260, 280) sts. Work back and forth for 3 ridges of garter st (k every row), then join, being careful not to twist, and place marker (pm) for beginning of rnd. **Begin 20-st F&F chart** Work rnd 1 of chart 11 (12, 13, 14) times. Continue to work through rnd 5 of chart, then work 5-rnd rep 2 or 3 times more, increasing to 224, (244, 264, 284) or [K] on the last rnd. (Mark the "side seam" sts in case you want to do any shaping, insert sets of short rows across the back only, or add Phony Seams. All three are optional.) Work even in St st to wanted length to underarm

In perusing one of my mother's knitting journals, the page reproduced here caught my eye. You may see that Elizabeth wrote "Pink one," so I chose Dusty Rose Shetland wool and did my best to interpret the notes shown here. I was unable to make the scribbled numbers work without unbalancing the motif, so I have reworked the yoke. Also, I added Feather and Fan to the lower edge of the body and deep cuffs, blousing the sleeves.

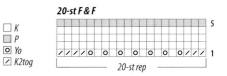

20-st F&F

□ K
▨ P
⊙ Yo
☑ K2tog

20-st rep

17-st F&F

17-st rep

(sample measures 18"), then place 19 (19, 21, 23) sts (8% of [K]) each side onto a holder, centered directly above your "side seam" markers.

SLEEVES

Using CC and dpn, cast on approx 20% of [K]—51 (51, 68, 68) sts. Join, pm, then k 1 rnd and p 1 rnd. **Begin 17-st F&F chart** Work rnd 1 of chart 3 (3, 4, 4) times. Continue to work through rnd 5 of chart, then work 5-rnd rep 10 times more (or fewer if you don't want such a deep cuff), then change to MC and St st. K 1 rnd. *Next rnd* Inc 25 (25, 22, 22) sts evenly around—76 (76, 90, 90) sts. Continue in St st until you are about 5–6" shy of wanted length to underarm. For a quasi-gusset (eliminate for smallest size), mark 3 center underarm sts and M1 each side every 6th rnd, 0 (5, 4, 7) times—76 (86, 98, 104) sts, or approx 35% of [K]. Work straight to wanted length at underarm. Put 8% of [K]—19 (19, 21, 23) sts—on a holder, centered directly above underarm seam line. Knit second sleeve to match.

Body/Sleeve Joining

Amalgamate sleeves and body onto 24" circular needle, matching underarms (see drawing) and keeping underarm sts on hold. You now have 300 (340, 376, 400) sts altogether: 93 (103, 111, 119) each on the front and back and 57 (67, 77, 81) on each sleeve. Work even in St st for 3 rnds, then work short row shaping for back neck and shoulders as foll: knit to 17 sts past left front sleeve/body join. Wrap and work back (either by turning and purling or by knitting backwards) to the same spot on the right front. *Wrap and work to 6 sts shy of the first wrap, then wrap again and work back; rep from* once more (6 extra rows on back and sleeves). Work a complete rnd, knitting all the slipped sts together with their wraps then, except for the two smaller sizes, work three more complete rnds.

YOKE

Change to CC. K 1 rnd then p 1 rnd, inc 0 (0, 4, 0) sts evenly spaced—300 (340, 380, 400) sts. **Begin Yoke Dec chart** Work rnd 1 of chart 15 (17, 19, 20) times. Continue to work chart as established through rnd 64 to approx 36% of [K]—75 (85, 95, 100) sts. If you determine that the neck is too wide, you may work final evenly-spaced dec's on rnd 65 to obtain the circumference you want. Continue through rnd 69 of chart, then change to MC and k 1 rnd, p 1 rnd. Bind off using Elizabeth Zimmermann's beautifully elastic Sewn Cast-Off.

Weave Underarms Slip held sleeve sts to dpn; slip corresponding body sts to a second dpn. With fabric coming from three different directions, the corners are a bit stressed. To cope with that, pick up a loose thread at each end of each needle, twist it into a stitch and add it to the needle—you will now have 2 additional sts on each needle. This move will eliminate the automatic hole that forms at each end of the woven join. Graft sleeve sts to body sts, and if you still have a small hole, work a duplicate st around the hole. Pull it snug and darn it in. Weave in ends and block.

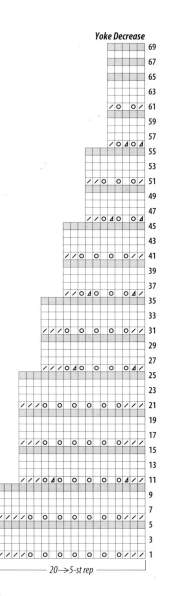

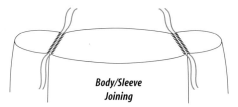

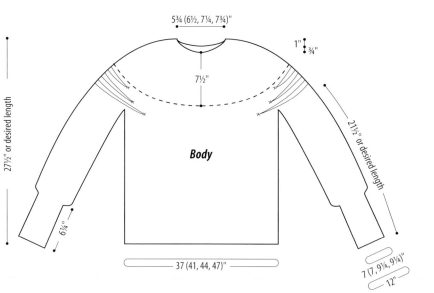

Feather & Fan Pullover

The bedjacket was intricate,

involving sixteen rows to each

feather-and-shell design.

Executed in pale pink

three-ply wool

it had taken Miss Fogarty

many hours of fiddling work—

and some of unpicking—

to complete the garment.

Miss Read,

The Sad Affair of the Bedjacket

Skill level

Intermediate

Sizes

XS (S, M, L, XL). Shown in size S.

Finished measurements

Underarm: 39 (42, 45, 48, 51)",

buttoned

Length: 19½ (20, 21, 22, 23)"

Yarn

Garnstudio Cotton Viscose

(1¾oz/50g; 120yds/110m;

54% cotton, 46% viscose)

11 (12,14, 15, 17) balls Gold #4

(shown below; Light Olive shown on

next page is not available)

Needles

Size 3 (3.25mm) needles and circular,

32" (80cm) long for neck edging

or size to obtain gauge

Extras

Stitch markers

Five ⅝" buttons

Blocked gauge

28 sts and 39 rows to 4"/10cm in St st

using size 3 (3.25mm) needles.

Edging St (multiple of 12 + 4, decreasing to multiple of 10 + 4 sts after Row 3) *Row 1* (WS): Purl. *2* K3, *k1 then sl this st back to LH needle, pass the next 9 sts, one at a time, over this st and off LH needle, yo twice, then k this st again, k2; rep from*, end last rep k1. *3* K1, *k3, drop 1 yo, [k in front and back of yo] 3 times, k in front of yo; rep from*, end last rep k3. *4 and 5* Knit.

Purse St (over an even number of sts) *All rows* *Yo, p2tog; rep from*.

NOTES *1* When dec or inc in Purse St, work single sts in purl. *2* When dec at right front v-neck, be careful that ssk's of Vine chart are considered separate from v-neck dec's. *3* See *Techniques*, p. 162, for cable cast-on and double yo.

BACK

Using cable cast-on, cast on 184 (196, 208, 220, 232) sts. **Begin Edging St** Work 5 pat rows—154 (164, 174, 184, 194) sts. *Next row* (RS) Dec number of sts to 127 (135, 143, 151, 159) as foll: (k1, k2tog) 1 (2, 2, 3, 4) times, *k4, k2tog; rep from* to last 7 (8, 6, 7, 8) sts, (k1, k2tog) twice, k1 (2, 0, 1, 2) sts. **Begin Vine Chart and Purse St** (WS) P2, work 12 (16, 16, 20, 20) sts in Purse St, *p1, begin with row 2, work 13 sts of Vine Pat, p1, work 6 (6, 8, 8, 10) sts in Purse St, rep from* 4 times more, end last rep with 12 (16, 16, 20, 20) sts in Purse St, p2. Continue in pats as established until piece measures 11 (11, 12, 12½, 13)" from beginning to underarm, end with a WS row.

Shape armhole

Continuing in pats, bind off 6 sts at beginning of next 2 rows—115 (123, 131, 139, 147) sts. Dec 1 st each side of this and every foll RS row 7 (11, 11, 15, 15)

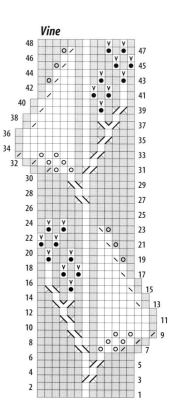

Vine

□ K on RS, p on WS

▨ P on RS, k on WS

⊙ Yo

▨ K2tog

◥ Ssk

▨ P2tog on RS, k2tog on WS

▽ Slip 1 purlwise

● *Make bud* Cast on 3 sts, p4, sl 2nd, then 3rd, then 4th st, one at a time, over first st on RH needle and off RH needle

▨▽▨ K into F of 2nd st on LH needle then p into F of first leaving 2nd st rem on LH needle, yb, sl this rem st-k1-psso

▨▨ *1/1RT* K 2nd st on LH needle, then k first st; sl both sts off needle

◥◥ *1/1LT* With RH needle behind LH needle, k 2nd st on LH needle through back loop, then k first st; sl both sts off needle

▨▨ *1/1RPT* K 2nd st on LH needle, then p first st; sl both sts off needle

◥◥ *1/1LPT* With RH needle behind LH needle, p 2nd st on LH needle, then k first st; sl both sts off needle

Pipit sate upright in her chair

Some distance from where

I was sitting;

Views of the Oxford Colleges

Lay on the table, with the knitting.

T. S. Eliot,

A Cooking Egg

times as foll: k1, ssk, work to last 3 sts, k2tog, k1—101 (101, 109, 109, 117) sts. Work even in pats until piece measures 7½ (8, 8, 8½, 9)" from beginning of armhole shaping.

Shape neck and shoulder

Bind off 8 (8, 9, 9, 10) sts at beginning of next 2 rows. Bind off 8 (8, 9, 9, 10) sts at beginning of next row, work until there are 17 (17, 19, 19, 21) sts on RH needle. Place center 35 sts on holder. Working each side separately, turn and bind off 1 st at neck edge, work to end. Bind off 8 (8, 9, 9, 10) shoulder sts, work to end. Bind off 1 st at neck edge, work to end. Bind off remaining 7 (7, 8, 8, 9) shoulder sts. Beginning with a RS row with no bind-offs, work second shoulder to correspond to first.

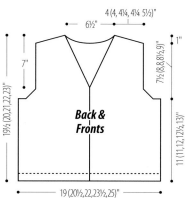

RIGHT FRONT

Using cable cast-on, cast on 100 (100, 112, 112, 124) sts. **Work Edging St as for back**—84 (84, 94, 94, 104) sts. **Next row** (RS) Dec number of sts to 62 (66, 70, 74, 78) as foll: *XS size ONLY* K2tog, *k2, k2tog; rep from* to last 2 sts, k2tog. *S size ONLY* K2tog, k1, k2tog, *k3, k2tog, rep from* to last 4 sts, k2, k2tog. *M size ONLY* K1, k2tog, *k2, k2tog; rep from* to last 3 sts, k1, k2tog. *L size ONLY* K2tog, *k3, k2tog; rep from* to last 2 sts, k2tog. *XL size ONLY* K1, k2tog, *k2, k2tog; rep from* to last st, k1. **Begin Vine chart and Purse St** (WS) P2, work 12 (16, 16, 20, 20) sts in Purse St, *p1, beginning with row 2, work 13 sts of Vine Pat, p1, work 6 (6, 8, 8, 10) sts in Purse St; rep from* once, ending rep with 10 (10, 12, 12, 14) sts in Purse St, p2. Continue in pats as for back until piece measures same as as back to underarm, then shape armhole at side edge as for back—49 (49, 53, 53, 57) sts. Work even in pats until piece measures 12½ (13, 14, 15, 16)" from beginning, end with a WS row.

Shape Neck

Place marker at neck edge. *Dec 1 st at beginning of next 2 RS rows by working k1, ssk. Work 1 RS row without dec; rep from* until 31 (31, 35, 35, 39) sts remain. Work even in pats and when piece measures same as back to shoulder, shape shoulder at side edge as for back.

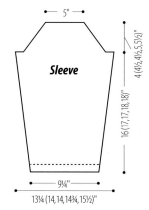

LEFT FRONT

Work to correspond to right front, reversing all shaping and pat placement.

SLEEVES

Using cable cast-on, cast on 88 sts. **Begin Edging St** Work 5 pat rows—74 sts. **Next row** (RS) Dec number of sts to 50 as foll: *k1, k2tog, rep from* to last 2 sts, k2. **Begin Purse St** (WS) P2, work 46 sts in Purse St, p2. Continue in pat as established, keeping 2 edge sts each side in p2, inc 1 st each side every 12th row 9 (11, 11, 13, 15) times, working inc sts into Purse St—68 (72, 72, 76, 80) sts. When piece measures 16 (17, 17, 18, 18)" from beginning, end with a WS row.

Shape Armhole

Bind off 6 sts at beginning of next 2 rows—56 (60, 60, 64, 68) sts. *Dec 1 st each side of this and next 3 RS rows as foll: k1, ssk, work to last 3 sts, k2tog, k1. Work 1 RS row without dec; rep from* until 24 sts remain, end with a WS row. Bind off 4 sts at beginning of next 2 rows. Bind off remaining 16 sts.

FINISHING

Block pieces. Sew shoulder seams. **Work neck edging** With RS facing, circular needle, and beginning at lower right front edge, pick up and k 9 sts for every 10 rows to marker; work k1-yo-k1 at marker; pick up and k 1 st for each row to shoulder; pick up and k 5 sts along back right neck shaping; from back neck holder, k and inc 5 sts evenly spaced (40 sts); pick up and k 5 sts along back left neck shaping; pick up and k 1 st for each row to marker; work k1-yo-k1 at marker; pick up and k 9 sts for every 10 rows to lower left front edge. **Next row** (WS) K all sts, placing markers every 50 sts for ease in counting. Count sts. Determine the nearest multiple of 12 + 4. **Next row** (RS) K all sts, inc or dec as needed to achieve the determined multiple. **Begin Edging St** Work Rows 2 and 3 of Edging St. Bind off all sts in knit. Sew underarm and side seams. Sew buttons to left front, the first at the beginning of neck shaping, the last just above lower edge, and 3 spaced evenly between, placing buttons opposite the loops of edging which will function as buttonholes.

Skill level

Intermediate

Sizes

P (S, M, L). Shown in M.

Finished measurements

Underarm: 38½ (43, 48, 53)"

Length: 24 (25, 26, 27)"

Yarn

Grignasco Flavia (1¾oz/50g;

220yds/200m; superwash wool)

10 (11, 13, 15) balls Off-white #901

Needles

Size 2 (2.75mm) needles and

double-pointed (dpn) or circular,

16" (40cm) long for neck,

or size to obtain gauge

Extras

Cable needle (cn)

Stitch markers

Stitch holder

Blocked gauge

40 sts and 42 rows to 4"

in cable portion of chart pat, using

size 2 (2.75mm) needles.

K2-p2 rib
Row 1 (RS) K2, *p2, k2; rep from*.
Row 2 (WS) P2, *k2, p2; rep from*.

BACK
Cast on 190 (214, 238, 262) sts. Work in k2-p2 rib for 1 (1¼, 1½, 2)", end with a WS row.
Begin chart: Row 1 Work first 4 sts, work 24-st rep 7 (8, 9, 10) times, then work to end. Continue to work chart as established, and when chart is completed, rep the last 2 rows of chart for remainder of piece, AT SAME TIME, when piece measures 16½ (16,17,16½)" from beginning, inc one st each side (for armhole seaming) and place markers at inc's. Work new st in St st. Work even on 192 (216, 240, 264) sts until piece measures 22½ (23½, 24½, 25½)", end with a WS row.

Shape neck
Work 65 (77, 89, 101) sts, place marker (pm), work 11 sts, place center 40 sts on a holder. Join new yarn, work 11 sts, pm, complete row. Work a WS row, working both sides at same time. *Dec row* (RS) Continuing in pat, work to 2 sts before marker, p2tog, work remaining 11 sts before neck edge. On opposite side, work 11 sts, p2tog, work to end. Continue as established, working dec row every RS row 7 times more—68 (80, 92, 104) sts remaining each side. Work even and when piece measures 24 (25, 26, 27)" from beginning, bind off all sts.

FRONT
Work as for back until piece measures 21 (22, 23, 24)". Work neck shaping as for back. Work even in pat on remaining 68 (80, 92, 104) sts each side until piece measures same as back to shoulder. Bind off.

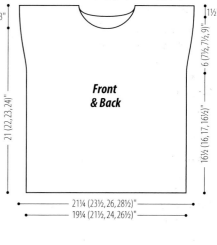

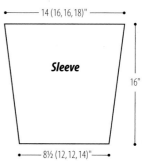

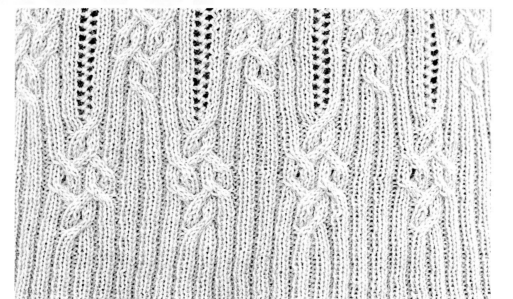

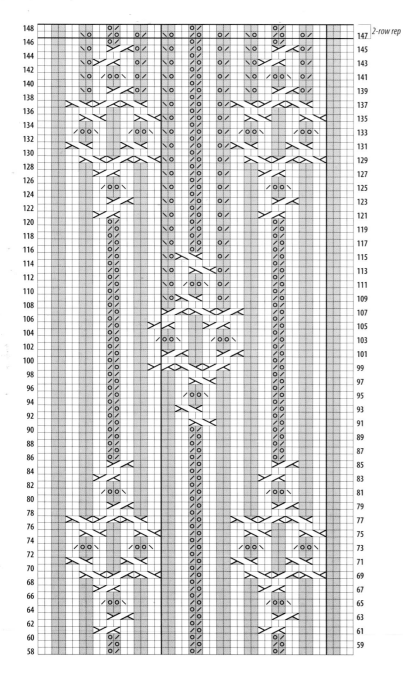

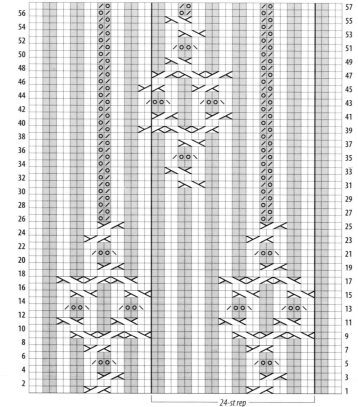

SLEEVES

Cast on 84 (118, 118, 142) sts. Work in K2-p2 rib for 1", end with a WS row. **Begin chart:** *Row 1* Work first 4 sts, work 24-st rep 3 (4, 4, 5) times, then work to end. Continue to work chart as established, AT SAME TIME, inc 1 st each side—working inc sts into chart pat—every 6th (8th, 8th, 8th) row 27 (20, 20, 20) times on RS rows as foll: K2, yo, work to last 2 sts, yo, k2. Work even in pat on 138 (158, 158, 182) sts until piece measures 16" from beginning. Bind off.

FINISHING

Block pieces. Sew shoulder seams. (NOTE If you knit the shoulders together, I recommend stabilizing the seams with yarn or seam tape.)

NECKBAND

With circular needle or dpn, RS facing, and beginning at back neck holder, p1 then work k2-p2 rib across sts from holder, end p1. Pick up and k 40 sts to front neck. From front holder, p1 then continue in chart pat as established for 38 sts, end p1. Pick up and k 40 sts to back neck—160 sts. Pm and join. Beginning with p1, work k2-p2 rib in rnds, keeping center front neck in pat as established. When neckband measures 3", bind off in rib.

Set in sleeves between markers. Sew side and sleeve seams.

□ K on RS, p on WS
▨ P on RS, k on RS
◦ Yo
◺ Ssk
◿ K2tog
◣ Ssp
◢ P2tog

2/2 LPC Sl 2 sts to cn, hold to front, p2, k2 from cn
2/2 RPC Sl 2 sts to cn, hold to back, k2, p2 from cn
2/2 LC Sl 2 sts to cn, hold to front, k2, k2 from cn
2/2 RC Sl 2 sts to cn, hold to back, k2, k2 from cn

Fascinators, nightingales,
and zephyrines—the language of
yesterday's knitted lace intimate
apparel is as sibilant as silk,
alluring, yet cloaked in secrecy,
suggesting a feminine mystique
of days gone by.
The hard lives of many women
were doubtless softened by knitting
something precious and dainty.

Shirley A. Scott,
*Canada Knits: Craft and Comfort
in a Northern Land*

Ribbed Lace Pullover

Skill level

Experienced

Sizes

S (M, L). Shown in M.

Finished measurements

Underarm: 42 (45, 48½)"

Length: 25 (26½, 28)"

Yarn

Kimmet Croft Fibers Fairy Hare

(2oz/56g; 300yds/270m; 40%

angora, 60% merino),

4 (5, 6) skeins Natural white

Needles

Size 4 (3.5 mm) needles in

double-pointed (dpn) and circular,

16" and 24" (40 and 60 cm),

or size to obtain gauge.

Extras

Stitch marker

Stitch holders

Waste yarn for cast-on

Blocked gauge

23 sts and 35 rows to 4"/10cm

in Chart B using size 4

(3.5mm) needles.

Construction notes

The sweater is knit from the neck down, increasing through the yoke, then the sleeve sts are put on holders, additional sts are cast on for the underarm, and the body is knit down to the hem. Finally, the sleeves are picked up and knit down to the cuff.

NOTES *1* Change to 24" needle when necessary on yoke; change to dpn when necessary on sleeves. *2* Only odd rnds are charted. On even rnds, all sts are knit. Follow appropriate A chart for chosen size. *3* Beginning of rnd marker will be moved as yoke progresses. *4* Chart B is used for all sizes, working different numbers of sts for each size as indicated. *5* See *Techniques,* p. 162, for double yo, invisible cast-on, and sl2tog-k1-p2sso.

YOKE

With 16" needle, invisibly cast on 84 sts. Place marker (pm) and join, being careful not to twist. K 6 rnds. *Next rnd* (picot rnd) *K2tog, yo; rep from*. K 6 rnds, p 1 rnd, k 1 rnd. **Begin Chart A (A1, A2):** *Rnd 1* Work 12-st rep 7 times around, pm between repeats if desired—91 sts. Continue to work chart as established through rnd 26. *Rnds 27–80* Work chart 14 times around—336 (364, 392) sts.

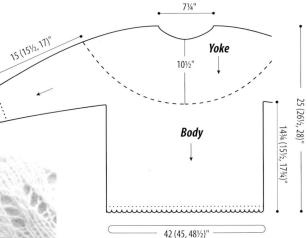

A GATHERING OF LACE

…and forward leans to catch the sight
Of a man's face,
Gracefully sighing through the white
Flowery mantilla of lace.

D. H. Lawrence,
Drunk

Chart A

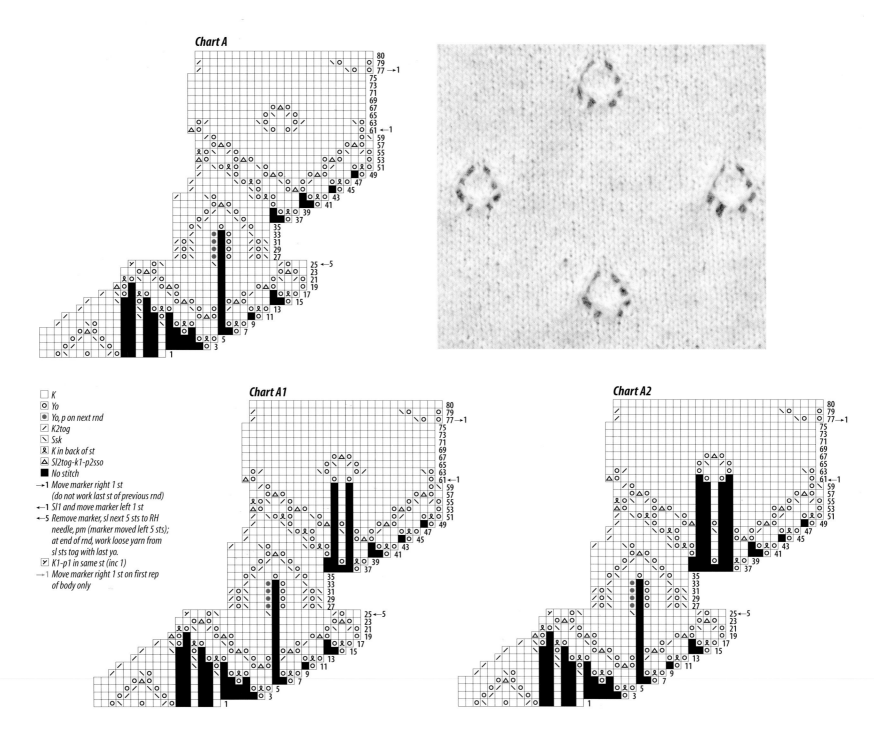

☐ K
◉ Yo
◉ Yo, p on next rnd
◢ K2tog
◣ Ssk
⅃ K in back of st
△ Sl2tog-k1-p2sso
■ No stitch
→1 Move marker right 1 st
   (do not work last st of previous rnd)
←1 Sl1 and move marker left 1 st
←5 Remove marker, sl next 5 sts to RH
   needle, pm (marker moved left 5 sts);
   at end of rnd, work loose yarn from
   sl sts tog with last yo.
⅄ K1-p1 in same st (inc 1)
→1 Move marker right 1 st on first rep
   of body only

Chart A1

Chart A2

Divide for body and sleeves
Begin Chart B: *Rnd 1* Remove marker, work next 2 sts (yo, k2tog), pm for beginning of rnd, work 24 (26, 28)–st rep 4 times, k1, place 71 (77, 83) sts on holder for sleeve, cast on 23 (25, 27) sts for underarm, work 4 reps of chart, k1, cast on 23 (25, 27) sts for underarm, place on holder for second sleeve all remaining sts—71 (77, 83) sts, including 2 sts from moving marker—240 (260, 280) sts in body.

BODY
Continuing with Chart B, k 1 rnd, work 32-rnd rep of chart 3 (4, 4) times, then work rnds 1–25 (1–5, 1–19).

Decrease for hem
Next rnd: K4, *k2tog, k8; rep from*, end last rep k4—216 (234, 252) sts. P 1 rnd. K 6 rnds. *Next rnd* (picot rnd) *K2tog, yo; rep from*. K 6 rnds. Turn hem to inside on picot rnd and sew to body through loops of sts.

SLEEVES
Place 71 (77, 83) sts from holder onto 16" needle, pick up and k 11 (12, 13) sts from underarm cast-on, pm. **Begin Chart cast-on B:** *Rnd A* Pick up and k 14 (15, 16) additional sts from underarm cast-on. Begin with 2nd st of chart, work to end of chart, work chart twice more, k 11 (12, 13)—96 (104, 112) sts in sleeve. Knit 1 rnd. *Rnd 1* K14 (15, 16), begin with 3rd st of chart, work to end of chart, work chart twice more, ending last rep with k1 instead of yo, k11 (12, 13). *Rnds 2 and 3* Knit. *Rnd 4* (dec rnd) K3, ssk, work to last 2 sts, k2tog. Work dec rnd every 6th rnd 20 (21, 23) times more—54 (60, 64) sts remain; AT SAME TIME, continue to work chart as established for 130 (136, 148) rnds total, eliminating lace motif if it conflicts with dec's, ending with a rnd 3 (9, 21) of chart. *Next rnd* Knit, dec 4 (6, 6) sts evenly around. P 1 rnd. K 6 rnds. *Next rnd* (picot rnd) *K2tog, yo; rep from*. K 6 rnds. Turn sleeve and neck hems to inside and sew as for body.

Chart B

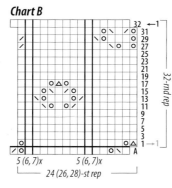

NOTES *1* Tam is worked from hem to center of crown. *2* Tam achieves its distinctive shape by blocking. *3* See *Techniques*, p. 162, for invisible cast-on.

Tam

With circular needle, invisibly cast on 90 sts. Place marker and join. K 12 rnds. P 1 rnd (turning rnd for hem), then k 11 rnds. **Inc rnd** *K, inc 36 sts evenly spaced—126 sts. **Begin Tam Body chart: Rnd A** (set-up) Work 18-st rep of chart 7 times around. Work rnds 1–8 of chart four times as established, then work rnds 1–3 once. **Begin Tam Decrease chart** Work rnds 1–28, changing to dpn when needed. Break yarn, leaving an 8" tail. With tapestry needle, draw end through remaining sts, then draw through first st again. Pull up snugly. Fasten off.

Finishing

Fold hem to inside of band on turning rnd and sew loosely in place, removing waste yarn. Dampen tam by misting with fine spray and block by stretching over 10½" diameter cardboard circle or large dinner plate.

Skill level

Intermediate

Size

One size fits most;

tam is 10½" in diameter.

Yarn

Kimmet Croft Fibers Fairy Hare

(2 oz/56g; 300yds/270m; 40%

angora, 60% merino)

1 skein Red

Needles

Size 2 (2.75 mm) needles in

double-pointed (dpn) and 16"

(40cm) circular

or size to obtain gauge

Extras

Stitch marker

Waste yarn

Cable needle (cn)

Tapestry needle

10½" circle of cardboard or

large dinner plate for blocking tam

Blocked gauge

20 sts to 4"/10cm in St st using

size 2 (2.75mm) needles.

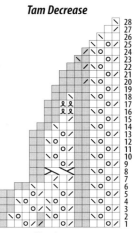

Tam Decrease

17→1-st rep

Tam Body

18-st rep

☐ K
▨ P
⊙ Yo
╱ K2tog
╲ Ssk
▧ P2tog
◣ Ssp
⚇ K in back of st
⧓ **2/2 yo LC** Sl 2 to cn, hold to front, k2, then yo, ssk from cn

By the eleventh century A.D.
Spain had become the centre of
hand knitted lace and silken hose,
and the craft spread rapidly
to the rest of Europe...
The art of knitted lace must have
begun even earlier, some believe
in India and perhaps in Greece.

Sarah Don,
The Art of Shetland Lace

NOTES *1* Only odd rnds are shown for Lacy Zig-Zag pat. Knit all even rnds. *2* Casting on over 2 parallel dpn helps keep the cast-on edge from being too snug.

LEFT HAND

Cast on 60 sts loosely. Divide sts evenly over 4 dpn. Place marker (pm) and join, being careful not to twist. P 1 rnd. K 1 rnd. **Begin rib and Lacy Zig-Zag chart** Work p1-k1 rib over 22 sts. * P2, work rnd 1 of chart; rep from* 4 times more, end p2, k1. *Next rnd* Continue to work p1-k1 rib over 22 sts. [P2, k5 for rnd 2 of chart] 5 times, end p2, k1. Continue to work rib pat and 16-rnd rep of chart pat as established for a total of 24 rnds, then discontinue p1-k1 rib, working these 22 sts in St st instead for 4 more rnds.

Thumb Gusset

Next rnd *K22, pm, yo, work to end of rnd as established. Work 3 rnds even in pats, working the yo into St st on next rnd. Rep from* 5 times more, working yo after the marker—66 sts. Continue until piece measures 2½" from top of cuff (or desired length to thumb opening), end with an even chart rnd.

Thumb Opening and Hand

Next rnd Continuing in pat, work 24 sts, place the next 12 sts onto waste yarn and cast on 10 new sts in their place. Work to end of rnd. Continue on these 64 sts as established, purling the last cast-on st and knitting the rest. Adjust sts so there are 16 sts on each dpn, but do not change position of beginning of rnd. When hand measures 1½" from cast-on thumb sts, begin little finger.

Little Finger

Place the first and last 9 sts of the rnd onto dpn. Place all remaining sts onto waste yarn. Work across the 9 palm sts, then cast on 7 new sts and work across the 9 pat sts on top of hand—25 sts. Work one rnd even in pat, working cast-on sts in St st. On next rnd, dec the 7 cast-on sts to 5 as foll: sl1-k1-psso, k3, p2tog—23 sts. (On following rnds for this and all other fingers, continue to p the p2tog.) Adjust sts so there are 11 pat sts (k1, p2, 5 chart sts, p2, k1) on first dpn and 6 sts each on 2nd and 3rd dpn. Work in pat until finger measures 2" or desired length to center of fingernail. *Shape finger tip beginning with first dpn* Sl1-k1-psso, k7, k2tog, sl1-k1-psso, k8, k2tog. Continue to work dec's every rnd at the beginning of first and 2nd dpn and at the end of first and 3rd dpn until 7 sts remain. Break yarn and with tapestry needle, thread the end through these 7 sts and pull them up snugly.

Lacy Zig-Zag

			o	∕		15
		o	∕			13
	o	∕				11
o	∕					9
∖	o					7
	∖	o				5
		∖	o			3
			∖	o		1

5-st rep

☐ K
o Yo
∕ K2tog
∖ Sl1-k1-psso

Vanalinn means Old Town in Estonian. It is a part of Tallinn, the capital of the country, which is just as a traveler would imagine towns to be in this northern part of the world. This oldest part of Tallinn, now surrounded by a modern city, began as an Estonian settlement on the hill called Toompea. Danish, German, Swedish, and Russian influences added to the town as it grew down the hillside and spread out toward the sea. Many of the buildings have survived since Hanseatic times, when Tallinn was an important trading community. Today a traveler can walk the cobbled streets and imagine time long past, stop in cafes hundreds of years old and shop for knitting in an outdoor market nestled into the walls of a monastery near one of the old town gates. I named these gloves for Tallinn's old town because for me it is a place of magic, of such history and beauty. It has a quiet elegance that is always enchanting. I imagine these gloves worn for a special occasion, perhaps to a wintertime concert or for a walk on a frosty afternoon.

Skill level

Intermediate

Size

Woman's medium

Yarn

Schoolhouse Press Satakieli (3½oz/100m;

357yds/325m; wool)

1 skein Natural # 003

Needles

Set of 5 double-pointed

needles (dpn) in size 0 (2mm),

or size to obtain gauge

Extras

Stitch marker

Tapestry needle

Waste yarn

Blocked gauge

16 sts and 23 rnds to 2"/5cm in St st

using size 0 (2mm) dpn.

A GATHERING OF LACE

...I knew her by the

broad white hat,

All ruffled, she had on.

By the dear ruffles round her feet,

By her small hands that hung

In their lace mitts,

austere and sweet,

Her gown's white folds among.

Edna St. Vincent Millay,

The Little Ghost

Vanalinn Gloves

NANCY BUSH

Continue Hand

Replace held sts onto dpn. Attach yarn to the left of little finger at palm side. Continue to work as established, and at the end of the first rnd, pick up and k 7 sts into the cast-on sts at the base of the little finger. *Next rnd* Work to last 7 sts, then dec these 7 picked-up sts to 5 as foll: p2tog, k3, k2tog. When 5 rnds are completed, begin ring finger.

Ring Finger

Place the first and last 7 sts of rnd plus 5 picked-up sts onto dpn. Place all remaining sts onto waste yarn. K 7 from palm side, then cast on 7 new sts, work to end of rnd in pat—26 sts. Work 1 rnd even in pat, working cast-on sts in St st. On next rnd, dec the 7 cast-on sts to 5 as foll: sl1-k1-psso, k3, p2tog—24 sts. Adjust 11 sts on 1st dpn as for little finger, dividing the remaining 13 sts between 2nd and 3rd dpn. Work in pat until finger measures desired length to center of fingernail. Shape fingertip as for little finger, drawing end through remaining 8 sts.

Middle Finger

Place next 7 sts from each end of waste yarn onto dpn, leaving remaining sts on waste yarn. Attach yarn to the left of ring finger at palm side, k7, cast on 7 sts, work 7 sts in pat, then pick up and k7 sts into the cast-on sts at the base of the ring finger. On next rnd, k the cast-on sts and dec the 7 picked-up sts to 5 as foll: p2tog, k3, k2tog—26 sts. On next rnd, dec the 7 cast-on sts to 5 as foll: sl1-k1-psso, k3, p2tog—24 sts. Work as for ring finger to desired length.

Index Finger

Place remaining 18 hand sts onto dpn. Attach yarn to the left of middle finger and work in pat across all sts. Pick up and k7 sts into the cast-on sts at the base of the middle finger—25 sts. On next rnd, dec these 7 sts to 5 as foll: p2tog, k3, k2tog—23 sts. Work as for little finger to desired length.

Thumb

Place the 12 held thumb sts onto a dpn. Attach yarn, pick up and k 14 sts across back of thumb opening where 10 sts were cast on—26 sts. Finish rnd, keeping in pat as established. On next rnd, begin p2tog, k3, k2tog, work to end of rnd—24 sts. Adjust sts and complete as for other fingers.

RIGHT HAND

Cast on 60 sts loosely. Divide sts evenly over 4 dpn. Place marker (pm) and join, being careful not to twist. P 1 rnd. K 1 rnd. **Begin rib and Lacy Zig-Zag chart** Begin k1, p2, *work rnd 1 of chart, p2; rep from* 4 times more. Work k1-p1 rib over 22 sts. *Next rnd* Begin k1, p2, [k5 for rnd 2 of chart, p2] 5 times. Continue to work k1-p1 rib over 22 sts. Continue to work in rib and chart pats as established

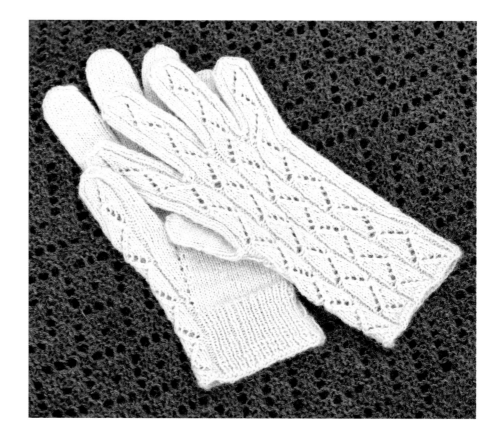

for a total of 24 rnds, then discontinue k1-p1 rib, working these 22 sts in St st instead for 4 more rnds.

Thumb Gusset

Next rnd *Work to last 22 sts, yo, pm, K22. Work 3 rnds even in pats, working the yo into St st on next rnd. Rep from* 5 times more, working yo before the marker—66 sts. Continue until piece measures same as left hand to thumb opening, end with an even chart rnd.

Thumb Opening and Hand

Next rnd Continuing in pat, work 30 sts, place the next 12 sts onto waste yarn and cast on 10 new sts in their place. Work to end of rnd. Continue on these 64 sts as established, purling the first cast-on st and knitting the rest. Adjust sts so there are 16 sts on each dpn, but do not change beginning of rnd position. When hand measures 1½" from cast-on thumb sts, begin little finger.

Little Finger

Place the first and last 9 sts of the rnd onto dpn. Place all remaining sts onto waste yarn. Work across the 9 pat sts on top of hand, then cast on 7 new sts and k across the 9 palm side sts—25 sts. Work one rnd even in pat, working cast-on sts in St st. On next rnd, dec the 7 cast-on sts to 5 as foll: p2tog, k3, k2tog—23 sts. (On following rnds for this and all other fingers, continue to p the p2tog.) Adjust sts so there are 11 pat sts (k1, p2, 5 chart sts, p2, k1) on 1st dpn and 6 sts each on 2nd and 3rd dpn. Work in pat until finger measures 2" or desired length to center of fingernail. *Shape finger tip beginning with first dpn* Sl1-k1-psso, k7, k2tog, sl1-k1-psso, k8, k2tog. Continue to work dec's every rnd at the beginning of first and 2nd dpn and at the end of first and 3rd dpn until 7 sts remain. Break yarn and with tapestry needle, draw the end through these 7 sts and pull them up snugly.

Continue Hand

Replace held sts onto dpn. Attach yarn to the left of little finger at the top of hand side. Continue to work as established, and at the end of the first rnd, pick up and k 7 sts into the cast-on sts at the base of the little finger. *Next rnd* Work to last 7 sts, then dec these 7 picked-up sts to 5 as foll: sl1-k1-psso, k3, p2tog. When 5 rnds are completed, begin ring finger.

Ring Finger

Place the first and last 7 sts of rnd plus 5 picked-up sts onto dpn. Place all remaining sts onto waste yarn. Work across the 7 pat sts on top of hand, then cast on 7 new sts and k the remaining 12 sts—26 sts. Work 1 rnd even in pat, working cast-on sts in St st. On next rnd, dec the 7 cast-on sts to 5 as foll: p2tog, k3, k2tog—24 sts. Adjust 11 sts on first dpn as for little finger, dividing the remaining 13 sts between 2nd and 3rd dpn. Work in pat until finger measures desired length to center of fingernail. Shape fingertip as for little finger, drawing end through remaining 8 sts.

Middle Finger

Place next 7 sts from each end of waste yarn onto dpn, leaving remaining sts on waste yarn. Attach yarn to the left of ring finger at the top of hand, work in pat across 7 sts, cast on 7 sts, k7, then pick up and k7 sts into the cast-on sts at the base of the ring finger. On next rnd, k the cast-on sts and dec the 7 picked-up sts to 5 as foll: sl1-k1-psso, k3, p2tog—26 sts. On next rnd, dec the 7 cast-on sts to 5 as foll: p2tog, k3, k2tog—24 sts. Work as for ring finger to desired length.

Index Finger

Place remaining 18 hand sts onto dpn. Attach yarn to the left of middle finger and work in pat across all sts. Pick up and k7 sts into the cast-on sts at the base of the middle finger—25 sts. On next rnd, dec these 7 sts to 5 as foll: sl1-k1-psso, k3, p2tog—23 sts. Work as for little finger to desired length.

Thumb

Place the 12 held thumb sts onto a dpn. Attach yarn, pick up and k 14 sts across back of thumb opening where 10 sts were cast on—26 sts. Finish rnd, keeping in pat as established. On next rnd, begin sl1-k1-psso, k10, p2tog, work to end of rnd—24 sts. Adjust sts and complete as for other fingers.

Finishing

Weave in all ends and block gloves under a damp towel.

NOTES *1* The needle diagrams show the arrangement of sts on the dpn. Red numbers indicate the first dpn of the rnd. *2* See *Techniques,* p. 162, for sl2tog-k1-p2sso.

Leg

Cast on 72 sts. Divide sts evenly over 4 dpn. Place marker (pm) and join, being careful not to twist. Work 3 rnds of k2-p2 rib, then knit 1 rnd, dec 4 sts by knitting tog the last 2 sts on each dpn—68 sts. *Rnd 1* Work rnd 1 of Leaf Pat chart on dpn #'s 1 and 2, work rnd 1 of Rib Pat chart on dpn #'s 3 and 4. Work Leaf Pat on front of leg through rnd 30 then continue to work 20-rnd rep; work ten 4-rnd reps of Rib Pat on back of leg—40 rnds. *Rnd 41* Continue in pats as established on leg front, but change to St st on back of leg, keeping first and last sts of back leg in purl as established, until sock measures 7" or desired length for leg.

Divide for heel

The heel flap is worked directly below the St st at the back of leg on dpn #'s 3 and 4. The sts on the other 2 dpn will wait until the heel has been turned. The first st of each row of the heel flap is slipped, creating a chain down each side of the flap. **Next row* (WS) Sl 1, p33. *Next row* (RS) (Sl 1, k1) 17 times. Rep from* until 35 heel flap rows have been worked, ending with a WS row—17 chain sts each side.

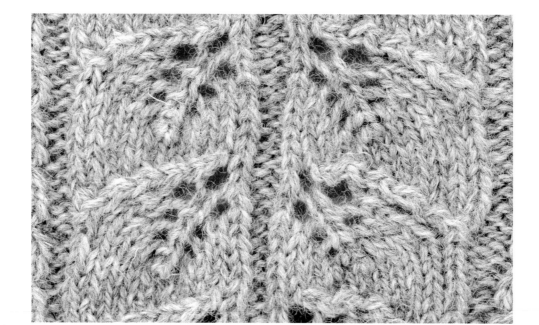

Skill level

Intermediate

Size

Woman's medium

Yarn

Schoolhouse Press Satakieli

(3½oz/100g; 357yd/325m; wool)

1 skein Gray #901

Needles

Set of 5 double-pointed needles

(dpn) in size 0 (2mm),

or size to obtain gauge

Extras

Stitch marker

Tapestry needle

Blocked gauge

16 sts and 23 rnds to 2"/5cm in

St st using size 0 (2mm) dpn.

And next I saw

she'd piled her raiment rare

Within the garde-robes,

and her household purse,

Her jewels, and least lace

of personal wear;

And stood in homespun....

Thomas Hardy,

The Burghers

NANCY BUSH

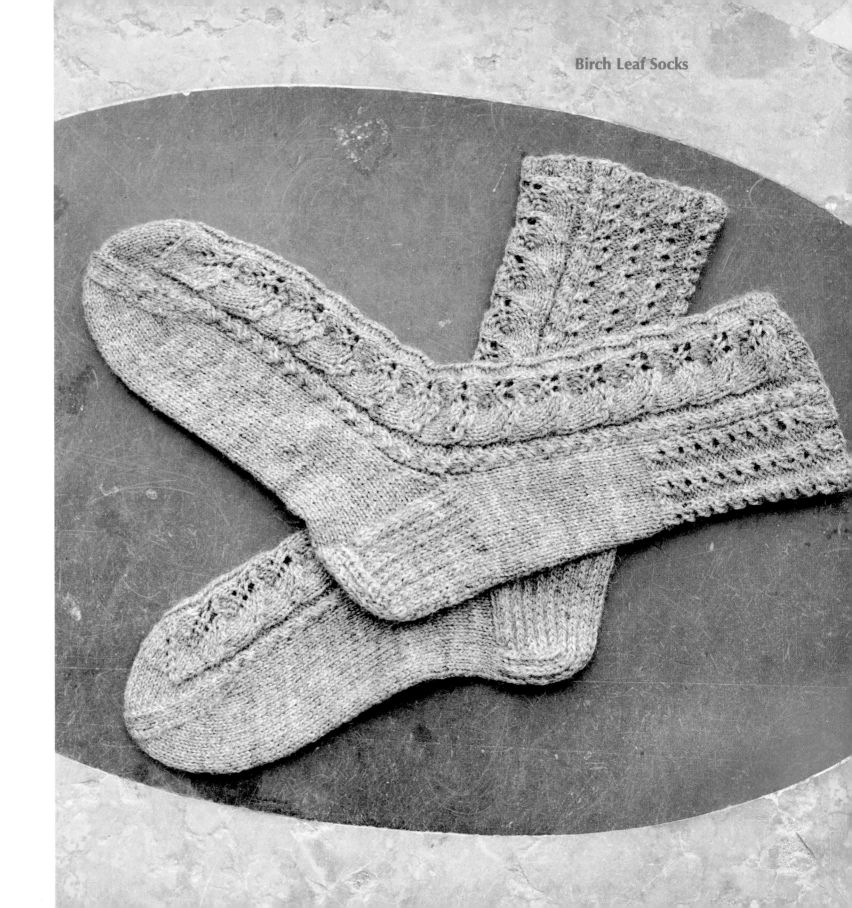

Turn Heel

Next row (RS) (Sl 1, k1) for 21 sts (the 21st st is a sl 1), sl 1-k1-psso. *Next row* (WS) Sl 1, p8, p2tog. *Next row* (RS) (Sl 1, k1) for 9 sts, sl1-k1-psso. Rep from* until all the waiting heel flap sts have been used, end with a WS row—10 heel sts remain.

Gusset

Next row (RS) Knit across the 10 heel sts. Pick up and k17 from right side of heel flap. Work across the 34 instep sts on 2 waiting dpn, continuing to work 20-rnd rep of Leaf Pat. Pick up and k17 from left side of heel flap, then k5 from heel. Beginning of rnd is now at back of heel. *Next rnd (dec rnd)* Work St st to last 3 sts of dpn #1, k2 tog, p1. Work across instep sts, keeping in pat. At the beginning of last dpn, p1, sl 1-k1-psso, work St st to end. Work next rnd even in pats, continuing to keep the first and last sts of back leg in purl as established until beginning of toe. Work dec rnd every other rnd until 17 sts remain on each of the back leg dpn—68 sts.

Foot

Work even in pats until foot measures approx 2½" less than desired length from heel to toe, end with a rnd 20 or 30 of Leaf Pat.

Toe

Next rnd (dec rnd) K to last 3 sts of dpn #1, k2 tog, k1; work rnd 31 of Leaf Pat on next 2 dpn; k1, sl1-k1-psso, k to end of rnd (toe dec's are incorporated in charts). Work next rnd even in pats, continuing to work Leaf Pat chart as established. Work dec rnd every other rnd until 9 sts remain on each dpn, then work dec rnd every rnd until 2 sts remain on each dpn. Break yarn, leaving an 8" tail.

Finishing

With tapestry needle, draw the end through the remaining sts and pull them up snugly. Weave in ends. Block socks under a damp towel or on sock blockers.

Leaf Pat

22   22

17   17

51
49
47
45
43
41
39
37
35
33
31
29
27
25
23
21   20-rnd rep
19
17
15
13
11
9
7
5
3
1

dpn #2 (3)   dpn #1 (2)

Rib Pat

4
3
2
1   4-rnd rep

dpn #4 (1)   dpn #3 (4)

NOTE Dpn #'s in parentheses represent beginning of rnd change at gusset

☐ K
▨ P
⊡ Yo
◣ Sl1-k2tog-psso
◪ Ssk-sl to LH ndl, pass next st over-sl back to RH ndl (dec 2 sts)
◣ Sl1-k1-psso
◿ K2tog
◭ Sl2tog-k1-p2sso
✕ 1/2 RT K into 3rd st on LH needle, then work into 1st and 2nd sts.

Skill level

Intermediate

Size

Woman's medium (wide)

Yarn

Schoeller-Esslinger Fortissima Cotton

(1¾oz/50g; 231yds/210m;

75% cotton/25% nylon)

or comparable sock yarn.

2 balls Black #02

Optional: Reinforcing yarn

for heel and toe.

Needles

Set of 5 double-pointed needles

(dpn) in size 2 (2.75mm),

or size to obtain gauge

Extras

Tapestry needle

Blocked gauge

14 sts to 2"/5cm in St st

using size 2 (2.75mm) dpn.

A 13-st rep of the feathered

chart pat measures approx 2½".

The inspiration for these socks was a pair of store-boughts that I positively wore out, and when replacements could not be found, the gauntlet—or, I should say, the socklet—had been thrown.

The process of inventing a suitable lace pattern taught me about a characteristic of lace vs. St st: if there is very much lace (yo's and their compensatory dec's), the fabric will gain a good bit of sideways stretch and won't fit a narrow foot and leg very well, so I needed fewer sts than usual. I also discovered that the locations and types of decreases affected the fabric. I chose the arrangement for this sock that would cause the fabric to lay the flattest: the *feathered* dec's. However, I've included a chart that gives a bold, almost 3-dimensional result, as well as expanded charts for those who'd like to knit socks for very wide feet or thick ankles.

NOTES *1* The needle diagram shows the arrangement of sts on the dpn. Red numbers indicate the first dpn of the rnd. *2* Directions are for medium size with wide size in parentheses. *3* Only even chart rnds are shown. Knit all odd rnds. *4* See *Techniques,* p. 162, for sl2tog-k1-p2sso.

Sock

Cast on 52 (60) sts loosely, and divide evenly between 4 dpn. Join and work in k1-p1 rib for 1¼"—approx 15 rnds. **Begin chart pat:** *Rnd 1* K 1 rnd. Work 4 reps of rnd 2 in whichever 13-st chart (15-st chart) you prefer (Feathered or Bold), then work through rnd 20 (24) of chart as established. Work rnds 1–20 (1–24) twice more, then work rnds 1 and 2 once.

Heel Flap

K across the first 2 dpn so that 26 (30) sts are now on 1 dpn, adding reinforcing yarn now if desired. The sts on the other 2 dpn will wait until the heel has been turned. The first st of each row of the heel flap is slipped, creating a chain down each side of the flap. *Next row* (WS) Sl 1, p25 (29). *Next row* (RS) Sl 1, k25 (29). Rep from* until 31 heel flap rows have been worked, ending with a WS row—15 chain sts each side.

Turn heel

Next row (RS) Sl 1, k 14 (16), ssk, k1, turn. *Next row* (WS) Sl 1, p5, p2tog, p1, turn. *Next row* Sl 1, k to 1 st before last turn, ssk, k1, turn. *Next row* Sl 1, p to 1 st before last turn, p2tog, p1, turn. Rep from* until all waiting heel flap sts have been used, end with a WS row—16 (18) heel sts remain.

Gusset

Next row (RS) K across all heel sts. If reinforcing yarn was used, break it off now. Pick up and k 15 chain sts from right side of heel flap. Continuing in chart pat, work across the 26 (30) instep sts on 2 waiting dpn. Pick up and k 15 chain sts from left side of heel flap, then k8 (9) from heel. Beginning of rnd is now at back of heel. *Next rnd* On first dpn, k to last 3 sts, k2tog, k1. Work chart pat on next 2 dpn. On 4th dpn, k1, ssk, k to end. *Next rnd* K on 1st and 4th dpn, continue in chart pat on 2nd and 3rd dpn (these should also be k on this rnd.) Rep from* until the sts on the 1st and 4th dpn have been reduced to the original 13 (15) sts. Continue to work even—the instep in chart pat and the sole of the foot in St st—until foot measures 2½" from end of longest toe. It is more important that the length be right than that you stop at the end of a whole repeat.

Toe

If reinforcing yarn is desired, add it now. Change to St st on all dpn. *For medium size* K 7 rnds. *Next rnd* *Ssk, k11; rep from*. K 5 rnds. *For wide size:* *Next rnd* *Ssk, k13; rep from*. K 6 rnds. *Next rnd* *Ssk, k5; rep from*. K 5 rnds. *For both sizes:* *Next rnd* *Ssk, k4; rep from*. K 4 rnds. *Next rnd* *Ssk, k3; rep from*. K 3 rnds. *Next rnd* *Ssk, k2; rep from*. K 2 rnds. *Next rnd* *Ssk, k1; rep from*. K 1 rnd. Ssk 8 times. Break yarn, leaving an 8" tail.

Finishing

With tapestry needle, draw the end through the remaining sts and pull them up snugly. Weave in end.

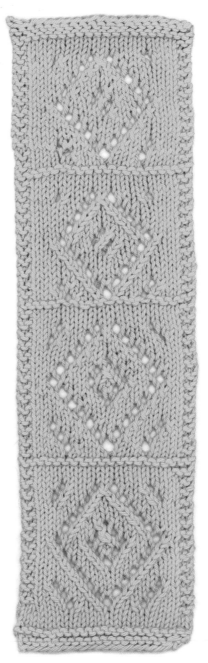

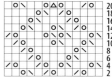

13-st Feathered

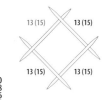

13 (15)   13 (15)

13 (15)   13 (15)

13-st Bold

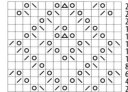

15-st Feathered

☐	K
⁄	K2tog
○	Yo
\	Ssk
▲	Sl2tog-k1-p2sso
◣	Sl1-k2tog-psso

15-st Bold

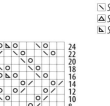

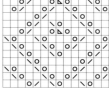

Old Mr. Saxby, a literary agent, is attempting to turn the heel on a sock while Cosmo Wisdom attempts to get some sense out of him about his book (which he didn't write, but Lord Ickenham suggested to Cosmo's uncle Beefy Bastable who did write it that it wouldn't ruin Cosmo's career to admit to it especially since Cosmo doesn't have a career and Beefy does) which has just appeared in serial form in the paper. Cosmo never does get any information out of him, but Old Mr. Saxby is perturbed, because it is so rude of someone to interrupt while one's trying to turn the heel—that is the trickiest part after all.

Regan Conley's summary
of a scene from *Cocktail Time*
by PG Wodehouse

Construction notes

This shoulder bag consists of two lace hexagons joined together on four sides by a double fabric gusset strip. The gusset continues and becomes the shoulder strap. The other two sides of each hexagon are finished with I-Cord and fold over to close the bag, with the outer flap secured by a decorative button. A washable fabric is used for the lining for easy care and to highlight the lace itself.

I-Cord Bind-Off Make 3 backward loops on RH needle, sl to LH needle, *k2, sl 1 knitwise, k1 from hexagon, psso, sl 3 sts back to LH needle; rep from*.

NOTES *1* Hexagon is knit from center out. *2* Only odd rnds are marked on the chart. Knit all sts on even rnds. *3* See *Techniques*, p. 162, for circular beginnings, sl2tog-k1-p2sso, and St st grafting.

Hexagon (make 2)

Using circular beginning and dpn, cast on 6 sts, distributing evenly between 3 needles. **Begin chart** Work rnd 1 of chart 6 times, placing markers between each rep of chart for ease of working. Use contrast color marker for beginning of rnd. Continue to work chart as established, changing to smaller circular needle when appropriate. When all 50 rnds are complete, bind off 2 of the 6 segments in I-Cord using larger needle, beginning and ending with a corner st. Leave sts from remaining 4 sides on smaller needle. Break yarn, leaving 6" tail. Work other hexagon same way to this point.

Gusset

With waste yarn, crochet a loose chain about 30 chains long. Leaving 6" tail of a new ball of main yarn and using larger needle, pick up and k 26 sts into chain. Transfer first 12 sts onto a 2nd size 8 circular needle and fold fabric so that purl sides are together. The 12 sts will be the inside of gusset; the 14 sts will be the outside of gusset with the st at each end "saddling up" with the fabric of the two hexagons.

Hexagon Set-up for joining to gusset (see drawing)

Lay hexagons on the table, knit side up and with the I-Cord flaps facing you. It's going to be tricky until we get established, so hang in there and don't be afraid of all the dangling needles.... This joining process, although seemingly unwieldy, is actually easier to knit than traditional double-knitting would be, with all its congestion and handling of every st twice on each pass.

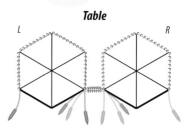

Table

L   R

Grab the other end of 12-st needle and, closing the gap to join yarn to the beginning, k across those 12 sts. Turn work and grab 14-st needle. With RS of hexagon facing, sl the first st of the hexagon on Table-R onto the left needle tip of front gusset needle; grab yarn and k these 2 sts tog (first saddle join made); k across gusset needle until 1 st remains, slip that st knitwise; grab Table-L hexagon and, with RS facing, k 1 st from its left-hand needle, psso (2nd saddle join made). Turn.* Drop front gusset needle. Pick up back gusset needle and k across the first few sts before you slip the front needle through to dangle out of the way, then finish knitting the rest of sts on needle. Turn, place next hexagon st from Table-R onto end of front gusset needle as before and, pulling yarn around, k 2 tog,

Skill level

Experienced

Finished measurements

12" wide x 10" high x 2½" thick,

with a 2" strap about 36" long.

Yarn

Tahki Yarns Cotton Classic

(1¾oz/50g; 108yds/98m; cotton)

4 skeins Purple #3945

Needles

Size 4 (3.5mm) needles in double-pointed

(dpn) and two 20" (50cm) circulars

Two size 8 (5mm) circulars, any length

or sizes to obtain gauge

Extras

Size F/5 (4mm) crochet hook

Tapestry needle

1 button, 1" to 1¼" in diameter

1 yd cotton canvas in Cream for lining

Sewing thread in yarn and lining colors

Stitch markers, 5 in one color

and 1 in contrasting color

Waste yarn

Freezer paper and protractor

for lining pattern

Blocked gauge

(NOTE Stitch gauge on smaller needles

must match row gauge on larger

needles. Adjust needle size if necessary to

achieve this.) 24 sts and 32 rows to

4"/10cm in St st using size 4 (3.5mm)

needles. 21 sts and 24 rows to 4"/10cm

in St st using size 8 (5mm) needles.

I thought it would be easy to work lace details into the six triangular sections of a hexagon, but a few surprises lay ahead.... As a visual aid, I folded a square of freezer paper in half, then into thirds around a center point and cut off the extra bits. So far so good. I've always liked eyelet raglans so I thought I could use the yo-k1-yo inc's every other rnd, along each spoke, and fill in with lace. It seemed a simple matter. I charted a lace triangle and gave it a try, figuring if I balanced all internal yo's with the same number of dec's, that the diagonal lines should widen the triangle at a suitable rate. The triangle looked good, but when I worked six of them in the round, the hexagon did not lie flat. I showed my results to daughter Medrith who remembered the specific requirements for a hexagonal shape from high-school geometry. She explained, "A hexagon is made up of six equilateral triangles, which means the last row of your knitted triangle should measure the same length as each of the two diagonal sides....

- to page 138

Knitting fancy laces in cotton,
linen, silk or worsted, was an
occupation not only 'fascinating
to the knitter, but also to
the beholders; for certainly no
other kind of fancy-work
displays a beautiful hand to
better advantage.

Anne L. Macdonald,
No Idle Hands

k across to last st, sl 1 knitwise, k next hexagon st from Table-L, psso. Turn. Rep from* until 4 sides of each hexagon have been joined, end with an inside gusset row. (NOTE Do not twist sts during joining or hexagons will not lie flat. Each time you turn, you may, after a few sts, adjust the circular needle you don't need anymore so that it dangles from its cable and stays out of your way.)

Shoulder Strap

Continuing with same ball of yarn and same size 8 needles, unknit last st and place on beginning of next needle. Sl 2 tog-k1-p2sso, work across to last 2 sts and place them on next needle; perform same double dec, k to end of needle—11 sts each needle. (The center st of each dec group should be the st that did the saddling, and these sts should be the first ones on both needles.) K in rnds, working EZ's Phony Seam on first st of each needle after 2" as foll: drop st down to st above double dec. With a crochet hook, hook up 2 ladders at a time (see illustration, p. 88). This will cause the strap to fold nicely and hold its shape. Work Phony Seam every 2" until strap measures 36" or desired length before laundering (NOTE Cotton knitted fabrics shrink about 10% in height, so allow for this), end with a rnd 2. *Next rnd* K1, M1 (by lifting running yarn between st just worked and next st, k into the back of this yarn), k10, M1, sl first st from 2nd needle onto this needle and k; on 2nd needle, M1, k10, M1—14 sts on outside strap needle and 12 sts on inside strap needle.

Graft Shoulder Strap to Gusset

Remove gusset sts from waste chain, placing 14-st group on one needle and 12-st group on another. Yarn should be coming from underside of strap, ready to form sts on outside of strap. Cut yarn, leaving 40" end. Thread this yarn into tapestry needle. Graft front gusset sts to front strap sts, then back gusset sts to back strap sts—connect end of tube to beginning. Adjust st placement if necessary to make folds line up. Secure ends of I-Cord bind-offs to base of each end of strap; work in all remaining ends.

Finishing

Button loop K a 2-st I-Cord about an inch long, leaving 4" ends. Attach ends to inside of flap so that it lies flat and hugs the innermost st of I-Cord at the point.

Lining

Wash shoulder bag and lining fabric separately, tumble dry to pre-shrink before cutting fabric to fit. Steam press fabric. To make hexagon lining pat on freezer paper, first draw a straight line 14" long, mark the center point, and then use a protractor to mark a radius every 60° degrees. Draw 7" lines from the center point through each of these marked positions. Connect all the outer points to complete the hexagon shape. Then add ½" seam allowance along entire

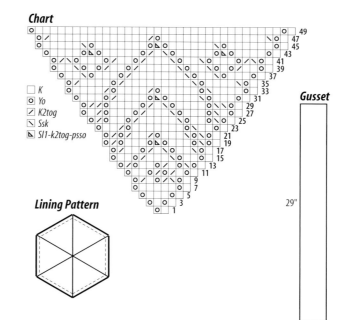

Chart

☐ K
⊙ Yo
⊘ K2tog
╲ Ssk
▧ Sl1-k2tog-psso

Lining Pattern

Gusset

29"

3½"

perimeter. Make gusset pat 29" x 3½". Place paper hexagon pat on canvas with straight grain of fabric lined up with one of the long spokes. Cut 4 hexagon pieces. Place gusset pat lengthwise along straight grain. Cut 2 gusset pieces. Sew 4 sides of one hexagon piece to edge of gusset strip, snipping seam allowances to turn corners easily. Attach 2nd hexagon to other long edge of gusset strip in same manner. As this is to be a double lining so that no seam allowances can show through the lace, rep this process with remaining hexagons and gusset strip. Press all seam allowances toward gussets. Tuck one lining inside the other, wrong sides tog. Hand stitch the hexagons tog next to stitching lines to keep seam allowances inside gusset space and stabilize the linings. Fold 2 remaining edges of lining pieces toward their wrong sides and press. (NOTE Turn under the inside layer at least ¼" more so that when sewn to outside layer of lining, the flaps will want to curl inward and will also draw the knitted fabric inward.) Press the folds and machine stitch tog. Hand stitch flaps of lining just inside I-Cord edges but leave lining unattached across inside of knitted gusset/straps. Sew button to front of shoulder bag through all 3 layers.

A raglan rate of inc (8 sts every other rnd) will give a nearly flat fabric, 9 or 10 sts every other rnd will be even flatter, but the hexagon spokes give you 12 sts increased every other rnd… and it flares. Also, since knit stitches are not square, you'll have to work with row as well as st gauge. You'll need extra rnds, so some rnds will need to have a net 'no change' in stitch count. In other words, there will need to be fewer stitches in the final rnd than there are increased stitches along the diagonals if you're to end up with equilateral triangles."
I was glad to know why it hadn't worked the first time. The need for extra dec's inside each triangle limited the amount of lace patterning that I could include, but I was able to come up with a petal-like composition that pleased me… and it all worked!

138

Notes *1* The sock is started at the toe. Short rows are worked in the sole to eliminate bulk at the front of the ankle, and the heel is also shaped with short rows. *2* A yarn-over (yo) is my preferred method of doing short rows. If you prefer, you may use the more common method of wrapping a st. The yo and wrap are identical when knit together with adjoining st. Knitting back onto my left needle (ndl) is also my preferred method, but if desired you may turn your work and purl back. *3* A functional rib hides behind the lace cuff. *4* Instructions are given for 3 different toe shapes. Shape 1, shown on the purple sock, has its inc's in a single line, similar to the toe found on commercial machine-knit socks (but without the seam across the top of the toe). Shape 2 is a common hand-knit toe shape with 2 sts between the inc's at the sides. Shape 3 will give you right and left foot socks. If you knit this toe shape, you must knit an extra half round before working the sole short rows on the second sock; otherwise, you'll find you have two socks for the same foot! *5* Only odd rnds are charted. All even rnds are knit. *6* See *Techniques,* p. 162, for EZ's Sewn Cast-off, knitting backwards, lifted inc, M1L, M1R, and sssk.

Skill level

Intermediate

Size

M (L)

Finished measurements

8 (9)" circumference around instep

Yarn

Schoolhouse Press Satakieli

(3½oz/100g; 360yds/325m; wool)

2 skeins Royal Purple #596 (MC)

1 skein Lavender #534 (CC)

Needles

Two 24" (60cm) circulars:

MEDIUM SOCK Size 0 (2mm)

LARGE SOCK Size 1 (2.25mm)

or size to obtain gauge

Blocked gauge

MEDIUM SOCK 32 sts and 45 rnds

to 4"/10cm in St st

using size 0 (2mm) needle.

LARGE SOCK 36 sts and 50 rnds

to 4"/10cm in St st using size 1

(2.25mm) needle.

If you are timid about knitting something large for your first lace project, or if you are a lace knitter and would like a small travel project, this pair of socks will fit the bill. This sock pattern includes innovative techniques that are useful in many knit projects. The variation of the Eastern European cast-on is an ideal way to start a circular knit shawl. Knitting with two circulars is useful for very large circumferences where stitches are crowded on one circular, as well as for small circumferences such as socks or gloves.

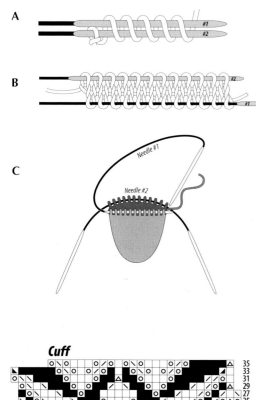

A

B

C

Needle #1

Needle #2

Cuff

35 →1
33
31
29
27 →1
25 →1
23 →1
21 →1
19 →1
17
15
13
11
9
7
5
3
1

□ K
○ Yo
△ Sl2tog-sl1-k3tog tbl
✔ M1R
↘ M1L
◪ K2tog
◩ Ssk
◢ K3tog
◣ Sssk
■ No stitch
→1 Move marker 1 st to right

Two Circular Needle Eastern European Cast-On
A Using 2 same-size circular ndls, make a slip knot on ndl #2. Hold tip of ndl #1 above and parallel with ndl #2. Bring working yarn from slip knot up behind ndl #1 and around the front of both ndls. Wrap the ndls in this direction as many times as necessary for cast-on. After wrapping, lightly hold down working yarn next to ndls with thumb and index finger, and slide ndl #2 so wraps are on the flexible part of ndl. *B* With opposite end of ndl #1, knit wraps off ndl #1, then slide ndl #1 so sts are on flexible part of ndl. Turn work, slide wraps on ndl #2 back to tip of ndl, remove slip knot, and knit wraps from ndl #2 with opposite end of ndl #2. Yarn for the first st will come from opposite needle, just as when knitting in the round with double points. *C* Continue as established, knitting all ndl #1 sts with ndl #1, and all ndl #2 sts with ndl #2, bringing the first st knit with each ndl up next to the st on the flexible portion of opposite ndl.

Using Two Circular Needle Eastern European Cast-On and MC, wrap needles 12 times. Knit one rnd. Work toe shape of your choice as foll: **Toe Shape 1:** *Rnd 2* On ndl #1, M1L, k to end, M1R. On ndl #2, k to end, M1R. *Rnd 3* On ndl #1, k to end. On ndl #2, M1L, k to end. (NOTE Work all inc's for Toe Shapes 2 and 3 using lifted inc.) **Toe Shape 2:** *Rnd 2* On ndl #1, k1, inc 1, k to last st, inc 1, k1. Work ndl #2 as for ndl #1. *Rnd 3* Knit. **Toe Shape 3:** *Rnd 2* On ndl #1, k1, inc 1, k to end. On ndl #2, k to last st, inc 1, k1. *Rnd 3* On ndl #1, k1, inc 1, k to last st, inc 1, k1. Work ndl #2 as for ndl #1.
For all Toe Shapes Rep rnds 2 and 3 until there are 36 sts each ndl—72 sts total. Continue to work even in St st to mid-foot.

Short-row Sole Shaping *K35 to last st on ndl #1. Yarn over left ndl, knit backwards or turn and purl 34 sts. If you purled, turn work. Yarn over right ndl, k34 to yarn over, k2tog. K across ndl #2. On ndl #1, ssk the first st and yo tog, k to end of rnd. K 5 rnds (approx 1"); rep from* until sole is approx ½" from total desired foot length.

Short-row Heel Shaping: *Row 1* K12, wrapping yarn over ndl from back to front (left sides of resulting sts are in front of ndl), k 12 as usual—24 sts. *Row 2* Yo left ndl from back to front, k12 onto *left* ndl. *Row 3* *Yo right ndl from back to front, k onto *right* ndl to yo, k2tog (the st following the yo and the yo). *Row 4* Yo left ndl, k onto *left* ndl to yo, insert tip of left ndl into left side of st following the yo and then into the yo, then k2tog onto left ndl. Rep from* until you have knit the last st on the needle tog with the yo. K across ndl #2. K2togtbl the first st and yo on ndl #1, then k to end of rnd. Work even in rnds in St st until sock measures 2" from end of heel shaping, then work k2-p2 rib for 2" more. On final rnd, work to last 6 sts on ndl #2. Slip these 6 sts onto ndl #1.

Turn for cuff (RS and WS reversed) Turn work, change to CC, and with WS facing and continuing with ndl #2, k36 (30 + 6 sts from ndl #1). K36 from ndl #1. K 4 rnds, p 1 rnd, k 1 rnd. **Begin Cuff chart** Work rnd 1 of chart 3 times around, placing markers between reps. Continue to work chart as established through rnd 36, working all even rnds in knit, then leave a tail approx 4 times the circumference of your sock and break yarn. Thread a tapestry needle with the tail, and bind off using EZ's Sewn Cast-off.

Finishing Weave in ends. Block, pinning out points of lace cuff. Wear or give with pride and pleasure.

Early impressions are hard

to eradicate from the mind.

When once wool

has been dyed purple,

who can restore it

to its previous whiteness?

Saint Jerome

Skill level

Intermediate

Size

Determined by size of hat form used in

blocking.

Yarn

Crochet cottton (size 5 or 10 pearl or

bedspread-weight cotton or fine linen),

approx 3½oz/100g

These hats can be airy or firm. The hat on

this page uses a fine cotton; the one on the

next 2 pages was worked with 2 strands of

a linen of similar weight—same size, but the

linen one is firmer. Starch and block swatch

to check that your choice is appropriate.

Needles

Size 3 (3.25mm) needles in

double-pointed (dpn) and circular,

20" to 24" (50 to 60cm) long

or size to obtain gauge

Extras

Size B/1 (2.5mm) crochet hook

Decorative ribbon

Rust-proof T-pins, string, hat form, foam

board and laundry starch for blocking

Blocked gauge

6 sts and 7 rnds to 1"/2.5cm in

St st using size 3 (3.25mm) needle.

NOTES **1** This hat is knit from the center of the crown outward to the brim, beginning on dpn and changing to a circular when necessary. It achieves its final shape through blocking. See suppliers listing, p. 173, for source for hat form. **2** All even rounds are knit. **3** See *Techniques,* p. 162, for circular beginnings, chain st, and sl2tog-k1-p2sso.

Hat

Begin Chart: *Rnd 1* Using circular beginning and dpn, cast on 10 sts and distribute evenly. Being careful not to twist sts, place marker for beginning of rnd and join. *Rnd 2* Knit this and all following even rnds. *Rnd 3* Work 10 times around—20 sts. Continue to work chart as established through rnd 88. Do not break yarn.

Edging

Using crochet hook and following markings at top of chart, crochet off edge sts with chain loops as foll: slip hook through bracketed group of 3 sts, yo and draw yarn through all sts, work 3 chain sts. After final chain, join to first st and fasten off.

Finishing

Dampen hat. Cook laundry starch to the consistency of gravy and put hat in warm solution. Roll in towel to remove excess starch. Thread string through eyelet on rnd 51.

The spinsters and the

knitters in the sun.

And the free maids that weave

their thread with bones,

Do use to chant it; it is silly sooth,

And dallies with

the innocence of love,

Like the old age.

Twelfth-Night,

William Shakespeare

Blocking Hat

Use hat form and foam board to block hat. Pre-mark board for pinning out the brim (1). Stretch crown over hat form and pin to board at base of form (2). Tie string tightly around base to keep crown from pulling away from form as the brim is stretched. Position hat with form on foam board and pin out brim 4½ to 5" wide (3). Allow hat to dry. Remove pins, hat form and string from rnd 51. Hand stitch ribbon band inside base of crown to maintain hat size. Decorate hat.

Chart

☐ K
⅄ K in back of stitch
╱ k2tog
△ Sl2tog-k1-p2sso
◣ Sl1-k2tog-psso
⊙ Yo
■ No stitch
←1 K1 then move marker left
   1 st before beginning rnd
→1 Move marker 1 st to right

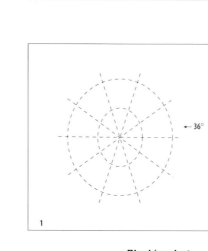

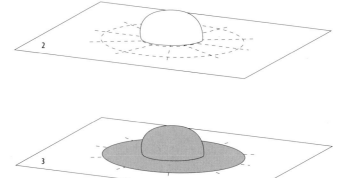

Blocking hat

NOTES *1* This purse is knit from top to bottom. *2* Only odd rnds are charted. Knit all even rnds. *3* See *Techniques,* p. 162, for 3-needle bind-off.

Purse

Using waste yarn, cast on 86 sts. Being careful not to twist, join and k one rnd. Change to main yarn. Leaving approx a 36" tail, k 1 rnd. *Next rnd* *K2tog, yo; rep from* to end. K 1 rnd. **Begin Purse chart: Rnd 1** Rep 43 sts of row twice, once for the front and once for the back of the purse. Continue to work chart as established through rnd 12, then rep rnds 1–12 six times more or for desired length. Close bottom of purse with 3-needle bind-off.

Finishing

Place first row of main yarn sts back on needles, removing waste yarn. Using tail, bind off all sts. Divide ribbon into 2 equal lengths. Beginning at one side, thread one length of ribbon through all eyelets at top of purse, ending at same side. Knot ends of ribbon together. Beginning at opposite side, repeat threading process with second length of ribbon. Adorn bottom of purse with beads if desired.

Purse

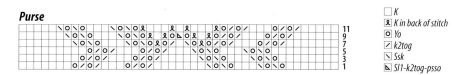

11
9
7
5
3
1

43 sts

☐ *K*
ℛ *K in back of stitch*
○ *Yo*
╱ *k2tog*
╲ *Ssk*
▲ *Sl1-k2tog-psso*

As an example of how lace designs mercurially slip around the globe, this heart pattern was found by Sidna Farley in Dorothy Read's *25 Original Knitting Designs*, 1968 USA, and Sidna originally designed this charming purse for *Knitter's Magazine*, issue #23.

When Rachel Misgades was searching for a suitable motif for her daughter Katherine's wedding purse, she found the same design in Marianne Kinzel's *Second Book of Modern Lace Knitting*, 1961 UK. As she was plotting her pattern, she saw Sidna's purse in *Knitter's Magazine* and used those instructions to knit the item shown here.

Skill level

Easy

Finished measurements

Width: 5"

Height: 6½"

Yarn

DMC Size 5 Perle Cotton

(1oz/28g; cotton)

Needles

Size 2 (2.75mm)

double-pointed needles (dpn)

or size to obtain gauge

Extras

1½ yds ⅜" satin ribbon

Waste yarn

Optional: Beads for decoration

Blocked gauge

39 sts and 48 rows to 4"/10cm

in St st.

NOTES *1* The child and doll sizes use different yarn and needles, but are made in exactly the same way. *2* Beads, shown here on doll's pinafore, are optional; make sure the hole is the right size for the yarn. *3* Yoke and straps are worked by double-knitting: working both sides of the fabric at the same time. *4* See *Techniques*, p. 162, for sssk.

Stringing the Beads

Beads are strung in reverse order onto the yarn before knitting. The single-bead "dots" in the upper skirt are strung first, followed by the "flower" bead groups in the lower border. (NOTES *1* If stringing beads for doll's pinafore, string all beads on single ball of yarn. For child's pinafore, string first flower row on one ball, dot row 1 and 2nd flower row on 2nd ball, then dot rows 1 and 2 on additional balls. *2* To place beads, slide bead up close to needles, then form new st, pulling yarn with bead through old st. Position bead on either leg of st but be consistent through garment, then tighten new st firmly.) *Dot row 1* Thread *1 pink, 1 blue* 4 (5, 6) times. *Dot row 2* Thread *1 green, 1 pink* 4 (5, 6) times. Rep dot rows 1 and 2, 0 (1, 2) times more, then dot row 1 once again. *Flower row* **Thread 8 (10, 12) pink beads, then *1 blue, 1 green* 8 (10, 12) times. Rep from** once more.

Skirt

With larger needles, loosely cast on 174 (216, 258) sts. K 5 rows for lower garter st border. **Begin Pinafore chart:** *Row 1* (WS) Work first 3 sts, work 42-st rep 4 (5, 6) times, work last 3 sts. Continue to work chart as established through row 57, rep rows 34–57 0 (1, 2) times, end by working rows 34–47 once more.

Cut the yarn leaving a tail approx 5 times the width of the knitting, and put all sts on a string. The tail will be used to bind off the sts after blocking. The bind-off prevents the top edge from stretching. To block the skirt, wash and pin out or pin out dry and spray until damp. In both cases, cover with a towel until thoroughly dry.

After blocking, bind off top edge, RS facing, as foll: Bind off 2 (3, 4) sts, *bind off 2 tog, bind off 1, bind off 2 tog; rep from* to last 2 (3, 4) sts, bind off remaining sts—106 (132, 158) bound-off sts.

Yoke and Straps

With smaller needles and RS facing, pick up and k 1 st into the bottom loop of each bound-off st—106 (132,158) sts. K 2 rows. *Next row* (WS) K20 (25, 30) and place on holder for right back yoke, bind off 15 (19, 22) sts for right underarm, k36 (44, 54) and place on holder for front yoke, bind off 15 (19, 22) sts for left underarm, k20 (25, 30) for left back yoke.

Armhole Selvage 2 (3, 3) sts: At beginning of row, sl 1 knitwise, k1 (2, 2). At end of row, k2 (3, 3). *Center Back Selvage* 3 (4, 4) sts: At beginning of row, sl 1 knitwise, k2 (3, 3). At end of row, k3 (4, 4).

Left Back Yoke

Next row: *Row 1* (RS) Work Center Back Selvage, (k1-p1) in each st to last 2 (3, 3) sts, k to end—35 (43, 53) sts. *Row 2* (WS) Work Armhole Selvage, *k1, sl 1 purlwise wyif; rep from* to last 3 (4, 4) sts, k to end. *Row 3* (RS) Work Center Back Selvage, *k1, sl 1 purlwise wyif; rep from* to last 2 (3, 3) sts, knit to end. Rep rows 2 & 3 four (five, six) times more. *Next row* (WS) K2 (3, 3), ssk to last 3 (4, 4) sts, knit to end—20 (25, 30) sts. *Next row* (RS) Knit. Bind off all sts in knit.

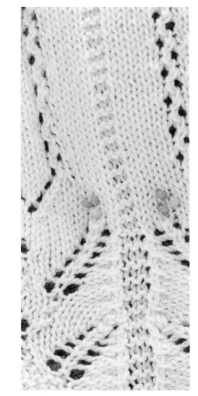

There is a tranquil beauty

about white cotton

lace knitting....

Furze Hewitt,

Classic Knitted Cotton Edgings

Classic Pinafore

Front Yoke

Work as for Left Back Yoke, working Armhole Selvage both sides.

Right Back Yoke

Work to correspond to Left Back Yoke, reversing Center Back Selvage and Armhole Selvage placement.

Straps (make 2)

With smaller needles, cast on 6 (7, 8) sts. K 2 rows. **Next row** K1, (k1-p1) in each st to last st, k1—10 (12, 14) sts. **Strap row** Sl 1 knitwise, *k1, sl 1 purlwise wyif; rep from* to last st, k1. Repeat strap row until at least 120 (160, 180) rows have been worked [60 (80, 90) rows each side of strap]. **Next row** K1, ssk to last st, k1—6 (7, 8) sts. **Next row** Knit. Bind off all sts in knit.

Pinafore

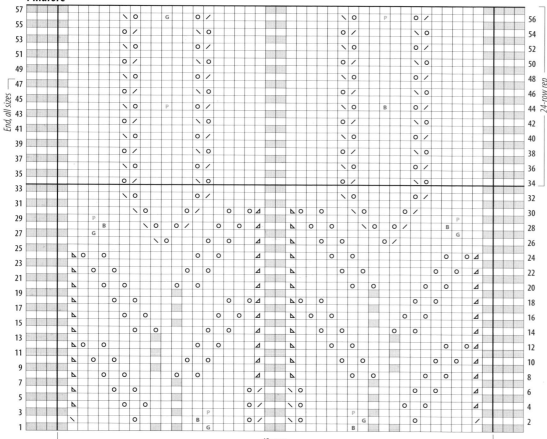

42-st rep

24-row rep

End, all sizes

☐ K on RS, p on WS
▨ P on RS, k on WS
○ Yo
╲ Ssk
╱ K2tog
◣ Sssk
◢ K3tog
B Blue bead on this st
G Green bead on this st
P Pink bead on this st

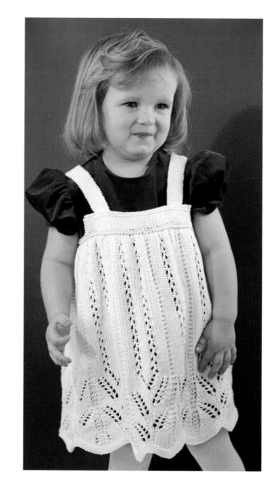

Finishing

Sew two pairs of snaps to top and bottom edges of back yoke at center back. Try pinafore on the lucky recipient and mark position of straps. Sew straps on inside of front yoke, bottom edge of strap level with bottom edge of yoke, and tack strap down firmly all around where it comes in contact with yoke. You can do the same on back yoke, but I recommend making straps a little too long and using snaps to attach straps to back yoke to allow for future growth.

This pattern shows that lace can be elegantly simple.

NOTES *1* Pillow cover is cast on invisibly and knitted, then beginning and end are grafted together, accommodating the pattern's tendency to wave. Side edges are seamed. *2* See *Techniques,* p. 162, for grafting, invisible cast-on, and sl2tog-k1-p2sso.

Pillow Cover

Invisibly cast on 69 sts. **Begin Tailored Lace chart:** *Row 1* (WS) Working chart from left to right, work first 6 sts, work 20-st rep 3 times, work last 3 sts. Continue to work through row 8 of chart as established, then work 8-row rep 15 times more—128 rows. Do not bind off.

Finishing

Place cast-on sts on spare needle, removing waste yarn. Graft beginning and end together. Block to 12" x 16" (double thickness). Beginning at one side of grafted seam and working 1 st in from edge, sew one side seam. Insert pillow form and sew remaining seam.

Skill level

Intermediate

Finished measurements

To fit 12" x 16" pillow

Yarn

Schoolhouse Press Satakieli

(3½oz/100g; 360yds/325m; wool)

1 skein Teal #770

Needles

Size 5 (3.75mm) needles

or size to obtain gauge

Extras

A few yards of heavier waste yarn

for invisible cast-on

Covered pillow form, 12" x 16"

Gauge

21 sts and 30 rows to 4"/10cm

in St st (steamed but not stretched).

To test gauge, cast on 29 sts and work

1 rep of pat for 32 rows;

steam and pat out.

It should measure 5" wide x 5" long.

	K on RS, p on WS
	P on RS, K on WS
o	Yo
∕	K2tog
∖	Ssk
△	Sl2tog-k1-p2sso

Tailored Lace

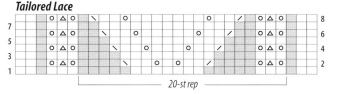

20-st rep

Being very much a cat person, I've loved Dorothy Reade's Peruvian Cats (*25 Original Knitting Designs*) for a long time, and this was a great opportunity to use them. Laceweight Shetland comes in several natural shades, including this silver that reminds me of our Abbi, so pick your favorite "catly" color and have fun!

NOTES *1* This lace overlay for a pillow front is cast on with dpn at the center and worked outwards in rnds, changing to increasingly longer circular needles as needed. *2* If your pillow form has rounded corners, work chart as given. If the corners are square, eliminate the indicated ssk's and k2tog's at the beginning and end of rnds 66–74. Note that you will, in this case, have more sts on the final rnds than the graph indicates. *3* Only even rnds are charted. Knit all sts on odd rnds. *4* See *Techniques*, page 162, for circular beginnings and sl2tog-k1-p2sso.

Pillow cover

Using circular beginning and dpn, cast on 8 sts, divide sts among 4 needles and work with 5th. Mark beginning of rnd. Knit 1 rnd. **Begin Catspaw charts** *Work rnd 2 of Catspaw I, work rnd 2 of Catspaw II; rep from* once. Continue to work pats in rnds as established, remembering to knit all odd rnds. (NOTE It may be helpful to place additional markers at the beginning of each chart section when changing to circulars.) When all chart rnds have been completed, bind off loosely in purl.

Finishing

Block piece to fit pillow top, weave in ends and sew lace to front of pillow.

Catspaw I

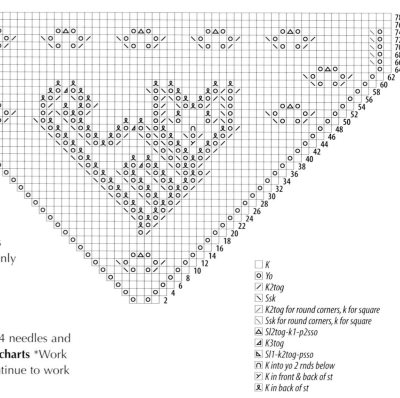

Catspaw II

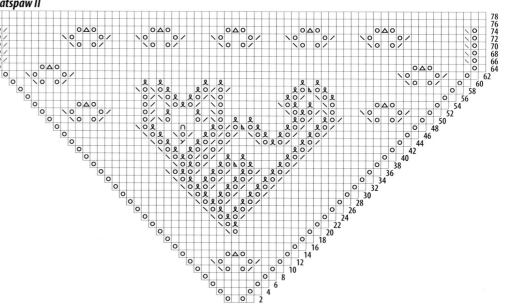

□ K
⊙ Yo
⟋ K2tog
⟍ Ssk
⟋ K2tog for round corners, k for square
⟍ Ssk for round corners, k for square
△ Sl2tog-k1-p2sso
⟑ K3tog
⟓ Sl1-k2tog-psso
∩ K into yo 2 rnds below
⋎ K in front & back of st
⋏ K in back of st

The modern woman,
in spite of her crowded
programme, still loves to
grace her surroundings
with fine needlework,
and a luxurious piece
of lace in the form
of a doily or tablecloth,
curtain or bedspread,
was never
surpassed in beauty.

Marianne Kinzel,
*First Book of
Modern Lace Knitting*

When Meg asked me if she could
use one of the lace shawls that I had
designed in an upcoming book, I
answered, "Sure! I'd love it. But, you
should know that I really don't
design lace." I'm like a historian
writing a book about Abraham
Lincoln. He borrows a little bit from
a lot of different sources. So do I.

One of Eleven
Dallas Cahill

Continued on p. 159

PHOTOS BY D. B. COBEY

We express ourselves by what we wear,
  what we make.
Wedding dresses usually hark back
  one hundred years.
Knitting, I make a seamless coating.
The plastic is nacreous.
It challenges, drapes, shines, confuses.
The shoulders are shaped like woolen
  overcoats, like daily wear.
The front opens and closes—
  but no buttons.
Its exaggerated, fringed opening,
  its lace, intends to flash.
The length preens, invites itself to dances,
  steps out of carriages,
  becomes an outskirt.
Beneath its froth,
  we point a plastic slipper.
This yarn is made by cutting
  shopping bags into strips.
They become continuous
  by knitting the overlap.
It is a take off, a cover up.
It is not waterproof, nor warm.
It rustles.
It is fantastic knitting, a real 'mirage.'

Mirage
Katharine Cobey

I had not knit lace since I was a child, but Meg said, "Never mind, you'll think of something." This project came to mind when we were living on a boat on the English canals last summer; we were passed by another boat toting a coracle—I was captivated. Its owner showed me how he had built it and gave me a demonstration of boat handling, which calls for skill and daring. In my youth, Australian children were raised on British history, which seemed to start each year with the coracle. This was always about the time I clicked out, so the coracle is actually my sole knowledge of the history of the world. Well, what could I do but knit a lace coracle? I made a mock-up of one while still in England using some black sheep's wool that I had on hand. I left it with a fellow at the marina who had greeted the project with considerable enthusiasm and had drawn up a number of plans for me which included elaborate bailing and flotation assists. (You will be surprised to hear that this venture has run into some technical difficulties along the way.) I decided to knit swirling lace as this is a rather swirly craft. I knit it out of fine Merino laceweight, which I then planned to dunk in fiberglass resin. After quite a lot of knitting was done, I tried out a sample only to find that the white wool became completely transparent in the resin. I really wanted the lace to be white against the dark water, but I had to dye it dark. Cotton would have remained white, but I didn't want to redo what I had done—maybe for my next coracle.

Coracle
Debbie New

The center section of this shawl is the center of an afternoon tea cloth from Marianne Kinzel's *Second Book Of Modern Lace Knitting.* The design is called *Rose of England.*

A Rose is a Rose Shawl
Robert Powell

Continued on p. 159

Growing roses and knitting have been my claim to fame since 1978. So I had a great desire to knit this shawl when I saw it pictured in the Winter '92 issue of *Knitter's.* All I had to go by was the designer's name: Robert Powell. Bob very graciously sent me the pattern for the lettering, along with his encouragement. The only thing that he wanted in exchange for the pattern was a photograph of the finished shawl. The finer yarn and gauge enabled me to include the beautiful rose leaf pattern, which is used in the Rose of England Dinner Cloth version, knitted beyond the lettering. I incorporated extra repeats to make sure the outer edge of the shawl would have enough diameter so the shawl could be worn comfortably, thus making the final blocked measurement a full 70 inches in diameter.

Sheryl Hill

My daughter Liesl was getting married,
and I began to search for a suitable
wedding shawl design. I found a
lovely doily pattern in a booklet,
Tapetes de Punto, which my mother
had brought from Spain. To make a
full-sized shawl, I repeated portions of
the chart several times—rather guessing
at the rate of increase—and finished it
off with a sideways border pattern from
Barbara Abbey's Knitting Lace.
Knitting by the seat of my pants, I kept
very sketchy notes on what I had done,
so your version will most likely look
quite different.

Spanish Peacock Shawl
Meg Swansen

Continued on p. 161

Thom Christoph's circular beginning

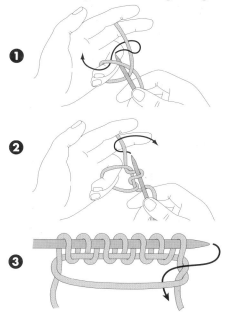

Emily Ocker's circular beginning

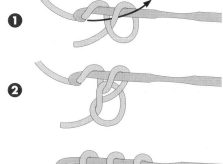

2 …and bringing it under the front of the thumb loop. Slip thumb out of loop, and use thumb to adjust tension on the new stitch. One stitch cast on.

THOM CHRISTOPH'S CIRCULAR BEGINNING

1 Make a loop at end of yarn and knit up one stitch.

2 *Yo, knit up another stitch in the same place, repeat from* until you have the desired number of stitches (for an odd number of sts) or until one fewer than desired (for an even number); both knits and yo's count as stitches. Divide stitches on 3 or 4 needles and close loop by pulling on the tag end of the yarn.

3 Yo before beginning the first round to make up that last stitch for an even number, if necessary. Knit into the back loop of each stitch around (including that last yo, if you have an even number of stitches). Place marker and continue.

EMILY OCKER'S CIRCULAR BEGINNING

Make a ring with the short end below. (This ring can be roomy; it will be tightened later.)

1 Chain through the ring.

2 Chain through last chain (chain B). Chain B is the first stitch and waits on the crochet hook.

3 Repeat steps 1 and 2 until there are as many loops on the crochet hook as stitches to be cast on. Distribute the loops on 3 or 4 double-pointed needles. After working around in pattern for several inches, you may pull on the short end to close the ring.

EZ'S SEWN CAST-OFF

1 *Slip needle into first stitch as if to knit and slip stitch off needle.

2 Slip needle into next 2 stitches as if to purl and pull through, leaving stitches on needle.

GRAFTING

St st grafting

With stitches on two knitting needles, thread a blunt needle with matching yarn (approximately 1" per stitch).

1 Working from right to left, with right sides facing you, begin with steps 1a and 1b:

    1a Front needle Yarn through first stitch as if to purl, leave stitch on needle.

    1b Back needle Yarn through first stitch as if to knit, leave on.

2 Work 2a and 2b across, adjusting tension to match rest of knitting.

    2a Front needle Yarn through first stitch as if to knit, slip off needle; through next st as if to purl, leave on needle.

    2b Back needle Yarn through first stitch as if to purl, slip off needle; through next st as if to knit, leave on needle.

Garter st grafting

Work as for St st graft, arranging so stitches on lower needle come out of purl bumps and stitches on upper needle come out of smooth knits.

1–2 Work as for St st graft except: on 1b, go through the stitch as if to purl. On 2b, go through first stitch as if to knit, and through next stitch as if to purl.

Grafting open stitches to edge

When grafting open stitches to bound-off or cast-on edge, match stitch for stitch.

EZ's sewn cast-off

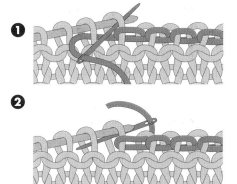

Grafting, St st

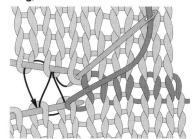

Grafting, garter st

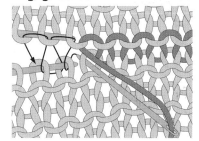

Grafting open stitches to edge

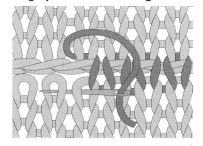

163

k1tbl

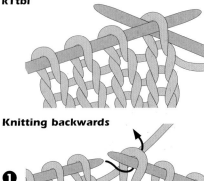

Knitting backwards

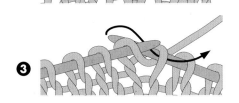

Purling backwards

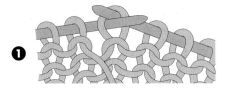

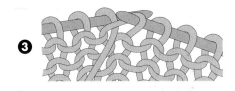

KNITTING THROUGH THE BACK LOOP (k1tbl or k1b)
To knit into the back of a stitch, insert the needle into the stitch from right to left.

KNITTING BACKWARDS
1 Enter back loop with left needle tip.
2 Wrap yarn from back to front over left needle tip.
3 While lifting right needle tip, draw wrap through and onto left needle to form new stitch.

PURLING BACKWARDS
1 With yarn in front, pass point of left needle from left to right through back of stitch on right needle.
2 Wrap yarn counterclockwise around left needle; draw under right needle and through loop to make stitch.
3 Drop stitch on right needle; new stitch is now on left needle.

MAKE 1 (M1) A single increase.
1 With right needle from back of work, pick up strand between last stitch knitted and next stitch. Place on left needle and knit through back (or purl through back for M1 purlwise).
2 This increase can be used as the left increase in a paired increase (M1L).
3 Another method: with left needle from back of work, pick up strand between last stitch knitted and next stitch. Knit.
4 This increase can be used as the corresponding right increase in a paired increase (M1R).

LIFTED INC
Knit into right loop of stitch in row below next stitch on left needle (1), then knit stitch on left needle (2).

SHORT-ROW WRAP Each short row adds two rows of knitting across a section of the work. Since the work is turned before completing a row, stitches must be wrapped at the turn to prevent holes. Work a wrap as follows:
1 With yarn in back, slip next stitch as if to purl. Bring yarn to front of work and slip stitch back to left needle as shown. Turn work.
2 When you come to the wrap on a right-side row, make it less visible by working the wrap together with the stitch it wraps.

SSK A left-slanting single decrease.
1 Slip 2 stitches separately to right needle as if to knit.
2 Knit these 2 stitches together by slipping left needle into them from left to right. 2 stitches become one.

SSSK A left-slanting double decrease.
Work same as SSK except:
1 Slip 3 stitches separately to right needle as if to knit.
2 Knit these 3 stitches together by slipping left needle into them from left to right. 3 stitches become one.

Make 1 (M1)

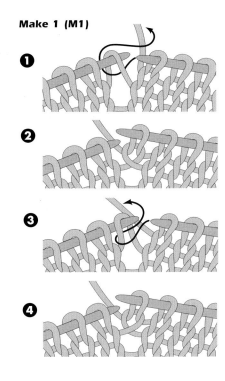

Lifted inc

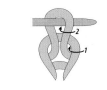

Short-row wrap

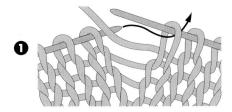

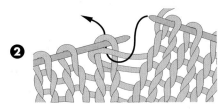

ssk

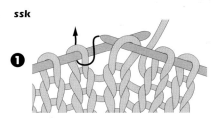

❶

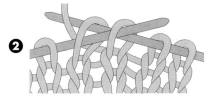

❷

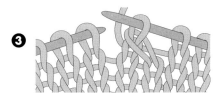

❸

sl2tog-k1-p2sso

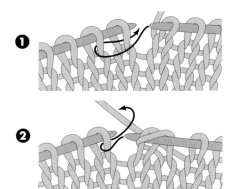

❶

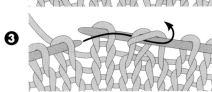

❷

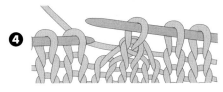

❸

❹

SL2TOG-K1-P2SSO A centered double decrease.

1 Slip 2 stitches together to right needle as if to knit.

2 Knit next stitch.

3 Pass 2 slipped stitches together over knit stitch and off right needle. 3 stitches become 1; the center stitch is on top.

SSP A left-slanting single decrease.

1 Slip 2 stitches separately to right needle as if to knit.

2 Slip these 2 stitches back onto left needle. Insert right needle through their back loops, into the second stitch and then the first.

3 Purl them together.

DOUBLE YARNOVER
Wrap yarn twice around needle between stitches.

ssp

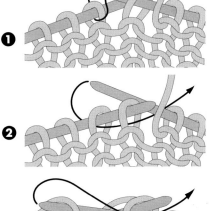

❶

❷

❸

Double yarnover

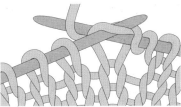

Yarn Weights

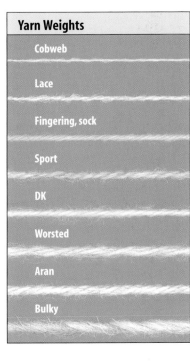

Yarn Weights
Cobweb
Lace
Fingering, sock
Sport
DK
Worsted
Aran
Bulky

Metrics

To convert inches to centimeters,
multiply the inches by 2.5.
For example: 4" x 2.5 = 10cm

To convert feet to centimeters,
multiply the feet by 30.48.
For example: 2' x 30.48 = 60.96cm

To convert yards to meters,
multiply the yards by .9144.
For example: 4 yds x .9144 = 3.66m

Abbreviations

approx approximate(ly)
b back
beg begin(ning)(s)
CC contrasting color
cn cable needle
cm centimeter(s)
dec decreas(e)(ed)(es)(ing)
dpn double-pointed needle(s)
foll follow(s)(ing)
g gram(s)
" inch(es)
' foot(feet)
inc increas(e)(ed)(es)(ing)
k knit(ting)(s)(ted)
lb pound(s)
LH left hand
M make one
m meter(s)
mm millimeter(s)
MC main color
no stitch skip to next square on chart
oz ounce(s)
p purl(ed)(ing)(s)
pat(s) pattern(s)
pm place marker
psso pass slipped stitch(es) over
rep repeat(s)
RH right hand
RS right side(s)
rnd round(s)
sl slip(ped)(ping)
st(s) stitch(es)
St st stockinette stitch
tbl through back loop
tog together
WS wrong side(s)
wyib with yarn in back
wyif with yarn in front
yd(s) yard(s)
yo yarn over

Eugen Beugler

It seems that I have always knitted. I learned when I was 8 years old—not from Mom, or any beloved aunt or grandmother, but from books. Learning by myself has stood me in good stead—I can usually figure my way through a pattern without help.

I began collecting lace patterns in the 40's. At first I just admired their ethereal beauty—and then one day I sat down and knitted one of them. It was like magic; I was hooked. I gave up all other forms of knitting and concentrated on lace. My collection has patterns from Germany, Italy, France, Denmark, and Spain, and I'm always looking for more. So far, my fascination with lace knitting has not abated. Long may it flourish!

Nancy Bush

From the beginning of a career which has taken me from knitter to shop owner to designer and writer, I have been passionate about knitting history, traditional patterns, and techniques. How knitters were inspired, what motivated them, and how they solved the mysteries of construction fascinate me.

My interest in lace early when I studied the history of bobbin and point laces in college. I learned about knitted lace by working a long sampler scarf in traditional Shetland patterns. When I began to work with Estonian knitting, I discovered a wealth of lace there too, from lovely shawls to small items such as the socks and gloves offered here.
Author: *Folk Socks, Folk Knitting in Estonia.* Owner: **The Wooly West,** mail order, Salt Lake City. Teacher

Hazel Carter

Born in Cambridge, I was brought up mostly in Beckenham, Kent. My mother taught me to knit before I went to school, age 5. Mother also told me I could never do cables as they were too difficult, so making my first cabled jersey was something of a victory over childhood brain-washing.

My love of lace began when a cousin brought silk bobbin lace back from Malta. The distinction between 'real' and machine-made lace was clear,

and lace was still being smuggled. Every well-dressed baby had a Shetland shawl, and the hap ("covering:" an everyday shawl) was popular with ladies, so I was aware of the islands' knitting traditions.

I developed a charting method, not realizing that I was re-inventing the wheel. It speeded up the process, and I could understand the way the pattern elements fitted together. The human eye-span can grasp a larger segment of a row in charted form.

Until retirement I was a university professor of African languages and literature; in later years I specialized in the influence of African languages on the Caribbean Creoles. My publications had such riveting titles as *Syntax and Tone in Kongo* and *Three Creole Pitch Systems* and curiously did not make money. The one that did was my knitting book.
Author: *Shetland Lace Knitting From Charts.* Teacher

Amy Detjen

I grew up in Eau Claire, Wisconsin, the youngest of three girls. My Grandma Giles would knit wonderful dresses and jackets for our dolls. Christmas and birthdays brought surprises for both Barbie and Midge, with the occasional Aran pullover for Ken.

Mom taught me to knit when I was 8 or 9. When I tried again, years later, my hands seemed to know what to do. I suddenly wanted to know everything about knitting, and started collecting tips, techniques—and purple yarn. I was hooked for life. When I joined a class from Ann Swanson and Katie Nagorney, Ann told me that I "belonged" at Meg Swansen's Knitting Camp, so I applied. Ann was right.

I found my true mentor. Meg taught me to think about knitting not as a hobby, but as a passion. That has made all the difference.

Maureen Egan Emlet

I was born to a military family. When my mother taught me to knit when I was five. I had an immediate affinity and love for it. I knit my first sweater when I was eight and tackled an Aran at age ten.

My professional career began in Alaska. After

we moved to the lower 48, I continued custom knitting for boutiques. I have worked as a knitwear and crochet designer and teacher, am married, and have three fabulous children.

An extraordinary knitter, Melva Rhuhaak, introduced me to the beauty of lace knitting and helped me to unlock the secrets of designing lace.

I knit every day and everywhere. I am never impatient in line and sometimes find myself hoping for longer red lights. I have even been photographed knitting while floating on the Dead Sea in Israel—proof that a person can and should knit wherever they are!

Sidna Farley

It's amazing what desire and sibling rivalry can do. I started to knit in high school after eyeing my younger sister's growing pile of hand-knit sweaters. I said to myself, "If my stupid sister can knit, so can I."—and so I could!

The first sweater I knit was a yoke sweater. I followed the pattern and knit four flat pieces, but the yoke was knit on a circular needle. That gave me the information I needed to figure out how to knit without seams and I've been knitting circular even since.

A few years later when I went to Elizabeth Zimmermann's knitting camp, she gave me the inspiration to design my own sweaters. I love it when my own camp encourages others the way she encouraged me.
Author: *Seamless Sweaters, Farley Footwear,* and *Critter Classics.*

Norah Gaughan

This sounds weird to me, but the truth is, I've been knitting for over 25 years! I loved it from the start. Well, there was a shaky period right after my first teacher sent me home and I ended up in tears trying to read the directions. Mom rescued me with a copy of Elizabeth Zimmermann's *Knitting Without Tears.* The encouragement of flexible thought and intelligent explanations were exactly what I needed.

I have been designing hand knits professionally

for over 15 years. Producing over 60 garments a year (with the help of professional knitters) the first five years seemed like an intense graduate school. Working with talented editors expanded and challenged my concepts of garment design, and the sheer bulk of the work meant I was learning loads—about technique, about psychology, about writing things down. My specialty (and passion) has become developing pattern-stitches, in particular cable-stitches. When I was producing up to 20 new pattern-stitch swatches a month, one idea (good or mediocre) led to another and another (some of them really good), until I couldn't notate them on paper fast enough. This is where the lace shown on p. 115 comes in. I was experimenting by cabling stitches not commonly cabled. In this pattern, the ribs make the transition into a more and more open lace.
Design Director of Knitting Yarns at JCA

Medrith Glover

It seems I've been thinking about knitting all my life... As a designer, I've never been particularly prolific; I seem to have many back burners and there's something on every one of them, but there's no telling when a process will be "done."

I opened my shop in 1983 and have enjoyed everything connected with it...the lovely knitters, enduring friendships, access to superior yarns and tools and books, and the positive role I've been able to play in my community and the larger world community. The annual Knitters' Retreats I have done with Karen Yaksick have been some of the most joyful times of my knitting life.

My mother felt Elizabeth Zimmermann to be her mentor through the years, and I've always felt Meg Swansen to be mine. We treasure the hours spent together at their Knitting Camps, but there are many others who have influenced our thought processes too; inspiration comes at us all the time and there are overlaps and spin-offs and even eurekas once in a while as we draw encouragement from each other.
Owner: **The Wool Room,** Quincy, CA. Teacher.

Diana Hrvatin

My first introduction to lace was in my late teens. I remember being impressed with a lace doily in a knitting magazine. I met the challenge and knitted my first lace doily.

I taught mathematics on the secondary level for 10 years, then opened a preschool/child care center.

When I was diagnosed with an allergy to wool, I looked to other fibers to satisfy my knitting compulsion. I knitted a lot of lace because cotton was locally available and in 1992, opened my shop to provide a source of a variety of fibers and lace-weight yarns.

Owner: **Gossamer Threads & More!**, Durango, CO
Teacher

Debra M. Lee

Knitting gives me a creative channel to combine color, texture, and structure into silhouette-flattering styles. I've been knitting since 1986—taught by my (now) mother-in-law.

After winning an amateur design contest, I've been paying more attention to how I create so that I can share the process with other knitters. I'm president of our guild and have started teaching.

I'm an American-born Chinese from the Washington, DC metropolitan area; have a B.S. in Business and Management and an M.B.A. in Information Systems Technology; and work in software sales. I'm married to a wonderfully supportive husband, George McLennan.

Susanna Lewis

I was educated in fine art, music, and biology, and have worked professionally in all these fields.

In the early 1970's, pursuing a desire to find an innovative tapestry technique, I chanced to see a knitting machine in a shop window and, after a

brief demonstration, realized that I had found my technique for tapestry; but it took several years of practice and experimentation to produce the fabrics I wanted.

Commissions for architectural hangings followed, as well as participation in the growing "art to wear" movement during the 1970's. My wearable art works are preserved in museum and private collections around the world and can be seen in such publications as *Ornament* magazine and the book *Art To Wear* by Julie Schaffler Dale. As a professional knitter, I now teach and write.

I am currently having a wonderful play period knitting prototype quarter-scale garments by hand and machine for my Sasha® dolls. The dolls are always patient, show their appreciation by looking terrific, and never complain about anything you make for them!

Author: *A Machine Knitter's Guide to Creating Fabrics* (co-authored with Julia Weissman), and *Knitting Lace.* Teacher

Dale Long

I grew up in Walla Walla, Washington. If variety is the spice, I have certainly had a well-seasoned life, being at various times a Western Union messenger boy, a shoeshine boy, a movie theater doorman and marquee changer, a sailor, a police radio dispatcher, an undersheriff, an actor, a stage manager, a legal secretary, and a paralegal. I am now the office administrator of a small law firm in New Orleans.

I have been knitting pretty steadily since 1962 when my sister, who is left-handed, asked me to help her figure out how to knit. Now this isn't generally known, but Lavonne and I invented the continental style of knitting. She was working from a little Coats and Clark booklet. It showed the British style of carrying the yarn in the right hand, and since she was left-handed, it only seemed natural to hold the yarn in the left hand and pick at it with the right-hand needle. I could make holding the yarn in the right hand work, but I could tell that she was making much faster progress, so I adopted the continental style too. Since Mr. Coats and Mr. Clark didn't seem to be of much use to either of us, we figured out a strange way of purling by grabbing the yarn beween left thumb and forefinger

and wrapping it around the working needle. I still use this method today.

When I came across a copy of *Knitting Without Tears*, it was a wonderful revelation. I could do things on my own, design my own patterns, and be the boss of my own knitting. Since then, knitting has taken on a new dimension for me and is so much more exciting and satisfying. I re-read Mary Thomas and Elizabeth Zimmermann every couple of years and try to pretend it is for the first time.

Sally Melville

Most of us are, to some degree or other, self-taught knitters. As much as we pick up from other sources—mentors and resource books—it is what we teach ourselves that we learn best.

When I look back at the things I mis-taught myself, I see a number of quite hilarious mistakes, but the lessons I learned from these mistakes were learned very well. I took nothing for granted, and I came out of each knitting experience with a greater understanding of the craft. And this is something I try to impart when I teach.

Working stitch patterns in combination is a class I love to teach, so, when asked to do something for this book, I decided to combine the simplest lace stitch pattern we know (sometimes called purse stitch) with another stitch pattern (the vine panel) which I designed myself. The result is the Vine Lace Cardigan on p. 112.

For the edging, I wanted to avoid two things: a crocheted edge and a lengthwise knitted edging. I ended up modifying the 'Scalloped Shell Edging II' in the second *Harmony Guide to Knitting Stitches*. It is a lovely, lacy edging, with the advantage that it produces its own buttonholes! Also, while it is cast on and worked up at the bottom edge, I found that when I picked up along the front edge and worked the edging out from the piece (hence, working it upside down), it still looked quite like itself!

Author: *Sally Melville Styles.* Teacher

Katharine Misegades

I learned to knit from mama, Rachel Misegades. I can hardly remember when I didn't know how to knit. I knit mittens and a lot of leper bandages (garter stitch, three inches wide and as long as a large ball of bedspread cotton would allow).

In my twenties, while I was in college and as an officer in the Navy Nurse Corps, I despaired of knitting garments that fit properly so I started knitting lace. I enjoyed using fine needles, and the fiber was less expensive.

While my children were small, I pursued a variety of activities—needlepoint, cross-stitch and other embroidery techniques, tatting, crochet, needle-made lace, quilt-making, woodcarving, weaving, painting, and drawing. I designed charted patterns and dreamt of sharing these with others. When the opportunity arose for me to return to college, I majored in graphic design and made a career change.

Several years ago, my mother asked me to take her to Knitting Camp. That experience focused me on developing my skills, freed me from my hesitation to experiment, and encouraged me to publish a collection of my designs.

As I watch a pattern grow, I often think that "sleep" (as Shakespeare proposed) is not the only thing that "knits up the raveled sleeve of care." Knitting is not only fascinating and productive, but it is, for me, therapeutic.

Author: *...And A Time to Knit Stockings* and *A Vested Interest*

Rachel Misegades

I was born in 1906. My younger sister and I grew up on a Kansas farm. My father was a gas engine specialist and good carpenter. My mother was a good cook. She knew how big a stick of wood was needed to finish baking a pie and did the breakfast biscuits while she milked two Jersey cows. We girls didn't know there was anything we couldn't do.

I learned to knit from a grandfather when I was six and made squares for the Red Cross during World War I. I shocked my parents on the eve of high school graduation when I asked to go to college. My major was Art with a minor in History. So many doors of knowledge opened that I was overcome. In two years I could teach in rural schools.

When I married Harold Misegades, I had started work on a Masters degree and had a teaching job at the university, but we decided I should trade my Master for a Mister. I was never sorry.

No craft or fiber subject does as much for an ailment—mind or muscle—as does knitting.

Debbie New

After knitting for a large family for many years, I turned to it as a medium of expression when my husband became seriously ill. I then began to knit seriously (and in jest). I think it has been explored less than other fiber arts and I am excited by its non-traditional possibilities.

I have taught and given presentations across Canada, the US, and Austrailia. In 1999 I was named Visual Artist of the Year in my region, surprising recognition for a knitter.
Teacher

Cheryl Oberle

I received a B.A. in philosophy and in psychology from the University of Denver, studied art and architecture at Harvard, and did graduate work at Northwestern University.

I learned to knit at the age of four and at present am a free-lance designer and knitting instructor in Denver, Colorado; give classes and workshops around the country; design for magazines and yarn companies; and have my own line of designs and hand-painted yarns.

I've been knitting for 40 years, but it was the discovery of Elizabeth Zimmermann's books that really brought me "out of the closet." I decided about 12 years ago to learn everything that I could about knitting and I'm still learning something amazing every day! Knitting is meditative for me,

proof that spiritual pursuits can be incredibly sensuous as well.

I still remember that first time I tried to knit lace. I got so frustrated that I put my knitting down for a whole week! One of my goals as a teacher and designer is to get knitters to try lace and to present them with projects that are appealing and accessible. Hence the Sampler Tabard (p. 90).
Author: *Folk Shawls.* Teacher

Emily L. Ocker

When I was eleven years old (in 1931), I happened to see directions for knitting basics in the back of a ten-cent crochet book. I managed to follow the diagrams, taught myself to knit, then went to the library and borrowed every knitting book that was available.

During World War II, *Woman's Day* magazine came on the scene at 2 cents a copy. Direction sheets for lace edgings and doilies were offered for a few pennies. I sent for every one, and that was the start of my collection.

While my children were young, I had a home business of knitwear repair and alteration....I must have shortened at least 200 knit skirts! My knitting career includes teaching adult education classes at the YWCA and at senior citizen recreation centers.

After corresponding with Elizabeth Zimmermann for many years and acquiring every pattern and article I could find by her and about her, finally in 1981 I went to her knitting camp. What a revelation! We were all encouraged to be designers and to trust ourselves!

I moved to California to be near my daughter Medrith, and I participate in every class at her shop. I always have several projects on the needles and am eager to learn something new. If I can't take my knitting with me, I'm not leaving!

Robert Powell

I was born in a small coal mining town in West Virginia. I am 39 years old, I have been 39 for sev-

eral years, and I will remain 39 for what I hope will be several more years.

When I was 12 or 13, I taught myself to knit. I worked for 10 years in a double-knit factory as the assistant to the women's wear stylist, Jane Harvey. I translated her design ideas into computer data that ran the patterning mechanisms of the electronic knitting machines. That taught me about pattern coordination, repeats, color combinations; instilled in me an appreciation and love of good design; and developed my sense of aesthetics.

Next I did color separation work for textile printing. Samu Tof taught me how computers really worked, what they could do, and how to make them do what they weren't supposed to be able to do. When the market took a downturn, I turned to graphic arts, where I have worked since.

Knitting is here to stay. It has endured the test of time.

Gayle Roehm

My mother taught me to knit as a child, but I wasn't truly dedicated until I needed a stress reliever for a demanding job. Once started, I never stopped.

My work involved a lot of travel, and I've knitted my way across five continents, always alert for yarn and for other knitters. During several years in Asia, I discovered Japanese knitting patterns. Later I prepared the Japanese section of Margaret Heathman's book *Knitting Languages* and wrote an article in *Knitter's* about understanding Japanese knitting patterns.

I'm intrigued by unusual construction methods. In my two designs, I've experimented with a new joining technique and created curves by short rows. I knot, spin, dye, and sew in Bethesda, MD.

Bridget Rorem

Having knitted since grade school, I credit a life-long dedication to insomnia for the completion of so many projects, and the boredom that comes with indifferent lecturers for my penchant for designing. It is easier to appear rapt and engaged if

you are mentally deciding whether a lacy Shetland wrap or a boat-neck Guernsey would look better on the dreary professor in front of you. I caution, however, that mentally dressing authority figures in finely knit garments is best not practiced on a policeman approaching your pulled-over car. It is hard to wipe the silly smile from your face after you have decided that fluffy magenta mohair numbers would make better uniforms.

I live with my husband, Chip, and youngest son, Eli, in a very small town in Illinois. In other aspects of my life, I am an environmentalist and peace and justice activist.

Joan Schrouder

It can be truthfully said that pure orneriness and sheer, pig-headed stubbornness have fueled my quest into knitting design. I can be challenged by remarks such as, "Oh *that* can't be done in knitting!" or "Don't bother trying that stitch in circular knitting." even when uttered by knitting mavens whom I respect. Some of my favorite results have come at such instigation. When Elizabeth Zimmermann said, "Don't try this [her Wishbone Sweater from *Knitter's Almanac]* in lighter weight yarns; the formula won't work," I dropped from super bulky to knitting worsted weight, changed from stockinette to garter, and it worked! (I'm sure that she was just baiting me....)

Knitting is a major focus of my life, leading me to part-time designing and teaching careers.
Teacher

Joy Slayton

I learned to knit from my grandmother around age nine, but didn't really get into knitting seriously until I encountered Elizabeth Zimmermann's *Busy Knitter* series on PBS. A copy of *Knitting Without Tears* opened a whole new world to me: I didn't have to follow long, written instructions and make someone else's design.

In the '70s, I answered an ad in a writers' magazine for a knitting columnist for a now long-gone magazine. Nothing came of it, and I pretty much

forgot about the whole thing—until a letter arrived saying the company was starting a new magazine, *Knitting World,* and was I interested in doing a column for it. I was and had a column in every issue from December 1978 until it was discontinued in September 1993. Since that time I have designed for a number of publications and self-publish a line of patterns
Owner: **JoyKnits**

Ann Swanson and Katie Nagorney

The road to our partnership as 'designing women' began during our primary life choice—stay-at-home motherhood.

During the endless gymnastic sessions with our daughters it was, perhaps, fate that we would each note another stay-at-home mom knitting across the gym. Lots of conversation and yarn road trips later, we had become partners in a multi-owner yarn/needlework store.

After some creative soul-searching, we determined we wanted to walk away from knitting shop models and daily store activities. Our design business was born.

We began our patterns with directions we used when teaching community education classes. Taking cues from our students, we recognized that there was a need for patterns that gave precise details about the technical aspects of knitting construction. The growth of the business side of our partnership has been gradual, by design, and our maturation as knitters has been rapid and personally gratifying.
Owners: **Wool You Order**

Meg Swansen

My lace knitting days started when my mother began importing the works of Marianne Kinzel from England. One of lace knitting's strongest appeals to me is that it feels as if I am engaged upon a separate discipline; I use it to take a break from knitting.
Author: *Handknitting with Meg Swansen, Meg Swansen's Knitting*

Owner: **Schooolhouse Press.** Teacher

Sandy Terp

College studies have been in literature, writing, and architecture, and my career has followed the same eclectic path. But I have always knitted—don't remember when I learned how. I'm so fortunate to do it for a living now. My business sells books, kits, and tools for knitting. I teach at every opportunity and have self-published two books—more on the way. My greatest joy has been to see many of my students go on to success in the knitting field.

Lace knitting is something I started to do when my children were small, (I have seven, five of them girls). But it wasn't until *Barbara Abbey's Knitting Lace* came into my life that I learned and started to teach Lace Shorthand.

I started designing knitted lace about 15 years ago. The copestone came for me when I read Margaret Stove's book. She freed me to work around a theme and use symbolism that expresses my spiritual beliefs and values. At the risk of sounding pretentious, this added art to my work, as well as personal fulfillment.
Owner: **Moonrise.** Teacher

Marilyn van Keppel

I was born in Kansas City, Missouri, and have lived there all my life, with the exception of my years away at college. While in college, I learned trivial things like nuclear physics and integral calculus, and one essential thing: how to knit. I started on socks, and presented my future husband with 24 pairs of argyles. When I returned to Kansas City, I could find no knitters—no guild, no friend or family member to whom I could turn for help. But it wasn't long before I discovered a mail-order business that a transplanted Englishwoman had started. She was, of course, Elizabeth Zimmermann. The yarns I ordered from her came with a generous sprinkling of advice and encouragement. And what great patterns were in *Wool Gathering*! One

Christmas every family member received a rib-warmer. I even made a pair of bright red long johns to wear while riding my horse on cold winter days. But I made no lace.

When my husband, the argyle sock guy, fell ill and died, I stopped knitting for about five years. A pattern for a charming lace shawl tempted me back to the needles. Next year, I discovered a book written in a strange-looking language, with lots of lovely shawls pictured. I set out to see if I could make one or two of these shawls, and ended by making all 19 of them, learning the language (Faroese) and translating the book in the process. Lace knitting is now a passion with me, satisfying both the scientific half of my brain, with the details of lace construction, and the artistic half, with the beauty of the finished piece.
Translator: *Knitted Faroese Shawls*

Joyce Williams

During World War II my entire second grade class in Sheboygan, Wisconsin was taught to knit. The class spent half an hour each day patriotically knitting khaki squares, which were later sewn into blankets by Red Cross volunteers and sent to the British armed forces.

I do not recall a time since the second grade that I have not been working on at least one knitting project. After reading *Knitting Workshop* and *Knitting Without Tears* by Elizabeth Zimmermann, I began to design my own knitted garments.

Although I like to share my ideas with others, I prefer learning to teaching. I have developed knitting techniques, primarily to avoid some of the knitting processes that I do not enjoy.

My husband Don and I have traveled extensively and have visited all seven continents. My hobbies include golf, skiing, reading, horseback riding, (obviously knitting), and walks on our beautiful farm.
Author: *Latvian Dreams: Knitting From Weaving Charts.*

Lois Young

I learned to knit when I was 10. No one told me that I should knit right-handed, so I sat opposite a friend and learned how to do it left-handed. She never taught me to purl, so all I could do was garter stitch, which I didn't consider "knitting." In college, someone said that purling was the opposite of knitting. It took me quite a while to figure out how those words fit the action of purling, but I did it, and I've been "knitting" ever since. My first sweater was a yoke sweater with bands of lace. I wrote the lace column for *Knitting World* magazine for 12 years. Later, I discovered Elizabeth Zimmermann's first book (which I think I memorized). I am a charter member of Elizabeth's Knitting Camp and have not missed a year so far.

There is a precision about lace that is very mathematical, but I design and memorize patterns as if they were living, growing things. In my other life, I teach calculus, garden and grow orchids, read mysteries, spoil my three cats, enjoy my family, and sing in our church choir.

Elizabeth Zimmermann (1910–1999)

Through nearly 50 years of steady contributions to the knitting world (unique sweater designs, magazine articles, books, television series, workshops, Knitting Camp, videos, and letter writing), this amazing woman has been a voice of clarity and encouragement to knitters all over the world.
Author: *Knitting Without Tears, Knitter's Almanac, Knitting Workshop, Knitting Around.*
TV Series: *Busy Knitter I and II, Knitting Workshop, Knitting Around.* Teacher

Perched on the California coast 45 miles south of San Francisco, Pigeon Point Lighthouse soars 115 feet into the sky. It has been lit since 1872 and has always been a beacon not just for mariners but travelers on nearby Highway 1. Today is no exception: our XRX photo crew goes to work surrounded by lighthouse visitors—and the wide Pacific.

This isn't just another shoot, and not just because of the breath-taking beauty of the location. For the first time we're working with a supermodel—the Gatherer of Lace herself, Meg Swansen. Meg has good-naturedly agreed to stand in front of my camera. We sneak away from Stitches West, head across the Bay Bridge, through San Francisco, and past green hillsides abloom with bright yellow mustard plants.

XRX Book Editor Elaine Rowley has joined our crew, along with Stitches Director Amy Detjen who has volunteered as the stylist. But it doesn't seem there's much for Amy to do. Stylists usually fuss with models and garments, nipping in with a clip here, tucking a front there. All Amy has to do is drape a shawl on Meg's shoulders and her job is done. Meg wraps it around herself, looks out to sea—and we have our shot.

The photography for *A Gathering of Lace* began on a different coast, a year earlier. On the shores of the azure Ionian Sea in a windy shore beneath the walls of a medieval monastery two of my friends hold Dale Long's 'Shetland Tea Shawl.' The resulting image, undulating, diaphanous lace contrasts against rocky shadow—and sets the tone for the photographs in this book (pp.30–31). And makes me realize that it isn't enough to

just show the structure of the lace; I also want to convey its spider-web transparency. And, just as important, show how lace moulds to the human body, providing a touch of elegance, and, on chilly days, a warm cocoon. So, amidst mounds of dried seaweed, a young Greek girl (p. 39) tosses Dale's shawl over her shoulders…

The blue Mediterranean backdrop gives way to deep-cut valleys, green hills bordered by dry-stone walls, and overcast skies as our team now finds itself in the Yorkshire Moors, during an Easter break while photographing Jean Moss' *Sculptured Knits.* "One of my fondest memories of that trip to England," says Amy, "was when the photographer said to me, 'Could you please give the model your shoes?' It had to be forty degrees—and we were standing in a sheep pasture generously fertilized with manure." Only Amy and our model were standing in the pasture, that is. Elaine and my friend, world-class photographer Alvis Upitis, stood on the firm, safe, ground of the road, amused at the scene unfolding before their eyes: in order to get the shot, I was now climbing on top of our white monster tour bus nicknamed Moby, heavy tripod and Hasselblad camera in hand!

No, that wasn't the toughest shot in the book. That distinction belongs to Debbie New's coracle (p. 156). Leave it to the fertile imagination of one of Canada's most talented designers to knit elegant lace—only to encase it in a bowl-shaped epoxy shell. Thus the 'Coracle' was born. But how to get the coracle in Ontario and the photographer in South Dakota together? You drive the former and fly the latter to Stitches East. And so, a stone's throw from George Washington's

(Counterclockwise from left:) Meg at Pigeon Point; Debbie New valiantly fighting the current of the Schuylkill River; mustard plants abloom on the California coast; Dale Long's 'Shetland Tea Shawl' billowing in the Mediterranean breeze; Meg taking a lace break; coracle lace closeup; photographing at Beningbrough Hall, an English country estate near York.

(From Top:) Draped in lace at Miami's Villa Vizcaya; Vizcaya's grotto transformed with lace webs; the lane at Beningbrough Hall; Vizcaya's coral-like walls acting as giant stretchers: Editor Elaine Rowley (second from left), Fashion Editor Nancy J. Thomas with photographer's assistant Andrew Holman, 'Gathering' photographer, and crew; Amy Detjen uses a reflector as a portable changing room; Norah Gaughan's 'Ribbed Lace Pullover'.

headquarters at Valley Forge, in the swift current of the Schuylkill River, we set Debbie and her coracle adrift. But not before giving her a lifeline (see photo, opposite page).

Debbie gamely paddled against the current, trying to keep the coracle from heading down to Chesapeake Bay. But paddling only made the coracle go in circles. When not disappearing under the stone bridge, that is. Thank God for that rope! We would drag Debbie and her little boat upriver, back to the starting point—and have another go. All the while, Debbie is worried about the rocks: it wouldn't take much to puncture the little craft's eggshell skin. Suddenly, the Coracle beaches itself on a sand bar, just long enough for me to snap a few pictures.

"Alexis, the rope!" Debbie's words made me jump from behind the camera, take the rope from my assistant's hands (who was holding on for dear life) and toss it to Debbie, who gave up paddling for just a second to grab it. I thought of letting David Xenakis and our pre-press wizards wave their magic Photoshop wand and make the rope disappear. But I realized how difficult a task that would be with a background of dappled light and moving water. Debbie quickly hid the rope beneath her, and went back to the oar—and I had my shot.

The waters of the Schuylkill were replaced by the Bay of Biscayne when photography for *A Gathering of Lace* resumed at Miami's Villa Vizcaya. This incredible estate, surrounded by ten acres of gardens and fountains, became our backdrop as our crew grew to include Fashion Editor Nancy J. Thomas and photo assistant Andrew Holman. With a gentle touch, lace would cling

to the coral-like weathered stone of the villa. This giant stretcher showed off the lace in all its glory (see photo, below).

Lace, of course, doesn't always look this beautiful—at least on the needles. "It's all shriveled and wrinkled," explains Meg. "You can't see any of the pattern. That's why I wanted the last photographs (p. 4 and opposite page). I felt strongly that there should be a representation of what the shawl looks like while you're knitting. If you've never knitted lace before, you'd only be disheartened and discouraged at what it looks like in its congested state hanging from your needle.

"Of course it looks better hanging on people! I love the garments on the models and the simplicity of the photographs. It's a clean, elegant, classy look. And shooting in different parts of the world, at different times of the year, added such a great dimension, excitement, and depth to the book. I love the daffodils, the spring flowers in the British garden.

"And how incredibly proud I am to be associated with the team that put it all together. Carol Skallerud, to mention just one name, was simply amazing. Elaine and I would come across a technique and say, 'We should have a drawing of this,' and rush and tell Carol what we wanted. We'd go back to Elaine's office, and about seven minutes later Carol would come in with a finished drawing of the technique we had just described to her! She's quite phenomenal. And Knitting Editor Ann Denton's gift with instructions is miraculous.

"My love for lace goes back to the 1960s when we started importing from England the Marianne Kinzel books, *(The First* and *The Second Book of Modern Lace Knitting,* now available through Dover). I had never seen a lace chart before, so on the first project I knit from that book, I followed the verbal instructions. But that gets tiring rather quickly, and before long I turned to the charts. I realized that I only had to memorize two or three symbols at most and I could read a lace chart the way one reads color pattern charts. I got hooked and have loved lace knitting ever since. The most beautiful part of the Kinzel books is that the charts

are done in such a way that the motifs are visible—it's like reading a book: you're reading the chart and you're reading your knitting. That's why I'm so pleased with Jay Reeve's incredible charts which so beautifully reflect the lace.

"The nugget of inspiration for *A Gathering of Lace* was all the knitters doing show-and-tell at Knitting Camp each year. I realized there are scores of undiscovered wonderful lace knitters out there. When Elaine and I began discussing the book, we knew we wanted a diversity of knitters and lace projects, but we didn't really know what to expect. We asked for submissions and ideas flooded in. I thought that ninety percent of the submissions would be shawls, and I was so pleased to see sweaters, vests, shrugs, tams, gloves, socks. I didn't anticipate any of that, and it was a wonderful surprise.

"Then the lace began to roll in. It was like Christmas. I opened the packages with great anticipation, and then sat back in stunned silence at the beauty of the lace. Then I put it all in the car and drove to Sioux Falls. Elaine and I spread everything out all over the Victorian living room of the XRX house. There was lace draped on the coffee table, over sofas, chairs, and staircase banisters. We stood in the middle and slowly turned, trying to take it all in. Then we tried to get a handle on how to divide it all into categories and knitting skill levels."

"All along, Meg's thought was of gathering a group of lace knitters and their work," Elaine says, "and that's how we present the material in the book. The hope was to make the book accessible to a lot of people, so there are the normal instructions, but we have also included wonderful techniques: keeping lace reversible, great joins, great beginnings.

"It was a challenge to make the book coherent visually due to the diversity of the material, and in that Art Director Bob Natz has succeeded admirably. It's a book of lace charts because none of us can imagine knitting most of these items from written instructions. We're hoping that knitters have learned that the pleasure of

lace is watching it grow on the needles and understand that the chart is essential to that process.

"For people who haven't knit lace we're giving blocked gauges. And we tried to indicate throughout the book that this gives the knitter a whole lot of leeway. A lot of these projects are not knit very firmly: they do get wet and they do get stretched, and that's what makes lace beautiful, that's what brings it to life. We wanted it to be a bit romantic and a bit timeless. But we wanted to give a fresh look at lace.

"It was really nice to see the models and stylists interested in our garments. It wasn't 'I'm wearing a curtain,' or 'I'm in costume.' They were real valid garments. And Alexis' photography celebrates the other qualities of lace: you can see through it; it forms patterns and shadows. It's been wonderful to have enough of those images to get that idea across as well as being able to show the details, the closeup shots. If we could have shown you every closeup we wanted to, the book would easily have 1,000—not 180—pages!

"The fact that a lot of the people in this book came up as knitters with Elizabeth Zimmermann's encouragement is a real celebration of Elizabeth's spirit. One of them, JCA Design Director Norah Gaughan, wrote to us about *Knitting Without Tears,* 'The encouragement of flexible fact and intelligent explanation were exactly what I needed.' That has always been Meg and Elizabeth's approach to their writing about knitting— and I'm so glad it comes across in this book."

While in my studio taking the last shots for *A Gathering of Lace,* I hear Meg's voice on National Public Radio. Elizabeth is no more. But she lives on: in our hearts—and in our gathering.

— Alexis Xenakis
Sioux Falls, South Dakota

(From top:)
Daffodils bloom by a stone bridge near Thirsk, Yorkshire; Elaine and Sarah out to pasture with Alexis on top of Moby; Amy Detjen's 'Beginner's Triangle' gracing a Villa Vizcaya model; Andreas, Zafeiris and Nandia in Greece.

"I wanted to do the easiest project with the least amount of shaping but the most amount of confidence building for a new lace knitter," Amy says. "It's very easy to tell if you're one stitch off— you'll know right away. You're basically counting to seven—so you always know where you are!"

BIBLIOGRAPHY

The Art of Shetland Lace, Sarah Don, Bell & Hyman, 1981

Barbara Abbey's Knitting Lace, Schoolhouse Press, 1993

Charted Knitting Designs, A Third Treasury, Barbara G. Walker, Schoolhouse Press, 1998

Classic Knitted Cotton Edgings, Hewitt & Daley, Kangaroo Press, 1987

Creating Original Hand-Knitted Lace, Margaret Stove, Lacis, 1995

Faroese Knitting Patterns, translated by Marilyn van Keppel, Schoolhouse Press, 1997

First Book of Modern Lace Knitting, Marianne Kinzel, Dover, 1972

Gossamer Webs, Galina Khmeleva, Interweave Press, 1998

Knitted Lace Doilies, Tessa Lorant, Thorn Press, 1986

Knitting Lace, Susanna Lewis, Taunton Books, 1992

Second Book of Modern Lace Knitting, Marianne Kinzel, Dover, 1972

A Second Treasury of Knitting Patterns, Barbara G. Walker, Schoolhouse Press, 1998

Shetland Lace, Gladys Amedro, Shetland Times Ltd, 1993

Shetland Lace Knitting From Charts, Hazel Carter, self-published, 1988

A Treasury of Knitting Patterns, Barbara G. Walker, Schoolhouse Press, 1998

25 Original Knitting Designs, Dorothy Reade, self-published, 1968

SOURCES

The yarns in A Gathering of Lace are available at fine yarn stores.
Use our online ShopFinder to find a shop near you www.knittinguniverse.com/athena/shopfinder
Or, write to these companies for a local supplier:

Cashmere America
PO Box 1126
Sonora TX 76950

DMC
10 Port Kearny
South Kearny NJ 07032

Fiber Fantasy
6 Hunters Horn Court
Owings Mills MD 21117
(For blocking wires)

Garnstudio Yarns
PO Box 3068
Moss Beach, CA 94038-3068

JaggerSpun
Water Street
Springvale ME 04083

Jamieson & Smith Shetland Wool Brokers LTD
90 North Road
Shetland Island ZE1 0PQ

JCA
35 Scales Lane
Townsend MA 01469-1094

Judith M Millinery Supplies
104 South Detroit Street
Lagrange IN 46761-1806
(For hat forms)

K1C2, LLC
2220 Eastman Avenue #105
Ventura CA 93003

Kimmet Croft Fibers
5850 Schudy Road
Wisconsin Rapids WI 54495

Morehouse Farm
141 Milan Hill Road
Milan NY 12571

Schoolhouse Press
6899 Cary Bluff
Pittsville WI 54466

Tahki•Stacy Charles Inc.
11 Graphic Place
Moonachie NJ 07074

ALSO
Many of the yarns and kits for some of the projects are available from shops
    on stitchesmarket.com

Tell us what you think:
by mail
    XRX Books
    PO Box 1525
    Sioux Falls SD 57101-1525

by phone
    605-338-2450

by fax
    605-338-2994

by e-mail
    erowley@xrx-inc.com

    on knittinguniverse.com
You may visit our XRX Books site on the World Wide Web:
    www.knittinguniverse.com/books

    on our Knitter's OnLine forums
Join the conversation and post your reactions and comments in our book discussion bulletin boards.

We look forward to hearing from you.